Preterism on Trial

Has All Biblical Prophecy Been Fulfilled?

Dr. Larry Spargimino

All Scripture quotations are from the King James Version of the Holy Bible.

© 2000, 2022 by Larry Spargimino. Previously published as *The Anti-Prophets: The Challenge of Preterism*. All rights reserved. No part of this book may be used or reproduced in any manner whatsoever without written permission of the publisher, except in the case of brief quotations in articles and reviews. For more information contact:

Beacon Street Press
500 Beacon Drive
Oklahoma City, OK 73127
1-800-652-1144
www.swrc.com

Printed in the United States of America

ISBN 978-1-933641-63-8

Preterism on Trial

Has All Bible Prophecy Been Fulfilled?

Dr. Larry Spargimino

To Kenneth C. Hill
Servant of the Lord, defender of the faith,
communicator of truth, faithful friend.

Contents

Introduction 9

Part One
The Challenge

Preterism: Its Leading Features. 19
Preterism: Its Leading Figures 32
Preterism: Its Leading Ally 53
Preterism and the Eclipse of Pre-millennialism 69
Preterism: Its Support of Replacement Theology. 91

Part Two
The Response

The Question of the "Time Texts" 135
A.D. 70 and Other "Preterist Texts" 162
Prophetic Multiple References 181
Was A.D. 70 Really "The End?". 191
Are We Really Living in the Kingdom Age? 205
Preterism and the Old Testament Law 233
"The Blessed Hope" or "The Blasted Hoax"?. 242
Prophetic Gaps. 256
How To Receive Jesus Christ 266

Introduction

This is not your normal kind of a book on prophecy. It doesn't focus on current events in the light of the Scripture, nor does it describe "the signs of the times." Instead, it deals with the critically important issue of whether or not there are prophecies in the Bible that are yet to be fulfilled.

Most Bible teachers would agree there are basically two categories of Bible prophecy: fulfilled prophecy and unfulfilled prophecy. Fulfilled prophecy refers to those ancient predictions of Scripture that have already been fulfilled in events that have already occurred. The virgin birth of Christ is an example. Isaiah 7:14 states: "Behold, a virgin shall conceive, and bear a son, and shall call his name Immanuel." Some seven hundred years later the angel of the Lord appeared to Joseph in a dream and told him that the woman to whom he was engaged had not been immoral. To be sure she was pregnant, but not through an immoral act. Matthew tells us that this was not some surprise happening, but rather, "all this was done, that it might be fulfilled which was spoken of the Lord by the prophet, saying, Behold, a virgin shall be with child, and shall bring forth a son, and they shall call His name Emmanuel, which being interpreted is, God with us" (Matt. 1:22–23). This prophecy was literally fulfilled some two thousand years ago.

There are many other examples of fulfilled prophecy in the Bible. The betrayal and death of Judas Iscariot was prophesied and fulfilled (Acts 1:16–20), and the resurrection of Christ, according to Peter, was a fulfillment of Psalm 16:8–11 (Acts 2:25–28). Certain events that were prophesied in Old

Testament times were also fulfilled in Old Testament times. The length of the Babylonian captivity was predicted to be a period of seventy years (Jer. 25:11; 29:10). Daniel evidently had a copy of this prophecy and by it knew when this period would end (Dan. 9:21).

The other category of prophecy is unfulfilled prophecy. These are biblical predictions concerning events that yet await fulfillment. The return of the Lord and the catching away of the saints (1 Thess. 4:13–18), for example, has not yet happened. The same can be said of the final conflagration in which the present world will be burned up with intense heat and transformed so that we are still looking "for new heavens and a new earth, wherein dwelleth righteousness" (2 Pet. 3:13).

Interpretive difficulties arise, however, regarding the time of the fulfillment of some prophecies. In Matthew 24:21 Jesus said, "For then shall be great tribulation, such as was not since the beginning of the world to this time, no, nor ever shall be." What did He mean by "then"?

There are two schools of thought giving widely divergent answers. Futurists believe that Christ was referring to a time yet future even from our point of view, a time of unprecedented woe that will affect the entire planet Earth. Because they understand prophecy in a literal way, futurists expect the references to the darkening of the sun and moon, and the falling of the stars described in the context, along with the coming of the Son of Man (vss. 29–30), to be literal predictions of worldwide disasters of such magnitude that it is totally impossible that this prophecy, and scores of others like it, could have been already fulfilled.

Preterism, on the other hand, says that futurists are totally in error. Futurism fails to understand how the biblical writers described prophetic events. By taking apocalyptic language too literally, says preterism, futurism expects events to happen in the future that have already happened in the past. "After all," says the preterist, "didn't Jesus state, 'Verily I say unto you, This generation shall not pass, till all these things be fulfilled' (Matt. 24:34)?" And if the futurist tries to make any kind of a reply that puts the fulfillment in the future, the preterist will remind him that Jesus made this prediction in the presence of His immediate disciples (Matt. 24:1–3). "This generation" must therefore mean "the generation of the disciples." Within their generation, argues the preterist, the entire Olivet Discourse will be fulfilled.

For some of my readers this will sound like a novel and farfetched interpretation. "What about the book of Revelation? Isn't that future?"

According to the preterist, not really. The preterist will be glad to remind the futurist that the opening verses of Revelation chapter one indicates a first-century fulfillment: "The Revelation of Jesus Christ, which God gave unto him, to shew unto his servants things which must shortly come to pass for the time is at hand" (vss. 1, 3). For the preterist, the book of Revelation was written around A.D. 68, and it has the same focus as the Olivet Discourse: some impending disaster in the immediate future that will affect the ancient Roman world. What might that be? Preterists unanimously point to the destruction of Jerusalem in A.D. 70. Citing contemporary sources, preterists will argue that more than a million Jews were slaughtered by the Romans under the leadership of Titus. It was a time of "great tribulation." The Jewish temple was destroyed, and the Jewish economy was forever terminated. This is "the end" mentioned in the prophetic scriptures, argues the preterist.

By now the reader can understand the significance of the title of this book: *Preterism on Trial*. Futurists look to the prophetic scriptures and see them as describing "last days" that are yet future, but preterists argue that "the last days" of prophecy are already "past days."

The reason for the subtitle is also becoming evident to the reader. If the last days of prophecy are already past, the church will see no significance in prophecy. Current events are not signs of the coming Tribulation—it has already taken place. Nothing that is happening today has any relationship to prophecy. Even the return of the Lord may be hundreds, or even thousands, of years in the future.

What will happen if large numbers of Christians embrace this view on the eve of the rapture?

We can at least partially answer that question by looking at how the growing popularity of preterism has affected the church today. Pre-millennialism has been greatly eclipsed and prophetic ministries have noticed a definite loss of interest in prophetic themes. And this is not surprising. If preterism is correct, we have all been "barking up the wrong tree" and "chasing the wind." Those who preach the imminent return of the Lord and the necessity of preparing for spiritual survival in an age of growing apostasy, are made to look like wild-eyed fanatics.

This is an issue that affects how Christians look at current events. While many Christians view the advances in science and technology, the establishment of the Jewish state, microchip technology, invasive surveillance techniques, and the continuing erosion of our liberties as relating to biblical end-time events, preterists are debunking the prophetic significance of these prophesied events.

A few words are necessary regarding my approach to this subject. I am a futurist and believe that futurism is the view taught by Scripture. Hence, I will seek to quote Scripture and show by a careful exegesis of biblical texts why I believe preterism is wrong.

I will also quote extensively from preterist authors. It is vital that the reader understand their arguments. Too many futurists don't. They act as if preterism will go away if ignored. It won't. Preterists have done their homework and the first step in dealing with preterism is to take it seriously. Most preterists point to Scripture to justify their position and hold to many of the essentials of the Christian faith. No serious-minded Christian ought to feel comfortable with dismissing their arguments without careful study.

There is another reason for the extensive quotations of preterist authors—so that no one can say that they have been misrepresented. It is all too easy, in any controversy, to demolish straw tigers, but doing that leads to a false sense of security.

Lastly, I need to say that one may be a preterist, or a futurist, and not be a heretic. Though I believe that this is an important issue, we are not talking about salvation. I was saved in an a-millennial church. The pastor was an avid preterist, openly denounced dispensationalism and futurism, and brought in speakers who taught that God is finished with Israel. Yet the message of salvation was clearly taught and affirmed in that congregation. I have found that while preterists allegorize prophecy, they take the rest of Scripture very seriously. The doctrines of the grace of God, the Triunity of the Godhead, the sufficiency of Scripture, biblical authority, the necessity of the new birth, and the substitutionary atonement of Jesus Christ, are all affirmed by most preterist authors. They would also affirm the literal, physical return of the Lord Jesus Christ.

Well then, if this is true, why write this book? I will answer that with a word of testimony that I think will illustrate the practical importance of this topic.

In the 1960s I served as a police officer with the New York State Police, and in the early and mid-seventies I was a caseworker with the New York City Welfare Department, later known as the Department of Social Services. That was a period of great turmoil and strife, both in the streets of our cities and towns, in homes and families, and in the highest branches of government. The Vietnam War was taking American lives at an alarming rate. America was portrayed as being on the wrong side. Crime, increasing problems in the homes of America, and welfare fraud were destroying morale. It was a time when America seemed to have lost its soul. Was all this some kind of bizarre coincidence, or was there more going on than really met the eye?

As a preterist, I could not understand the meaning of these events. I certainly did believe in the providential operations of God; being part of a denomination that held to Calvinistic doctrine of divine sovereignty, I did not believe that anything was happening by accident—certainly not based on "luck." History seemed to be going nowhere and the events that I was reading about in the newspapers seemed to have nothing to do with the Bible other than being a sad testimony to the depravity of the human heart. These events certainly did not seem to have anything to do with one of the major doctrines of the Bible—one that is mentioned some three hundred times in the New Testament—the return of Christ.

I came to sense that there was something drastically wrong with my eschatology, that is, my view of "last things." I was in a church that held to covenant theology and had heard, many times, of the errors and even "heresies of dispensationalism." So, dissatisfied with a-millennialism, my only viable eschatological option at that time seemed to be post-millennialism. At least it seemed to deal in a more biblically responsible fashion with a text that I had stumbled over many times as an a-millennialist—Romans 11.

Most of my readers associate post-millennialism with theological liberalism and the erroneous notion that man is evolving upwards. However, I found that many of the Puritans were post-millennial, along with other Reformed thinkers such as Jonathan Edwards, who looked forward to a "latter-day glory" on earth. These men were certainly not theological liberals.

Moreover, back in the seventies there was a new and exciting movement. It was thoroughly Reformed, academically respectable, and seemed to be biblically sound. I was impressed with the bombastic scholarship of Gary North, and the detailed studies of Old Testament law by Greg Bahnsen, Rousas John Rushdoony, and others in the Christian Reconstruction Movement.

Though I believed that post-millennialism deals with some important issues that are brushed aside by a-millennialism, I realized that it too has some major problems. For one thing, it allegorizes large portions of prophecy, and consequently has the church inheriting Israel's promises. It also puts what I believe is a misguided emphasis on Old Testament law. Reconstructionists believe that the law of "the Older Testament," to use a pet phrase, is ultimately to be imposed on all of society. It is only in this way, according to their view, that Jesus Christ can truly be "Lord of all."

There are other aspects of a Christian Reconstruction/post-millennial view that I believe is out of keeping with Scripture. By failing to see the distinctions between Israel and the church, those in this camp ultimately end up by Judaizing the New Testament. They fail to miss the distinctly unique characteristics of the present Church Age. Desiring to maintain one over-arching covenant of grace for all redemptive history since the fall, Israel loses its promises, the church becomes an extension of the theocratic kingdom, and the return of Christ is viewed in an anticlimactic manner. After all, when you have Christianized the entire world, the return of Christ is not really that significant.

I believe that pre-millennial dispensationalism has none of these shortcomings. It is the only eschatological position that avoids teaching that the present age is the kingdom. In this way it maintains the distinctive features of the kingdom of God as presented in Scripture and reminds us that one day soon the Messiah's New World Order will be established.

Part One

The Challenge

Chapter 1

Preterism: Its Leading Features

Gary North, a leading Christian Reconstructionist and avid preterist, wrote the publisher's preface to Kenneth Gentry's *The Beast of Revelation,* a well-researched volume that seeks to advance the view that "The Beast" of Revelation 13 was a first-century individual.

North opens his preface by writing, "'Oh boy! A new book on Bible prophecy!' It certainly is. But it is not a book about the future." North feels that this is a terribly important, and practical, subject. He states that if Gentry's

> ... thesis is correct, the "last days" are not ahead of us; they are long behind us. And if the "last days" are behind us, then all "futurism"—dispensationalism, most contemporary non-dispensational pre-millennialism, and the more popular forms of a-millennialism—is dead wrong. Anyone who says that "dark days are ahead of the Church because the Man of Sin is surely coming" is a futurist. Thus, this book is not simply an obscure academic exercise. If futurists prove incapable of refuting it and its larger companion volume, they have surrendered their intellectual position.

North believes that wrong thinking leads to wrong action which, in this case, means no action. Under a centered and bold heading that reads, "This Book Is About Hope," North explains:

> If the rapture is just around the corner, then the beast and the antichrist are in our midst already, preparing to take advantage of every opportunity to deceive, persecute, and tyrannize the world generally and Christians in particular. This would mean that all attempts by Christians to improve this world through the preaching of the gospel and obedience to God's Word are doomed. There would be insufficient time to reclaim anything from the jaws of inevitable eschatological defeat. This is precisely what dispensationalists believe, as I hope to demonstrate in this subsection.

North has definitely not misread the book in which his preface appears. After giving his "proofs" that Revelation 1:7—"and every eye shall see him"—is really a reference to the spiritual coming of Christ in judgment on Israel in A.D. 70, author Kenneth Gentry writes:

> This evidence removes any possibility of identifying the Beast with any figure beyond the first century. To assert that the Beast is any contemporary figure existing in our own time is to miss the total point of what John spoke about.

Gentry's view that Christ has already "come" is a common preterist view. Gary DeMar, author of *Last Days Madness*, which is perhaps the definitive work on preterism, pulls no punches.

> Jesus "coming" in judgment upon Jerusalem and His coming "up to the Ancient of Days" (Daniel 7:13; Matthew 24:30) were two events that occurred within the time span of the first generation of Christians. There is no future fulfillment of these events.

An oft-repeated sign in the Olivet Discourse that the return of Christ is near is the presence of false teachers. "For many shall come in my name, saying, I am Christ; and shall deceive many. ... And many false prophets shall rise, and shall deceive many" (Matt. 24:5, 11). With their view of prophecy, however, preterists are unmoved by the growing apostasy in the church and the increase in false teachers. We are not living in times of growing apostasy as prophesied by Scripture. Those days are long since gone. Preterist Gary DeMar explains:

> John offers evidence that it was "the last hour" (1 John 2:18): "They went out from us, but they were not really of us" (2:19). This is solid scriptural evidence, that the words of Jesus were fulfilled in the days of the apostles.

It is generally recognized that there are two brands of preterism: moderate preterism and extreme preterism. Moderate preterism claims that almost all prophecy has already been fulfilled in A.D. 70. This means that prophecies regarding the Beast and the Tribulation refer to past events. For the moderate preterist, the only prophecy that remains to be fulfilled is the physical return of Christ, something that is immediately followed by the end of the present order.

Extreme preterism, on the other hand, believes that all prophecy has been fulfilled, including those prophecies that speak of the physical return of Christ. Extreme preterism is sometimes known as "consistent preterism" because it consistently applies the principles of preterism to all prophecy. If moderate preterists were consistent, they unavoidably would be extreme preterists, and would have to deny the reality of the eternal state.

Preterists and the Book of Revelation

Preterists believe that the contemporary expectation of the human author of the book of Revelation controls the time of fulfillment. Ray Summers, a Southern Baptist and avowed preterist, objects to futurism on the grounds that it makes prophecy irrelevant for the generation in which the prophecy was given. In his commentary on the book of Revelation, Summers writes:

> One of the strongest objections to the futurist method is that it leaves Revelation altogether out of relation to the needs of the churches to which it was addressed, and which first received it. One of the basic principles of prophecy is that it takes its start with the generation to which it is addressed. Its first purpose is to meet an immediate need—to comfort, to instruct, to warn.

I don't believe that this is a valid conclusion. A prophecy can provide comfort, instruction, and warning by speaking of something that is still far in the future from the perspective of the readers. Second Peter 3:14 speaks of the final burning up of the universe, and yet Peter can write: "Wherefore, beloved, seeing that ye look for such things [things that are far yet in the future], be diligent that ye may be found of him in peace, without spot, and blameless." The argument that prophecy has to be fulfilled within the lifetime of the original recipients to have any meaning to the original audience doesn't stand the test of Scripture. If that were true, then there could be no meaningful prophecy about the return of Christ.

Consistent with this belief, preterists search first century "newspapers" to see what events fit in with their scheme of first-century fulfillment. Though futurists are often charged with practicing "newspaper exegesis," preterists are the real masters of the art. Interestingly, for the preterist, the closer we move to the time of the Lord's physical return, the *farther* we get from the events they believe are indicated in the book of Revelation.

Preterists do not believe that the book of Revelation is primarily about the Second Coming of Christ to earth or about eschatology, but rather that it deals with the destruction of Israel and the establishment of the church as "the New Covenant Temple." Though extreme preterists believe that Revelation chapters twenty-one and twenty-two have already been fulfilled, most preterists believe in a future fulfillment for those chapters and relate them to the eternal state. However, these chapters mainly "fill out" the picture. The main focus of the book, according to preterism, is on the events that were to shortly take place in the first century.

Preterism and Prophetic Themes

Preterists see prophetic events in a radically different way than futurists. The following presents a brief survey of how preterists understand key prophetic issues:

» *The Great Apostasy*—Preterists will argue that there has always been apostasy and that there is no distinct prophetic period that can be characterized as "The Great Apostasy." Preterists who are a-millennial believe that there will always be apostasy until the Lord returns. Preterists who are post-millennial, however, believe that the church will be progressively strengthened as the Holy Spirit is poured out in increasing measure. Rather than increasing, apostasy will decrease. Large numbers will be saved, and the church will be strengthened. Bible truth will be honored more and more "… for out of Zion shall go forth the law, and the word of the LORD from Jerusalem" (Isa. 2:3).

» *The Rapture*—While moderate preterists do believe that the saints will be resurrected and caught up with living believers at the return of Christ, they do not believe in a pre-Trib Rapture, or that anything follows this catching up other than the eternal state. They do not see a thousand-year period between the resurrection of the righteous and the resurrection of the wicked at the Great White Throne Judgment. "The Rapture" is a term preterists avoid because of its futuristic connotations. That the word "church" does not appear in Revelation chapters four through verse sixteen of chapter twenty-two, they say, does not indicate that the church has been removed from the earth but simply that it is not in God's purpose to mention it.

» *The Great Tribulation*—Tribulation and suffering has been the lot of faithful Christians since the ascension of Christ. Preterists contend that the period of tribulation that the Olivet Discourse and the book of Revelation speak of occurred in the first century, and there is no future Great Tribulation, abomination of desolation, or time of Jacob's trouble as envisioned by futurists.

» *The Antichrist*—Preterists want to identify some first-century individual, such as a Roman emperor, as the Antichrist. For them wicked, corrupt, and murderous Nero fits the bill quite well. Preterists believe that the passages in the book of Revelation concerning martyrs and the suffering of believers are fulfilled in first-century persecution of the first-century church. Preterists do not look for a future world leader who will be the biblical Antichrist.

» *The New World Order*—Preterists recognize the fact that there is a movement to unite the world, and that there is a growing economic and political interdependency between the nations of the world and a consequent loss of U.S. sovereignty. However, they do not view this as some kind of an indication that Tribulation prophecy is about to be fulfilled. It is simply the result of a growing technology that naturally causes the world to "shrink." For some preterists, this can be viewed as preparatory to the establishment of worldwide dominion by the church. The unification of the world into a global composite will open the way for the revivals of the future. Global Christian education and the universal acknowledgement of Jesus Christ as Lord and Savior make the post-millennial hope of a converted world prior to the return of the Lord much more feasible.

- » *The Millennial Kingdom*—Preterists believe that there is no future earthly millennial kingdom during which God's ancient promises to Israel are fulfilled. A-millennialists believe in a "gospel millennium," meaning that this present age of gospel preaching is identified with the thousand-year period of Revelation 20. In other words, we are now living in the "millennium." A-millennialists like to speak of "realized millennialism," indicating that the only millennium to be expected is what is currently being realized in the present day. Post-millennialists, on the other hand, believe that things will greatly improve. A-millennialists are therefore pessimistic preterists and postmillennialists optimistic ones.
- » *Israel*—It is the preterist view that God no longer has any special plans for the nation of Israel, though many post-millennialists believe that large numbers of Jews will be converted to Christ in the future and brought into the church.
- » *The Millennial Temple*—There is no literal, future earthly temple according to preterism. Since Christ is the fulfillment of the Old Testament types, there is no need for God to reinstitute the Mosaic system. This is one of their weaknesses. Millennial worship is not a reinstitution of the Mosaic system. There are many differences between the worship of Ezekiel forty through forty-eight, and worship in the Mosaic Age. At any rate, preterists apply these chapters in Ezekiel either to one of the historical Jewish temples that has already been built, or to the church. This is in keeping with their general practice of removing Israel from future prophecy.

Preterism and the Mark of the Beast

Preterists deny that the mark of the beast (Rev. 13:16–17) has anything to do with emerging technology. The idea that computer technology might be how the system of Antichrist is implemented is, according to DeMar, "nonsense."

He sees Revelation 13 as simply describing a tattoo, or a brand, that was used to brand slaves in the first century A.D. How could modern technology have anything to do with a Tribulation that is already in the past?

Futurists generally teach that the development of smart cards, global communications systems, microchips, and other high-tech devices show that, for the first time in the history of the world, the prophecies of the book of Revelation can now be fulfilled, and that everything is in place for the fulfillment of this Tribulation scenario.

Preterists ridicule this and argue that there was sufficient know-how in the first century to fulfill the mark-of-the-beast prophecy of Revelation 13. "A simple mark," writes DeMar, "for example a tattoo or a brand, could easily be made on the forehead and hand. Branding was a way to identify slaves and idolaters." To prove his point, DeMar cites 3 Maccabees 2:29 where we are told that Ptolemy Philopater enrolled the Jews of Alexandria and branded them with a red-hot iron, and that Philo mentions idolaters who acknowledged their idolatry by making indelible marks on their bodies. He argues that there is nothing new or especially high-tech about any of this. Ezekiel 9:4 speaks about a man clothed in linen who put a mark on the foreheads of the men who sigh and groan over the sins of Jerusalem. This mark was given for divine protection and is similar to the marks mentioned in Revelation 7:3; 9:4 and 14:1.

I believe that DeMar's examples do not prove what he hopes they do. Enrolling Jews in Alexandria is far different than enrolling the population of the world. Revelation 13:16–17 states: "And he causeth all, both small and great, rich and poor, free and bond, to receive a mark in their right hand … And that no man"—not just Jews in Alexandria or the idolaters mentioned by Philo—"might buy or sell, save he that had the mark, or the name of the beast, or the number of his name." All classes imaginable are included. There is status—the small and the great. There is property and possessions—the rich and the poor. There is the state of the individuals in society—free and bond. While a brand or tattoo might function adequately to keep track of a few hundred people, such a device is woefully inadequate for the multitudes described in Revelation 13.

Preterists seek to counter this objection by limiting the scope of the book of Revelation to the ancient Roman world. The fact that they must resort to this evasion, however, shows that they must radically alter the plain meaning of the text to support their theories. We will deal with this evasion in greater detail but suffice it to say for the time being that even if Revelation were limited to the ancient Roman world, there would probably still be more people involved than could be kept under surveillance using a tattoo or brand. Have you ever taken a church youth group on an outing and tried to keep track of just fifteen kids?

DeMar tries to make his most damaging point by looking at the particular Greek preposition used in Revelation 13. He cites a futurist writer who speaks about the mark being placed "in" the hand or forehead. The word "in" is explained by the futurist to be a reference to an embedded microchip or some similar device placed under the skin. DeMar objects to this, however. He observes that the Greek text uses the preposition *epi,* meaning "on" or "upon" instead of *en* usually translated as "in." Translated literally, Revelation 13:16 reads: "He causes all to receive a mark **on** their right hand or **on** their foreheads. ..." Both the Westcott-Hort text and the Textus Receptus read "on." However, while I admit that the preposition *epi* is used, this does not consign the futurist interpretation to sudden death.

If this mark were purely on the surface of the skin, the resultant loss of skin, as happens regularly in all people, would mean the mark would disappear. For this mark to have any degree of permanence it must, in some sense, be "in" the tissue. The use of *epi* doesn't really deny that. It is simply saying that the mark is visible to someone, or to some device such as a scanner. In fact, the word "mark" (*charagma*) comes from the verb *charasso* which means "to cut to a point, then to inscribe." It is really not farfetched to see the phrase as describing some kind of minor surgery—a "cutting to a point" for the insertion of a chip that will be "inscribed" with data.

The root issue is whether or not the mark is literal. DeMar feels that it isn't. He equates the mark of Revelation 13 with the mark that is given to the 144,000 by the Lamb. "Will Jesus implant a microchip in the foreheads of the 144,000?" he asks.

Here DeMar confuses things that must not be confused. As the eternal Son of God, Jesus Christ does not need some kind of a visible mark to help Him watch over the 144,000. The Antichrist and his minions, however, are not divine. They are mere creatures who are in rebellion against God. Mention of an invisible mark in one place of Scripture need not imply that the mark in all other places is invisible. "Water" that is drinkable need not imply that every reference in the Bible to "water" implies literal "water." The word "covet" is similar. It frequently has a negative meaning, but not so in 1 Corinthians 12:31 where we are told to "covet" the best gifts. Preterists often criticize futurists for what they call "selective literalism." They could be charged with the same thing.

Preterism spiritualizes Scripture, especially prophecy, by appealing to other scriptures to prove their point. In keeping with this tendency DeMar refers to "invisible" marks in the Bible which he claims were simply spiritual marks that are indications of God's special protection for that which is so marked. However, he creates the impression that the only marks in Scripture are invisible and symbolic ones, and that is not at all the case. Literal stones were piled up in the Jordan River to remind Israel of God's covenant mercy (Josh. 4:3) and would prompt the children to ask what they signified (vs. 6). In the same way, the literal Passover meal would lead the children to ask, "What mean ye by this service?" (Exod. 12:26; 13:13–15). Likewise, circumcision was not an invisible mark, but a very visible one, and involved the actual cutting of the foreskin of the male baby (Gen. 17). Covenant theologians love to spiritualize this by claiming that infant baptism is the sign and seal of the covenant of grace and is the New Covenant equivalent of an Old Testament ordinance.

Visible marks were not unusual in the ancient world and were described in Scripture. In Exodus 21:6, for example, we read that servants who refused to be set free but wanted to stay and serve their masters were to have their ears bored with an awl. This was to be done against a doorpost, evidently to assist in puncturing the earlobe. With so many literal and physical marks described in Scripture, why should we think that the mark of the beast is merely symbolic?

Preterism's Claim That Futurism Fails to Maintain the Integrity of Scripture

Preterism believes that futurism makes Jesus a liar and that only preterism maintains the integrity of Scripture over and against the charges of unbelieving sceptics.

> ... the integrity of Scripture is at stake. Critics of the Bible have studied Jesus' words in these passages and have concluded that He was wrong! Jesus predicted that He would return within a generation, as Matthew 24:34 clearly states, and He did not. The conclusion? The Bible cannot be trusted as a reliable book. It is filled with errors. The well-known atheist Bertrand Russell seized on what he perceived to be a mistake and concluded that the Bible was not trustworthy.

The integrity of Scripture is a serious issue, but it is highly doubtful if preterism can live up to its inflated claims about maintaining the integrity of Scripture before an unbelieving world. Do preterists think that Bertrand Russell, or anyone else who is antagonistic to the Christian faith, is going to be convinced that the Bible is God's Word by arguing that Jesus came in

A.D. 70? A preterist coming is a pathetic coming. It does no honor to Jesus Christ, or to the integrity of Scripture. Russell and company read in the New Testament of a coming described with the words:

> And they shall see the Son of man coming in the clouds of heaven with power and great glory. And he shall send his angels with a great sound of a trumpet, and they shall gather together his elect from the four winds …
> —Matthew 24:30–31

What happened in A.D. 70 can in no way match the event described by these words.

DeMar argues that it discredits the Bible to preach that "Jesus is coming soon." Someone could say, "Preachers like you have been telling us for decades that Jesus is coming soon. Why should we believe you now?" "Of course," DeMar quips, "if you cry 'last days' long enough, you might be the one to get it right, but by then there might not be anyone listening."

This charge, however, is not really a charge against futurism, but against Christ and His apostles. They presented the truth that "Jesus is coming soon, but no one knows just when." Even two thousand years ago the saints were "looking for that blessed hope, and the glorious appearing of the great God and our Saviour Jesus Christ" (Titus 2:13). James even writes, "the judge standeth before the door" (5:9).

Taking a highly allegorical approach to Scripture does nothing to make the Bible more credible in the eyes of non-believers. As a whole, evangelicals have generally taken Scripture in a literal, straightforward manner and continue to do so despite ridicule from the unbelieving world. The substitutionary atonement of Christ, the trinitarian nature of the Godhead, and many others, are all truths that come from Scripture, but also truths that invite the attack of agnostics, atheists, humanists, and secularists. Why is it, when we come to prophecy, that suddenly we must tailor our interpretation to suit non-believers? Paul Boyer's comments may shed some light on this strange inconsistency:

> Down to the Enlightenment, biblical apocalyptic was read with seriousness throughout Christendom, at all social and educational levels, for the clues it offered to God's divine plan. But as skepticism and rationalism gained ground in the eighteenth century, the academic and popular views of these texts gradually diverged. ... At the popular level, particularly in America, the apocalyptic texts remained what they had always been: a vital source of doctrine, reassurance, and foreknowledge. Ordinary believers continued to pore over their pages and to look expectantly for the events they found predicted there.

Preterism makes many bold claims about its own approach to Scripture and seeks to justify these claims by an appeal to the Bible. Where did preterism come from, and who are some of the leaders of the movement? We will seek to answer these questions in the chapter that follows.

Chapter 2

Preterism: Its Leading Figures

For those who are futurists, preterism seems unbelievably radical. But perhaps even more startling is the fact that some of the leading figures in American Christianity are preterists.

D. James Kennedy, for example, whose radio broadcasts and books have rightly won the hearts of many Christians is also involved in "reclaiming America," an endeavor which he finds perfectly consonant with his views on last things. According to Kennedy (who expects Christians to be actively involved in bringing every aspect of culture and society under the Lordship of Christ), Christians must work for victory. Hence Kennedy has been actively involved in confronting our decadent culture with the claims of Christ, something he feels is necessary in view of the so-called cultural mandate:

> I encounter far too many people who have a split personality about the authority of God. On the one hand, they believe the Great Commission and agree that they should support the work of evangelizing the lost. But when it comes to influencing the culture with Christian values—and when it comes to speaking out from a framework of Christian values in cultural, social, and political situations—they run for cover. If God is God, then He

is Lord of all. He is not just the Source of salvation but the very Wellspring of life. If God rules in our hearts, then He must also rule in our heads—every day and in every way. If you believe that God can save a lost soul, then you must believe that He can save our lost world. If Jesus Christ is the Lord of the Great Commission, then He is absolutely and without question the Lord of the *cultural mandate.*

Another leading figure on the contemporary Christian scene who is a preterist is R. C. Sproul. Well-known for his insightful analysis of false doctrine and the careful articulation of Bible doctrine presented in a Reformation garb, Sproul has influenced countless numbers of Christians in the direction of the "Reformed Faith"—Five Point Calvinism (TULIP) and covenant theology, something he shares in common with Kennedy.

Eschatologically, Dr. Sproul is a preterist. In his book, *The Last Days According to Jesus,* he argues from texts like Matthew 10:23 and Matthew 16:27–28 that the kingdom has already arrived. While Kennedy is more subdued in his preterism because he has such a broad evangelical audience and reaches them with the concept that "we can win this battle," Sproul's emphasis is more distinctively Reformed and covenantal. Sproul has dealt in a more forthright manner with issues such as predestination, infant baptism, and replacement theology, since he is less concerned with alienating evangelicals who might not agree with him on these items of Presbyterian theology and seeks to appeal to those who are ready to make the switch to "the Reformed faith." Even the name of Sproul's daily radio broadcast, "Renewing Your Mind," shows that his target group is narrower than that of Kennedy's broadcasts, more popularly called "Truths That Transform."

How Did We Get to This Point?

Preterism, covenant theology, post-millennialism, Kingdom Now theology, dominion theology, the Christian Reconstruction movement, and theonomy are all related concepts. They are older views going back to the Puritans and the Westminster Divines and are reappearing with some modification and with renewed vigor.

How did these beliefs gain popularity at the present time, and why are they so attractive to so many? In order to answer these questions, we want to look at the history of what has been a trend to "re-Christianize" America, and to develop churches that ultimately hold to an "eschatology of victory."

Our survey will begin in the middle of the twentieth century with a man by the name of Rousas John Rushdoony, an individual who has rightly been called "the father of the Christian Reconstruction movement." A prolific writer with a keen insight into the ongoing struggle between God and Satan, Rushdoony has turned out books, pamphlets, and articles on the relevance of the Old Testament law to culture, education, politics, and government. Rushdoony not only challenged Christians to drop what he considered to be a defeatist otherworldly attitude—a "Rapture escapism"—but sought to show the relevance of biblical law to government and how the application of biblical law would make America a better place to live. With the hippie revolution of the sixties, and the growing disenchantment of the Christian right with the anti-war protesters of the Vietnam War era, many conservatives in America were looking for a strong Christian voice that endorsed such concepts as a just war, capital punishment, and a strong work ethic that would do more for solving the welfare problem than liberal handouts to the poor.

At the time that Rushdoony's popularity was growing, many Christians were of the opinion that something needed to be done that would be both biblical and positive. Rushdoony's Reformed theology had certain strong affinities with Puritanism and the religious forces molding early American history. Was the real problem with America due to the fact that America had lost sight of its godly heritage? Many answered in the affirmative. Rushdoony provided Christians with what appeared to be a biblical plan for reforming America that was very similar to the ideas that made America great. Concepts of crime and punishment, justice, and equity, are all found in the Old Testament case laws. Can America become great once again by getting back to her theological roots? Dennis Woods, who writes from a dominionist point of view states:

> ... the Puritans believed that the equity (essential principle or meaning) of the Mosaic legislation applied directly to the administration of public justice. Even before their arrival in the New World, Elniff notes that they "began to search the Scriptures for the very forms and models they should use in reforming England, especially the church and its relation to the state, as well as the government of the church itself. ..."
>
> The Puritan allegiance to Scripture extended even to statutory Law. In describing the Puritan system of servitude, Morgan notes, "When a man stole from, or otherwise damaged another and could not make restitution in cash, he might be sold for a number of years to pay the bill." This is a direct application of Exodus 22:1–3.

The Puritans were heavily indebted to Old Testament law and felt that the application of the Old Testament case laws to the ethical and moral needs of society would solve many problems. In this sense, they were really seeking to institute a theocracy, or as reconstructionist like to call it, a "Christocracy." Later in this volume we will look at the ways in which Old Testament law is misunderstood, and misapplied, by preterists. Their use of the law is integrated with their eschatology.

At any rate, dominionists have a high view of the law and its applicability to contemporary society. Perhaps the work that projected Rushdoony into the arena of international acclaim is his massive *The Institutes of Biblical Law*, published in 1973 by the Craig Press. The subheading sounds impressive and was calculated to draw a readership of thinking Christians: "A Chalcedon

Study with three appendices by GARY NORTH." The book is 890 pages in length, well written, and extensively footnoted. It looks like a scholarly tome, and it really is. It is thorough, bold, and the many references to contemporary problems show that the author is familiar with contemporary issues. His commitment to the Old Testament and the New Testament, understood from a reconstructionist perspective, is also obvious.

Rushdoony deals with the question of "Christ and the Law" and seeks to remove the common evangelical misunderstanding of the use of the law in the present age. "The cross of Christ is often cited as being the death of the law, and it is commonly stated that in Christ the believer is dead to the law," writes Rushdoony. He seeks to counter this objection by reminding his readers that Ephesians 2:10 states that Christians are God's "workmanship, created in Christ Jesus unto good works." Rushdoony concludes, "Plainly, therefore, we are regenerated 'unto good works,' that is, unto obedience to God's law word. ..."

Appealing to many conservatives who are unhappy with the courts' "soft" attitude toward criminals, Rushdoony believes that a society based on biblical law would rectify this problem. "Self-confessed rapists and murderers have been freed on imaginary technicalities, in clear partiality to the criminal as against the victim." He quotes from a Los Angeles newspaper, appearing June 3, 1968, where it is stated that the Supreme Court "declared that 'The death sentence cannot be imposed by a jury from which persons with conscientious or religious scruples against capital punishment were automatically excluded.'" This is ludicrous for Rushdoony, who comments: "In other words, the court demanded that people who *deny* the validity of the law be asked to 'enforce' the law!"

Rushdoony, and a growing rank of followers, have had a tremendous appeal to evangelicals who feel that most Christians have lost sight of the majesty and glory of God, and who are careless in their walk with Christ. Because Christians have "made God after man's own image," many in the church have lost a sense of reverence for God, a note frequently sounded by others in the Reformed camp, such as R. C. Sproul. In discussing the third commandment—"Thou shalt not take the name of the Lord thy God in vain"—Rushdoony approvingly quotes John Calvin. In the following quotation from Calvin, note how the two elements of worship and divine majesty are brought together:

> It is silly and childish to restrict this [our understanding of the third commandment] to the name of Jehovah, as if God's majesty were confined to letters or syllables; but whereas His essence is invisible, His name is set before us as an image, in so far as God manifests Himself to us, and is distinctly made known to us by His own marks, just as men are each by his own name. On this ground Christ teaches that God's name is comprehended in the heavens, the earth, the temple, the altar (Matt. 5:34), because His glory is conspicuous in them. Consequently, God's name is profaned whenever any detraction is made from His supreme wisdom, infinite power, justice, truth, clemency, and rectitude. If a shorter definition is preferred, let us say that His name is what Paul calls " that which may be known" of Him (Rom. 1:19).

Preterism, and the other trends associated with it, has had such a marked increase in following because it provides apparently biblical answers to many of the problems in the contemporary evangelical church. The church has many shortcomings, and preterism and its allies can "fix" them.

Do we see the contemporary church consumed with a "millennial madness" and needless prophetic speculation? Preterism will certainly take care of that. Has the church lost sight of the majesty and glory of God, substituting mindless choruses for the great Reformation hymns of the past which were remarkable for their doctrinal content? Well, Reformed theology will take care of that.

And what about the empty results of "decisionism"? Hundreds of thousands of people make "decisions for Christ" at crusades and in local churches, yet most don't seem to "stick." What's wrong? Why isn't our society changed if all these people are really born again? Might Calvinism shed some light on this contemporary failing of the church?

Reformed preterists are Calvinists. Calvinism is the view that salvation is all of grace, and that grace is all of God. Even the faith to believe in Christ comes from God. Why does one person come to faith, and another reject the gospel? The Calvinist's answer is: "Because one is elect, and the other is not."

Historically, Presbyterianism teaches "double predestination." Some are predestinated to heaven, and some are predestinated to hell. T-U-L-I-P describes the whole system:

» **T**otal Depravity—Human beings are totally corrupted in all their faculties, including mind and will. Even when Christ is effectively presented to the lost person, because of this innate depravity, the lost person does what is consistent with his fallen nature—he rejects the solution to his problems. Calvinists believe that no one comes to Christ unless God first changes the will. Many evangelicals believe that regeneration follows faith. Calvinists teach that regeneration precedes faith.

» **U**nconditional Election—The elect are chosen to salvation purely on the basis of God's inscrutable will. Calvinists do not believe that God foresees the faith that the elect will exercise when presented with the gospel. It is not election on the basis of foreseen faith, but election solely on the basis of God's will. There is nothing in man that moves God to elect one and reject the other.

» **L**imited Atonement—Since God has His elect, Christ only died for them. C. H. Spurgeon, who was a "TULIP" Calvinist, calls this point "particular redemption." Christ died with a particular goal in view—to pay for the sins of the elect, and no one else. The death of Christ did not make possible the salvation of those who believe. Ultimately, the death of Christ was to secure the redemption of those whom God has elected unto salvation from before time began.

» **Irresistible Grace**—Grace is given to the elect. But can't they reject the grace of God? The Calvinist answers in the negative. Because they are elect, God changes their will so that they will want to receive the grace of God. Remember, regeneration, in this scheme, precedes faith. When a person is regenerated, that person does what he or she wants to do—receive Christ.

» **Perseverance of the Saints**—All those whom God has chosen in eternity past will come to faith in Christ and, because of the operations of God's grace, will persevere in that faith. Calvinists dislike the phrase "eternal security," though, in principle, they would agree with it. "Eternal security" connotes someone making a "decision" for Christ—signing a card, walking an aisle, raising a hand—who follows the teachings of the Christian faith for a short time, but then, suddenly, drops out of church and out of sight spiritually speaking. Is that person saved? Many evangelicals would say "yes"—"once saved, always saved." Calvinists, however, would claim that to be a distortion of the grace of God. A person who is saved will persevere in the faith because of God's promises to His elect.

It is not surprising, then, with the many shortcomings of contemporary evangelicalism, that Calvinism is growing in popularity, along with its sister, preterism. Calvinists associate pre-millennialism with "easy believism," "decisional regeneration," and a popular brand of pre-Tribulational eschatology that allegedly has no basis in the Word of God. Quite often, when Christians move in the direction of Calvinism, they also move in the direction of preterism.

Though this volume is about eschatology, the growing popularity of preterism is tied in with the growing popularity of the so-called "doctrines of sovereign grace." Preterists, covenant theologians, postmillennialists, and their bedfellows, not only hold common views regarding eschatology but they hold common views regarding soteriology.

Dominionism in Another Camp

Christian Reconstruction is the staunchly Calvinistic, Presbyterian, and Reformed wing of the movement. However, charismatics have their own brand of Christian Reconstruction known as "Kingdom Now" theology. Barron observes that

> ... the idea of Christian dominion, though with less emphasis on biblical law, has been echoed within the charismatic movement, that segment of American Christianity identified by its free-spirited demonstrative worship and its practice of spiritual gifts such as tongues speaking and prophecy.

Moreover, Kingdom Now theology generally persuades its critics through music and "victorious praise services" and appeals to the emotions. On the other hand, Christian Reconstruction was born out of conflict, and reconstructionists are not afraid of theological conflict. In fact, some of them seem to relish the opportunity to parade their learning and look for opportunities to flaunt their ability to refute those who believe otherwise.

While many evangelicals who have a broadly pluralistic sociopolitical horizon are willing to be flexible in certain areas of theological differences, reconstructionists are far less willing to surrender any item of theological conviction. In this way "the dominionists have selected the path of resistance, openly confronting both the prevailing culture and the fellow evangelicals they accuse of having accommodated to that culture." This has led to bombastic, and often insulting, rhetoric that leaves the impression that reconstructionists are engaged in what they believe to be some kind of a "holy war."

Jabs at dispensationalists are everywhere, as in Gary North's dedication of his book *Rapture Fever: Why Dispensationalism Is Paralyzed,* which reads:

> This book is dedicated to Kenneth L. Genry, Jr. whose books would have paralyzed the dispensational theologians of this generation, had it not been for one thing: their constant revisions to the system had already paralyzed each other.

This utter contempt for dispensationalism can be seen throughout Reformed circles. R. C. Sproul's theological and spiritual mentor, John H. Gerstner, has authored a scathing critique of dispensationalism. Sproul, who has written the foreword, sees the book as a challenge to the vast majority of evangelicals who hold to some form of dispensationalism:

> This current work on Dispensationalism by Dr. John H. Gerstner will be equally explosive on the American evangelical scene. It is a hard book in that it strikes against a theological system that is the majority of report among current American evangelicals. Gerstner is convinced that nothing less than the gospel is at stake here and hence it is not a time for timidity.

Indeed, this is not an overstatement. Gerstner, along with most other Presbyterian and Reformed writers believes that dispensationalism is, ultimately, heretical and a serious perversion of the Gospel, as can be seen by some of the chapter titles and subheadings in Gerstner's book: "Dispensational Perseverance of the Saints Is the Preservation of the Sinner," "Dubious Evangelicalism: The Dispensational Understanding of 'Dispensation' Denies the Gospel," "Dubious Evangelicalism: The 'Kingdom Offer' to the Jews Undermines the Gospel …"

Dominionism and the Christian Right

We may chuckle at the thought that the Tribulation is past, and we are now in the Kingdom Age, and the belief that Christians will regain dominion over American society and eventually the entire world. However, "its intellectual substance, internal coherence, and heavy dependence on Scripture have helped reconstructionist philosophy win a hearing in many sectors of the Christian Right.

Dominionism and the Pluralism

Those who identify themselves with the Christian Right find strong ideological ties with the Christian Reconstruction movement. Both groups want to impact society and maintain strong biblical views. But though there are ties between the two, there is not an identity.

> Whereas the Moral Majority affirmed political pluralism, agreeing that persons of any religion or no religion have equal rights to participate in government, reconstruction just as openly rejects pluralism and cites "the moral obligation of Christians to recapture every institution for Jesus Christ."

Rushdoony, and others in his camp, see pluralism as a contradiction of basic Christian beliefs. To acknowledge pluralism as a valid societal dynamic is to infringe on the sovereign rights of God. It would be equivalent to supporting the presence of a Canaanite on the city council during the Mosaic era.

Reconstructionists support family values, industry and hard work, integrity, and honesty. But while there are many in America's conservative camp—Christians and non-Christians, Roman Catholics, Mormons, Jews, and others—reconstructionists, with their strong Calvinistic outlook on history and individual salvation, are not to be lumped into the conservative "stew," so to speak. A Christian reconstructionist is a Christian who wants to penetrate every area of life—political, scientific, and cultural—for the purpose of transforming society so that it ultimately becomes a society that is distinctly Christian and is based on the activity of Christians rather than the activity of conservative people who support so-called traditional values. "Many evangelicals want to change the world," observes Barron, "but only the dominionists insist that they must run it."

The Three Pillars of Reformed Dominionism

In this study I am going to primarily confine myself to Christian Reconstruction, which is the Presbyterian and Reformed brand of "Kingdom Now" theology. It is perhaps the fastest growing, most anti-dispensational, and most coherent form of preterism which, because of the literary and theological skills of its proponents, is having the greatest impact on Christians.

Biblical Law

Earlier I presented Rushdoony's *Institutes of Biblical Law*. Another work which is equally influential and perhaps more systematically polemical is Greg Bahnsen's *Theonomy in Christian Ethics*. The foreword is by Rushdoony. In the opening of the book, Bahnsen masterfully shows how, in his understanding of things, civil law, ethics, and eschatology are all part of the same package and thus relates the theonomic Christian state to the kingdom of God on earth. He writes:

> As the early church formulated its creeds it simultaneously reformulated civil law. Such a correlation was inevitable since, against the ancient pagan

> tradition that located the source of authority and immorality in the polis [city state], orthodox Christian creedalism asserted the sovereignty of the Creator over history and the incursion of the Messianic God-man into history. Thus, the early creeds were a declaration concerning, not only theology proper, but eschatology and ethics ...

Bahnsen faults Thomas Aquinas and other theologians from the Middle Ages because their inconsistent views of God, man, and revelation allowed certain areas of life to remain outside the purview of God's authority on earth. However,

> ... John Calvin broke with the view that the state was autonomous, arguing for the sole rule of Christ over both church and state. ... He reopened the way to a Christian view of the state, taking it to be subject, not to the church, but only to the laws of God.

Old Testament law is a major ingredient in the "eschatology of victory" associated with Reformed preterism. In fact, the Christian is not simply to personally obey every aspect of divine law in exhaustive detail, the Christian is also to work tirelessly to impose God's law on all of society and to demand obedience to that law. "The Christian must take it upon himself to encourage, exhort, and demand obedience to God's holy standards of morality in home, church, society, place of employment, and nation," writes Bahnsen; "otherwise these institutions or groups will be progressively degraded by sinful rebellion against God and His law."

Post-millennial Eschatology
Lest I misrepresent what they believe, I ought to emphatically state that the post-millennialism of the Christian Reconstruction movement is not the watered-down, rosy, optimistic post-millennialism of liberals and non-believing humanists.

Reconstructionists rightly point out that they are often misrepresented by evangelicals who equate post-millennialism with the belief of many liberal Protestants before World War I that man is, somehow, evolving upward, and with such a steady improvement that the world will eventually get better and better—a view that was, at least for the time being, dashed to pieces by a world engulfed in war. Quite to the contrary, reconstructionists, in keeping with their view of human depravity and the innate corruption of the human heart, believe that it is only through the regenerating work of God that there will be any improvement. They believe that it is in the will and "electing purposes" of God to convert more and more people through the preaching of the gospel, people who will themselves embrace a dominionist theology and be actively involved in transforming the world. Reconstructionists see dispensationalism as one of the greatest hindrances to this realization.

Reconstructionists believe that the Tribulation spoken of in the Olivet Discourse, and in chapters six through nineteen of the book of Revelation, was fulfilled in A.D. 70. The Beast of Revelation 13 is not a future individual, but rather a reference to someone who lived in the first century, perhaps the Roman emperor Nero. Consequently, the gloom and doom erroneously anticipated by futurists as coming upon the world in the near future, has already come and is long past. Revelation 20:1–6, with its binding of Satan for one thousand years, is not to be taken as a literal time period, nor is this period to be equated with any Old Testament prophecy of a future golden age on earth. Rather, Revelation 20 describes the present age in which more and more individuals are coming under the rule and reign of Jesus Christ. While pre-millennialists are sure that the "end" is near and that end-time events are beginning to unfold at the present time, post-millennialists believe that the real "end" could very well be many thousands of years in the future.

There are various views in reconstructionist circles regarding precisely how all of this kingdom growth will take place. Some have believed that there will be chaos and anarchy in the near future—such as we are seeing today—

but that Christians, by applying biblical law to political and social issues—will have such tremendous success that the unbelieving world will be convinced by the wisdom of Scripture and thereby put Christians in places of world leadership. Others have talked about some kind of a societal crisis—such as could be generated by a terrorist attack, a nuclear war, or a global pandemic-type crisis—that would leave the world in shambles but providing an opportunity for Christians to come and pick up the pieces and institute God's new world order through the application of biblical law.

Presuppositional Apologetics

The third pillar of dominionism is presuppositional apologetics. The word "apologetics" means "a defense." A Christian apologist is not someone who apologizes for the Christian faith, but rather someone who defends it against the attacks of those who are hostile against Christianity and who claim that there are errors in the Bible, inconsistencies and incongruities in biblical ethics, and various other problems that would render the Christian faith erroneous or even fallacious. Scripture states that Christians are to be "ready always to give an answer [*apologia*] to every man that asketh you a reason of the hope that is in you with meekness and fear" (1 Pet. 3:15).

Speaking in very broad terms, there are two types of apologetics: evidentialism and presuppositionalism. Evidentialists believe that the Christian apologist must appeal to logic and reason to show that Christianity is credible and reasonable. After all, evidentialists argue, didn't the apostle state: "Knowing therefore the terror of the Lord, we PERSUADE men" (2 Cor. 5:11). The evidentialist wants to use the evidence: historical, linguistic, and archaeological evidence that supports the reliability of Scripture. Scientific data showing a young earth, for example, would be considered "evidence" that confirms the biblical account that the earth was created in six days. That many of the Mosaic requirements regarding childbirth, health, and hygiene, and so on, conform to established scientific procedure accepted today would also be considered "evidence" that man did not write the Bible. In a day when the ancient Egyptians were applying the most bizarre "cures" to people, the Mosaic legislation shows an amazing understanding of health and hygiene. This is another strand of evidence that evidentialists would use to convince the nonbeliever that the Bible is God's Word.

On the other hand, presuppositionalists argue that all this evidence-gathering is really futile. Sinners are totally depraved—remember TULIP?—and therefore sinners will always misread the evidence and come up with the wrong conclusions. Moreover, no one will really change unless the apologist is able to understand their presuppositions—their core beliefs that are believed, not because of any logical reasons, but because of other factors. Presuppositionalists believe that all the conclusions people make from the evidence that is available to them is really based on their presuppositions about ultimate issues. If an individual, for example, presupposes that miracles just don't happen, all of the arguments showing that miracles do happen will be rejected. Even if the person is backed against a wall, he will still say something like: "While I can't explain how that happened, I still don't believe that it had a miraculous cause. I believe that there must be some logical explanation to it even if I don't know what it is."

One might wonder how a particular approach to apologetics is tied in with the Christian Reconstruction movement. Simply because it gives reconstructionists a theological basis upon which to deny the existence of natural law. Being strong Calvinists, reconstructionists want to emphasize that both man and nature are under the Edenic curse. To say that a lost person can look at nature and come up with "truth" about reality is to deny both the fallenness of man and the necessity of divine revelation.

Because of this, reconstructionists believe that there is no common ground from which both believers and non-believers may search for truth. "Presuppositionalism uses this radical denial of common ground to declare all humanly devised social systems invalid," writes Barron. "In place of these false systems, reconstructionists assert the divinely-revealed, binding nature of biblical law." It is for this reason that reconstructionists tend to reject the political efforts of the Moral Majority to appeal to common moral values. To do so represents a kind of philosophical incoherence leading to a compromise with the humanistic myths of pluralism and religious neutrality. Reconstructionists, because of their strong presuppositionalism, will affirm "there is no religious neutrality."

This is an important point with reconstructionists. They realize that much of what they believe is to be applied from Scripture to today's world will seem harsh and cruel to most people. Take, for example, the death penalty. Rushdoony observes that "the death penalty is required by Scripture for a number of offenses." Some of the offenses he lists include striking or cursing a parent, kidnapping, adultery, incest, bestiality, sodomy, unchastity, rape of a betrothed virgin, witchcraft, offering human sacrifice, incorrigible delinquency or habitual criminality, blasphemy, sabbath desecration, propagation of false doctrines, sacrificing to false gods, and others. He mentions the methods of capital punishment as outlined in the Bible: burning, stoning, hanging, and the sword. Rushdoony, who evidently approves of such methods for today's criminal, nevertheless realizes: "To the humanistic mind these penalties seem severe and unnecessary. In actuality, the penalties, together with the biblical faith which motivated them, worked to reduce crime." However, on the basis of the presupposition that natural reason is an unreliable guide, these "biblically-sanctioned" behaviors are no more unreasonable than the blood atonement of Christ.

Cornelius Van Til was perhaps the leading presuppositionalist and has had a tremendous influence on the Christian Reconstruction movement. Profoundly moved by the writings of two Dutch Calvinists, Abraham Kuyper and Herman Baninck, Van Til studied at Calvin College and Seminary in Grand Rapids, Michigan, the mecca of Dutch-Calvinistic thought in America. Van Til then went to Princeton and completed his seminary training with honors and became professor of apologetics at that institution in 1928.

In 1929, when the General Assembly of the Presbyterian Church reorganized Princeton Seminary's Board of Trustees and thereby frustrated the effort of the conservatives to bring a halt to the school's liberal trends, Van Til and three other Princeton professors resigned their professorship and joined the faculty of the newly formed Westminster Theological Seminary in Philadelphia. Van Til continued to teach there for almost half a century.

Van Til's approach to apologetics appealed both to those who wanted a philosophically-consistent, intellectually-credible approach to apologetics as well as maintaining Calvinistic distinctives such as absolute predestination, total depravity, and a covenantal view of history. Barron observes:

> Since God, Van Til argued with classic Calvinist logic, fully and sovereignly determines all history and defines all truth, humans can find truth not by thinking originally but only *analogically*—that is, by discovering and following what God has already thought. Christianity is the only belief system that makes sense of the world; all other systems, by introducing an element of human autonomy, negate the Christian principle that God has defined all things and imply instead that the universe is irrational, pervaded by chance. No mediating position is possible ... "a little autonomy involves absolute autonomy."

Rushdoony and His Followers

Rushdoony has had several followers, including Gary North, who married Rushdoony's daughter in 1972. In that year North, who has a Ph.D. in economic history, served for a short time on the Washington staff of Ron Paul, a Texas congressman who saw the dangers of big government, especially in terms of creating the potential for government intrusiveness.

In 1981, David Chilton, another one of Rushdoony's admirers, wrote a book entitled *Productive Christians in an Age of Guilt-Manipulators—A Biblical Response to Ronald J. Sider.* Sider had written *Rich Christians in an Age of Hunger* and lambasted well-to-do Christians in a way that led some evangelicals to consider Sider to be a "communist." Chilton's *Productive Christians* was dedicated to Pat Robertson, who was labeled by Chilton in the dedication as "'a productive Christian' who is leading God's people to victory." The cover of Chilton's book is satirical and features posters sporting statements, some of which read: "Foreign Aid for Canaanites," "Hail Seizer!" "Exhaling Pollutes," "Be Fruitful and Subtract," "Oppressive Taxation Builds Character," and several others. Chilton's "response" to Sider won the hearts of multiplied numbers of evangelicals because he aimed his book at those who demand complete government control over every area of life under the stated goal of "caring for the poor." Chilton ridiculed that and argued that what the government really wants is power. Rather than loving God's way, an oppressive government believes that a socialist state is morally better than free enterprise, charged Chilton.

Another follower greatly influenced by Rushdoony was Greg Bahnsen who, in a real sense, can be called "the high priest of biblical law." Bahnsen studied under Van Til at Westminster Seminary and became the first student in the history of that institution to complete both the M.Div. and Th.M. degrees within three years. In 1977, the Craig Press published Bahnsen's *Theonomy in Christian Ethics,* a scholarly, extensively footnoted, six-hundred-page defense of the applicability of Old Testament law to today's world. After the dedication page, Bahnsen quotes J. Gresham Machen (Presbyterianism's articulate defender of the orthodox Christian faith) who wrote that "a new and more powerful proclamation of that law is perhaps the most pressing need of the hour." Machen's statement, used by Bahnsen, goes on to state "a low view of law always brings legalism in religion; a high view of law makes a man a seeker after grace." There is also a quote from Van Til which reads:

"There is no alternative but that of theonomy and autonomy."

It is by including these statements by leading Reformed scholars in his book that Bahnsen sought to show that to be "truly Reformed," one must have a high view of the law of God. In the foreword to *Theonomy in Christian Ethics*, Bahnsen seeks to show the importance of a right (according to Bahnsen) view of **law** and ties this in with a dominion eschatology of victory:

> By redeeming and restoring man in God's image, Jesus Christ restored man to his creation mandate, to subdue the earth by means of science, agriculture, the arts, commerce and industry, education, and every other legitimate human pursuit, and to exercise dominion over all things under God. The purpose of the law has from the beginning been this task. Salvation is by the grace of God through faith, and sanctification is by law. Because God's law has been abandoned by the modern church, both evangelical and reformed, it has, first, restricted holiness to things personal. Clearly, sanctification inescapably begins in the heart of man, but it cannot rest there. The man who is being progressively sanctified will inescapably sanctify his home, school, politics, economics, science, and all things else by understanding and interpreting all things in terms of the word of God and by bringing all things under the dominion of Christ the King.

Bahnsen's case for the abiding validity of the laws of "the Older Testament" (to use his terminology) can be summarized in the following way:

1. The Law of God, as revealed to Israel under the old covenant is perfect.
2. Old Testament scriptures demonstrate that God judged the gentile neighbors of Israel according to the same standards revealed in the law.
3. While the cross of Christ cancelled certain "ceremonial" aspects of

the law, Christ confirmed both the moral and civil aspects of that law. This can be seen in a passage like Matthew 5:17 where Jesus stated that He came to "fulfill" the law.
4. Therefore, Old Testament law is binding upon all people today and must be enforced.

While it is true that Jesus Christ stated that He came to fulfill the law, this does not necessarily mean what reconstructionists want it to mean. Jesus fulfilled Old Testament law in several ways.

1. He obeyed it perfectly and satisfied its perfect demands.
5. Both by His life and His teaching, Jesus revealed its true meaning.
6. He is the anti-type of its types and shadows.
7. He offers a salvation that meets all the requirements of that law. Hence, those who put their faith in Christ have an "honorable pardon."

Bahnsen has had a tremendous impact on several individuals within the Presbyterian and Reformed community. In the years 1976 to 1978, while teaching at Reformed Theological Seminary in Jackson, Mississippi, Bahnsen made an indelible impression on Kenneth Gentry who, early in his Christian life, was a dispensationalist, but became very dissatisfied with what he considered to be its "Rapture escapism" and an antinomian view of the Christian life. Gentry has been an avid defender of historic post-millennialism and has written scholarly articles defending the pro-life position. In his book *The Beast of Revelation 666,* Gentry seeks to prove that the book of Revelation was written around A.D. 68 and uses this to support his view that "the end" came in A.D. 70 with the Roman invasion of Jerusalem.

Aside from the individuals I have already mentioned, other key figures in the Reconstruction movement are Joe Moorecraft, Gary DeMar, James Jordan, and George Grant.

Chapter 3

Preterism: Its Leading Ally

Once upon a time ...

One day a new Christian was speaking to a Christian friend. The friend told him that at his church they baptize infants because infants are included in God's covenant.

The young Christian protested. "How can you baptize infants when there is not a single example in the New Testament of an infant being baptized?"

"Infants have always been included in God's covenant," said the friend. "If God has changed this in the New Testament era, it is natural to expect that God would have told us. Since God hasn't told us not to baptize infants, we believe that they are still supposed to receive baptism as a sign and seal of the covenant of grace which, in the New Testament church, is baptism in water."

"Do you mean that you believe that infant baptism is right because God has not specifically forbidden it?" the new Christian asked.

"That's right," his friend said. "Once God revealed that the children of believers in the Old Testament are special to Him and that they were to be circumcised as a sign of His love to them, we believe that the children of believers are still special. Unless God tells us differently, we are going to still believe that and baptize them in recognition of His love for them."

The new Christian didn't quite know how to respond to this. It seemed to make sense, but it just didn't sound right. What did his friend mean by speaking of the "covenant of grace," and how are infants included in this covenant? He knew that the "covenant" had something to do with an agreement between God and man, but how is it that little babies are somehow involved in this agreement?

His friend interrupted his thoughts and said: "At our church, we believe the *whole Bible,* not just the New Testament. We believe that too many Christians cut the Bible up and take only some of it as being applicable to Christians, but other parts are ignored because they believe those passages were for Israel. We don't agree with that. The church is the new Israel, and what was written to Israel is really for us."

"That's not what my pastor said," responded the new Christian." He said that God still has a plan for Israel that has not yet been fulfilled. It will only be fulfilled in the Millennium, when the Lord Jesus Christ comes to rule and reign on earth."

"Our church and denomination doesn't believe any of that," his friend said. "We hold to reformational theology. Israel has been disobedient to God and has been cast off. Besides, all of God's promises to Israel were fulfilled under Joshua. Let me read to you from Joshua 21:43–45 Listen to what the Scripture says: 'So the LORD gave Israel all the land he had sworn to give their forefathers, and they took possession of it and settled there. The LORD gave them rest on every side, just as he had sworn to their forefathers. Not one of their enemies withstood them; the LORD handed all their enemies over to them. Not one of all the LORD's good promises to the house of Israel failed; *every one was fulfilled.*'"

Who Is This Ally?

The "friend" in the preceding story attended a church that holds to covenant theology. This is the system of theology that is one of the pillars of the Reformed faith. It teaches that infant baptism is scriptural based on the covenant of grace, excludes Israel from any future prophetic fulfillments, and—because of its unique features regarding God's covenantal dealings with mankind—supports preterism, post-millennialism, and the Christian reconstructionist view of Old Testament law.

Covenant theology is at the opposite end of the theological spectrum from dispensationalism. They are radically different ways of looking at the history of redemption. Unfortunately, while people in the covenant camp are acutely aware of these differences and have been aggressively attacking the other side, most dispensationalists have been slow to realize the differences or the threat. One of the strange and inexplicable mysteries to me is how dispensationalism could be so viciously attacked by those in the covenant camp, and yet for decades there has hardly been any response from dispensationalists. Covenant theologians take this as a tacit admission of guilt. Treating these differences as merely minor points of no real significance, dispensationalists have generally ignored these issues and continued to "preach to the choir." Predictably, the choir has been listening to some other voices.

One of the basic features of covenant theology is the concept of "the one covenant of grace." This one covenant of grace is something like a dispensation, but it includes God's dealings with mankind recorded in the Old Testament scriptures from the fall of the race to Malachi and includes all of the New Testament era. In other words, Christians living in the twenty-first century are in the same redemptive era as the Old Testament saints. Gerstner writes:

> Covenant theology recognizes two overarching covenants which frame God's dealings with man—the covenant of works and the covenant of grace. The covenant of works was established between God and Adam ... and promised eternal life on condition of obedience. That covenant of

works was broken in the Fall and is no longer in effect—it being replaced by the covenant of grace. Covenant theology traces this single covenant of grace throughout Scripture.

A dispensation is usually defined by dispensationalists as a period of time during which man is tested regarding some specific revelation from God characteristic of that particular period. Dispensationalists recognize anywhere from four to seven dispensations and emphasize that Scripture must be interpreted dispensationally. Each passage of Scripture has its dispensational context. It was written to a particular people at a particular point in time. Covenant theology, however, feels that such distinctions are wrong and even dangerous. Again, to quote Gerstner:

> ... although the covenant of grace was administered in various ways throughout the Old and New Testaments, covenant theologians agree on one crucial point—that there is only one covenant of grace ... and only one way of salvation.

Covenant theologians, consistent with their view of man's depravity, stress that since the fall, man has not been able to save himself. Therefore, salvation in every age must be by grace alone. Even in the Mosaic era, grace was the only way of entering into fellowship with God. In fact, covenant theologians strongly deny that the Mosaic period was a time when man was under a covenant of works. One Reformed theologian writes:

> For this reason, the covenant of law as revealed at Sinai would best be divorced from "covenant of works" terminology. The "covenant of works" refers to legal requirements laid on man at the time of his innocency in creation. The "covenant of law" refers to a new stage in the process of God's unfolding the richness of the covenant of redemption. As such, the law

which came through Moses did not in any way disannul or suspend the covenant of promise.

The Collective Aspect of Grace in Covenant Theology

We've all heard evangelists say, "Just because you were born in a Christian home doesn't mean that you are going to heaven. You have to personally put your faith in Christ to be saved." However, covenant theology not only emphasizes the unity and sameness of redemptive history, but also the collective nature of God's gracious dealings with people. He doesn't just work with individuals, but also with families and groups of people.

This collective aspect of grace is used to support the covenant baptism of infants. "The promises of God are given to the seed of believers collectively, and not individually," writes covenant theologian Louis F. Berkhof. When this collective understanding of grace and the idea of the single covenant of grace are combined, covenant theologians find a weighty argument for infant baptism.

The Unity of the Covenant of Grace and the "Christian" Sabbath

Covenant theologians like to speak of the "Christian" sabbath which, according to their theology, is Sunday. Just as the covenant circumcision of infants in the Old Testament "bleeds over" into the church and becomes infant baptism, the Jewish sabbath "bleeds" over into the church and becomes the "Christian" sabbath. Covenant theologians state that all ten of the Ten Commandments are moral and perpetually binding on individuals. Dispensationalists are faulted for violating the sabbath. Allegedly, the pernicious effect of dispensational antinomianism is ruining America. Covenant theologians argue that the Puritan view of strict sabbath-keeping is the only view that is consistent with the *entire* Bible. It is the only view that will bring America back to God.

But didn't Paul condemn the observance of special days in Galatians 4:9–10 and Colossians 2:16–17? Well, not really. The Jews of Paul's day—and Paul was a Jew—applied the term "sabbath" to their stated holy days. Since the "Christian" sabbath was not one of the Jewish holy days, Paul cannot possibly be speaking against *that* day, or so the argument goes.

The Unity of the Covenant of Grace and the Reconstruction Movement

Not all covenant theologians are reconstructionists, but all reconstructionists hold to a covenant position. As previously indicated, they are outspoken critics of dispensationalism.

The unity of the covenant of grace, as defined by covenant theology, allows reconstructionists to bring the Mosaic law into the church. In fact, reconstructionist and post-millennial advocate Greg Bahnsen has a chapter in his *Theonomy in Christian Ethics* entitled "The Abiding Validity of the Law in Exhaustive Detail." In the introduction of the book Bahnsen writes:

> In the pages that follow, my concern will be to show from God's Word that the Christian is obligated to keep the whole law of God ... and that this law is to be enforced by the civil magistrate. ... The Older Testament commandments are not mere artifacts in a religious museum. ... They are the living and powerful Word of God, directing our lives here and now.

The Old Testament law of God is an especially important item to the covenant theologian. If we really understand what the Bible is all about, we will see the necessity of preaching the law of God to nations as well as to individuals. Those who fail to do so are rank antinomians. Gary North explains:

Ah, yes; the commandments. The law of God. You know: the Old Testament. ... We find whole passages that promise social betterment in response to covenantal faithfulness, passages such as Leviticus 26:3–13 and Deuteronomy 28:1–14. This means that *Christians must preach God's covenant lawsuit to nations as well as individuals:* a covenant lawsuit in history that includes both law and sanctions. Problem: pre-millennialists deny the historical validity of God's sanctions in New Covenant history. They also have a tendency to deny the continuing validity of God's Old Covenant case law applications of the Ten Commandments. They are, in short, *antinomians*.

This alleged antinomianism leads twentieth century fundamentalism down the road of disobedience to God. In another book, North writes:

Virtually all twentieth-century fundamentalism and pietism has by implications and practice denied the existence of such [the "dominion"] covenant. The idea that men are responsible as faithful servants of God, to bring the whole world under the rule of God's law, is repulsive to the vast majority of professing Christians.

A Brief Evaluation of Covenant Theology

Covenant theology is correct in its assertion that after the fall, salvation must be solely by the grace of God. Perhaps some of the earlier dispensational writers made statements that seemed to deny this and maybe some did actually deny it. However, one can still be a dispensationalist and also affirm that the grace of God is operative in every dispensation, and that apart from divine grace there can be no salvation. Man, the fallen sinner, can offer nothing to God in payment for salvation. Indeed, our best works are as filthy rags (Isa. 64:6) and even our repentance needs to be repented of.

However, in setting forth the gracious nature of God's dealings with fallen mankind in all ages, covenant theology is blind to the valid differences that also exist in the different periods of biblical history. It only gives lip service to the unique features characteristic of the various periods of Bible history. In seeking to magnify the grace of God, covenant theology muzzles the prophets. I can only venture an educated guess as to why this happens. Perhaps they believe that an admission of these differences will ultimately lead to a denial of the grace of God. Hence, to shield the grace of God from such possible infringements, covenant theology constructs an artificial, overarching, all-embracing "covenant of grace." The outcome of this artificial construct is the Judaizing of the church and a denial of the progressive nature of God's revelation.

This is particularly seen in covenant theology's tendency to assert that God's requirements are revealed primarily through law. This clearly is unscriptural. Hebrews tells us that in past times God spoke in various ways but has "in these last days spoken unto us by his Son" (1:2). The teachings, life, and ministry of Christ reveal God's perfect will. Christ is not simply a messenger from God. He is the message of God. Hence his statement, *"as I have loved you,* that ye also love one another" (John 13:34). It is not that the law is wrong, or erroneous. Not at all, but when compared to the communicative power of the example of Christ it is simply inadequate.

The concept of the one covenant of grace is a man-made invention. The Bible never refers to God's dealings with mankind down through the centuries of redemptive history under the title of "one covenant of grace." Rather, it speaks of "the covenants [plural] of promise" (Eph. 2:12).

Covenant writers will quickly challenge this by citing Hebrews 13:20: "Now the God of peace, that brought again from the dead our Lord Jesus, that great Shepherd of the sheep, through the blood of the everlasting covenant, Make you perfect in every good work to do his will." The reference to "the everlasting covenant" is, allegedly, a reference to this "one covenant of grace."

It should be noticed, however, that the context deals with the issue of salvation. The context is not speaking about the relationship between circumcision and baptism, whether or not infants are included in the family of God, or the conditions and requirements for obedience to, and fellowship with, God in the various ages of divine history. It is speaking about the blood of the everlasting covenant. Christ and His blood are central in God's redemptive dealings with mankind. It is speaking about "covenant grace," not about "the covenant of grace."

Rather than speaking of one covenant of grace the Bible speaks of several covenants: the Abrahamic covenant (Gen. 15:17–21; 17:18), the Mosaic (Exod. 19:5; 24:1–4, renewed on the plains of Moab according to Deut. 29:1–15), the covenants at Mounts Ebal and Gerizim (Josh. 8:30–35), at Shechem (Josh. 24), the Davidic (2 Sam. 7), and the New Covenant with Israel and Judah (Jer. 31:31–40). Though these were gracious covenants, yet they are described by Scripture in the plural as "covenants" (Rom. 9:4). In Scripture, "covenant" is used to refer to a specific agreement with a specific people at a specific time. The word is never used to refer to some kind of an arrangement that does not have those specific limitations. Reformed theology has invented its own theological category that bears no resemblance to what is revealed in Scripture.

One and the Same Church?

Covenant theology holds that the church is the same in all ages. It therefore must conclude that rites and acts of worship—like circumcision and baptism—are essentially the same in all ages. Covenant theologian Charles Hodge writes:

> It was not mere faith or trust in God, or simple piety, which was required, but faith in the promised Redeemer, or faith in the promise of redemption

> through the Messiah. ... The covenant of grace, or plan of salvation, being the same in all its elements from the beginning, it follows ... that the people of God before Christ constituted a Church, and that the Church has been one and the same under all dispensations. It has always had the same promise, the same Redeemer, and the same condition of membership, namely faith in the Son of God as the Savior of the world.

According to covenant theology, the covenant of grace throughout the ages of history is "the same in all its elements." "The church has been one and the same," meaning that there was a "church" in the Old Testament era that is the same as the church in the New Testament era. There is even "the same condition of membership" in that same church that supposedly spans the Old and New Testaments. Nothing, according to this view, has changed. The changes and differences between Old Testament Israel and the New Testament church are merely minor and cosmetic.

The scriptural "proof" for this is found in Acts 7:38 where Stephen is speaking about Moses and the children of Israel and then calls the people of God "the church in the wilderness." Their argument is that the word "church" (*ekklesia*) is used to describe Old Testament Israel, thus indicating that the church "is one and the same" in all ages.

While it is true that in the New Testament the word "church" generally refers to the body of Christ, it is also true that the word was used for a group of townspeople gathered together for the purpose of carrying on official business, a citizens' forum. While *ekklesia* can have a specific meaning, it also can have a general meaning. It is clearly used that way in Acts 19:32 where it is applied to a mob of people in Ephesus who had been angered against Paul by Demetrius the silversmith. The use of the word "church" in Acts 7:38 to describe Israel does not indicate that Israel is to be considered part of the body of Christ, or that it shares in the unique blessings of the New Testament church. The word simply means "the congregation of God's people." The

New Testament church is distinctive and never to be thought of as synonymous with Israel for several reasons:

1. Through the Spirit of God Christ indwells the members of the church (John 14:17), but this is never said of Israel.
8. In the church, Jew and gentile are equals, but this was not true under the Old Covenant (Eph. 3:1–6).
9. The existence of the New Testament church is dependent upon the giving of gifts to the body of Christ which occurred at the Ascension of Christ, and not before. Christ led captivity captive and gave gifts to men (Eph. 4:8).
10. The existence of the church is tied in with the baptizing work of the Holy Spirit (1 Cor. 12:13).

To teach that the church is "the same in all ages" grows out of a desire to mold the Scripture to one's theology. It is not an example of building one's theology on the Scripture.

Scripture abundantly testifies that there are some major differences between old and new testaments. "For the law was given by Moses," we read in John 1:17, "but grace and truth came by Jesus Christ." No doubt, God was as gracious to Israel as He is gracious to the church, but that should not lead us to conclude that Israel and the church are one and the same. A far better position is one which deals with both biblical unity and diversity without allowing one to dominate the other. Ryrie explains the relationship between law and grace in this way:

> The Dispensationalist answer to the question of the relation of grace and law is this: The basis of salvation in every age is the death of Christ; the *requirement* for salvation in every age is faith; the *object* of faith in every age is God; the *content* of faith changes in the various dispensations. ... When

Adam looked upon the coats of skins with which God had clothed him and his wife, he did not see what the believer sees today looking back on the cross of Calvary. And neither did other Old Testament saints see what we can see today.

Why the "Covenant Baptism" of Infants Is Wrong

The reader may gain a better understanding of the presuppositions of covenant theology by considering the argument for the baptism of infants. John Calvin's apologetic for the baptism of infants is most revealing. In arguing from what he claims is the connection between Old Testament circumcision and New Testament baptism, Calvin states:

> Hence we may conclude, that everything applicable to circumcision applies also to baptism, excepting always the difference in the visible ceremony. ... For just as circumcision, which was a kind of badge to the Jews, assuring them that they were adopted as the people and family of God, was their first entrance into the Church, while they, in their turn professed allegiance ... to God, so now we are initiated by baptism, so as to be enrolled among the people, and at the same time swear unto his name. Hence it is incontrovertible, that baptism has been substituted for circumcision and performs the same office. ... But if the covenant remains firm and fixed, it is no less applicable to the children of Christians in the present day, than to the children of the Jews under the Old Testament. ... [God] is pleased that infants shall be formally admitted to the covenant. ... Wherefore, both the children of the Jews, because, when made heirs to that covenant, were separated from the heathen, were called a holy seed, and for the same reason, the children of Christians, or those who have only one believing parent, are called holy, and by the testimony of the apostle, differ from the impure seed of idolaters. ... The covenant is common, and the reason for confirming it

is common. ... Otherwise if the testimony by which the Jews were assured of the salvation of their seed is taken from us, the consequences will be that, by the advent of Christ, the grace of God which was formerly given to the Jews, is more obscure and less perfectly attested to us.

From this amazing statement we see that Calvin seeks to build his case for infant baptism from the alleged identity of circumcision with baptism, and that "the covenant remains firm and fixed" and is "no less applicable to the children of Christians in the present day, than to the children or the Jews under the Old Testament." From this, and from other statements from Reformed writers that we have examined thus far, it can be seen that there are at least five unscriptural assumptions made by those who baptize infants on the basis of the so-called covenant argument:

1. The commonwealth of ancient Israel and the New Testament church are the same.
2. The church consists of believers and their infant children.
3. The terms of admission into the Old Testament "church" are the same as the terms of admission into the New Testament church.
4. There is nothing intrinsic to baptism that makes it inappropriate to infants.
5. Jewish parents in Old Testament Israel who did not circumcise their children were guilty of sinning against God's covenant; therefore, Christian parents who do not baptize their children are likewise guilty of sinning against the same covenant.

Regarding this last point, Reformed theologian Charles Hodge makes an astounding admission:

They, therefore, sin against God and their own souls who neglect the command to be baptized in the name of the Lord; and their parents sin grievously against the souls of their children who neglect to consecrate them to God in the ordinance of baptism. Do let the little ones have their names written in the Lamb's book of life, even if they afterwards choose to erase them. Being thus enrolled may be the means of their salvation.

The Argument from Silence Silenced

Covenant theologians admit that the New Testament is silent when it comes to infant baptism. I would agree. Infant baptism is simply not mentioned. In fact, the silence of the New Testament in this matter is deafening.

Covenant theologians, however, use this silence to support the practice of infant baptism. Their argument is this: since children were included in God's covenant in the Old Testament era, in the absence of any particular statements to the contrary, it is reasonable to assume that they are still in that covenant in New Testament times. In other words, they believe it would take a specific command to not baptize infants, or statement showing that infants are no longer in the covenant, to cause them to renounce infant baptism.

There are two problems with this kind of thinking. First, the baptism of which the New Testament speaks in the Great Commission and elsewhere is an ordinance for those who are disciples. Baptism in water is a believers' ordinance. A disciple is someone who, regardless of age, consciously becomes a learner and takes up his or her cross and follows Christ. Unless those who support the covenant baptism of infants are willing to argue that the children of believers are born as Christian disciples, the New Testament forcefully silences the argument from silence.

Secondly, in Old Testament times the male children of Jews were circumcised because they were in the national covenant that God made with Israel. If a person was a Jew that person was, in some sense, in covenant with God. Such, however, is no longer true in the present dispensation. Being born in a Christian home doesn't make one a member of a "Christian nation." No such nation exists. God's covenant with Israel is not God's covenant with the church, nor is it God's covenant with America. Covenant theology has come up with erroneous conclusions in this because of its refusal to see the obvious distinctions between Israel and the church.

The covenant interpretation of Acts 2:39 is a case in point. In this verse, Peter states: "For the promise is unto you, and to your children, and to all that are afar off, even as many as the Lord our God shall call." This is a "proof text" for infant baptism. It says just what covenant theologians want to hear. The only problem is that the text has nothing to do with infant baptism nor does it have anything to do with the church.

Peter is addressing the physical children of Abraham. He addressed the crowd with the words, "Ye men of Judea, and all ye that dwell at Jerusalem" (Acts 2:14). In Acts 3 the same focus is evident: "Ye are the children of the prophets, and of the covenant which God made with our fathers, saying unto Abraham, And in thy seed shall all the kindreds of the earth be blessed. Unto you first God, having raised up his Son Jesus, sent him to *bless you"* (Acts 3:25–26). Peter was presenting a Jewish kingdom to Jewish people: "Repent ye [Jewish people] therefore, and be converted, that your sins may be blotted out, when the times of refreshing shall come from the presence of the Lord; and he shall send Jesus Christ" (Acts 3:19–20). Israel's repentance is tied in with the Lord's return. Scripture, however, never connects the repentance of gentiles with the Second Advent.

Once certain scriptural principles are understood, the argument from silence is meaningless. God does not have to tell us not to baptize infants if He doesn't want them baptized. The nature of the ordinance of baptism and the peculiarly dispensational nature of Old Testament circumcision and its relationship to the Jewish nation makes baptism totally unsuitable for infants in the Church Age. *If God wants infants baptized, He would have to specifically say so. The fact that the New Testament is silent on the baptism of infants means that they are not to be baptized.* Infant baptism, theonomy, Christian reconstruction all arise out of a failure to observe some basic principles of biblical interpretation.

Chapter 4

Preterism and the Eclipse of Pre-millennialism

Pre-millennialism has been the major eschatological position in America for over a century. Many, though not all, pre-millennialists are dispensational in their understanding of Scripture. Dispensationalism and pre-millennialism complement each other and are able to explain both the unity and diversity of Scripture and provide a sound basis for understanding God's promises to Israel. This is something that cannot be done with other approaches to Scripture and certainly says much in their favor.

Various developments on the world scene have done much to create an interest in prophecy. For many, the establishment of the Israeli State in 1948 was a confirmation of Bible prophecy. Added to that were a series of disasters—Bhopal, Chernobyl, AIDS, earthquakes, global warming, and others—that have created an "apocalyptic fever." Radical and far-reaching social changes such as the growing acceptance of the gay lifestyle, radical feminism, radical environmentalism, school shootings, and genetic experimentation, have all worked together to create the impression that "something momentous is going to happen soon." When life proceeds as usual and there is a general feeling of peace and safety, there is not much interest in biblical prophecy. But when the very foundations of a society are shaken and the bizarre becomes the norm, "millennial madness" spreads like a plague.

The Changing Spiritual Climate

In recent years, however, dispensational pre-millennialism has been losing followers. Opposing views—some of them having been around a long time but overshadowed by dispensational pre-millennialism—are appearing on the scene and gaining increasing numbers of adherents. Several factors can be offered to explain this phenomenon.

Some, for example, would point out that the events of the twentieth century seem to have mocked the pre-millennial understanding of history. Not only did Y2K not pan out as anticipated by many, but some believe that many events in the last half of the twentieth century have discredited a pre-millennial understanding of current events.

> For a while, current events seemed to bear out the pre-millennial view. But not everything went their way. There were obvious disconfirmations—especially Mussolini's fate. Instead of being a type of the Antichrist, he died a humiliating death, and the Roman Empire never revived. And Adolph Hitler's invasion of Russia in June 1941 shattered the prophetic expectation of a great northern confederation of Germany and Russia. How did pre-millennialism handle these apparent setbacks? Some were confused, others were dumbfounded. But for the most part there seemed to be just one big awkward silence.

Before we proceed, a few comments are in order. Yes, Y2K did not turn out to be a disaster. This is often used against prophetic teachers who taught that it could very well be a disaster. However, debunkers act as if the pre-millennial community actually created the idea of a Y2K disaster. That is patently false. The U.S. government along with a variety of organizations and utility companies were advocating taking appropriate measures. Consistent with this, millions of dollars were spent on preparedness. Those in prophetic ministries were simply reporting what was being stated on the media and from many other non-Christian sources.

And what about Kyle's statement about Mussolini's ignoble death and the revived Roman Empire failing to materialize? Yes, at the end of the Second World War, Europe was in ruins. But it is not that way today. No one who teaches that there will be a revived Roman Empire need apologize for that view. Both Scripture and current events amply testify to its reality. In the closing years of the twentieth century, events transpired in Europe that can only be explained in terms of prophecy. The European Union, the European Common Market, the euro-dollar, the vicious attack by NATO upon Yugoslavia in the spring of 1999, and the growing economic power of Europe that now possibly exceeds that of the United States are all harbingers of prophetic fulfillment.

And yes, Germany invaded Russia in June of 1941 as Kyle points out, but more than half a century later we know that the "expectation of a great northern confederation" is still in keeping with prophecy and being confirmed by current events. Russia has been through much turmoil, and we have all heard the rosy reports that "communism is dead." Recent developments, however, show that Russia and a great northern confederation cannot be dismissed with a wave of the hand.

Another complaint against pre-millennialism is that it often takes a negative view of society and culture. And that is true. Dispensational pre-millennialists have a deep-seated distrust of the world system. We believe that this distrust is what is taught in Scripture. However, some writers use this to demonize dispensational pre-millennialism. Richard Kyle explains when he writes:

Many dispensationalists are fundamentalists who tend to regard the world system and even culture in general as demonic. Thus they identify a variety of elements in the global order as forces of the Antichrist. Frequently targeted are Roman Catholicism, liberal Protestantism, the global economic system, modern technology, Jews, socialism, Communism, the New Age Movement, Islam, environmentalism, the Common Market, the Soviet Union, feminism, peace organizations, and rock music.

Critics of pre-millennialism who engage in such criticisms need to consider the categories "targeted" in the above quote. What about Roman Catholicism, liberal Protestantism, and the global economic system? Are these really the friends of biblical Christianity? Are we really to be demonized because we find that socialism, the New Age movement, Islam, environmentalism, peace organizations like the United Nations, and many other groups are more interested in destroying the testimony of Christ than preserving it?

Yes, I must agree with Kyle that "many dispensationalists are fundamentalists who tend to regard the world system and even culture in general as demonic." Yes, we even have problems with Halloween, Pokémon, Harry Potter, rock music, miniskirts, and crossdressing. But are we to be regarded as "the bad guys" because we recognize that Satan is "the god of this world" (2 Cor. 4:4)? Did not the Apostle Paul write that Christians are to be "casting down imaginations, and every high thing that exalteth itself against the knowledge of God, and bringing into captivity every thought to the obedience of Christ" (2 Cor. 10:5)? Are we to be faulted if we take seriously the many scriptural indicators that we are currently in a war of ideas, and that these ideas are all issues of critical concern because of what is at stake?

The Hunger for a Different Emphasis

Through much of prophetic teaching, multitudes have been mentally prepared to expect some kind of a dreadful apocalypse to shortly occur. A cloud of doom and gloom has cast its shadow.

While this kind of thinking is usually perpetrated by religious groups, even non-Christians and radical secularists were speaking of "doomsday." Carl Sagan, for example, wrote that "we may have only a few decades until Doomsday." "Religion no longer has a corner on eschatology," writes Kyle. Though not traditionally given to treating end-time scenarios, secular scientists began to speak of "The Secular Apocalypse." Science "has given us a depersonalized end: there will be no redemption, no survivors and no paradise. Scientists warn us that forces are at work that can literally blow us out of existence."

Futurists are often blamed with creating doom and gloom, but it is not just the prophecy preachers and conference speakers who are fanning the flames. Even Caspar Weinberger, when he was the U.S. Secretary of Defense, declared that this might be the last generation. In one interview, President Reagan looked at recent events and stated that they put him in mind of Armageddon. Reagan said:

> You know, I turn back to your ancient prophets in the Old Testament and the signs foretelling Armageddon and I find myself wondering if we're the generation that is going to see that come about ... believe me, they certainly describe the times we're going through.

It is in this midst of this growing pessimism, created by both the religious and secular thinkers, that Kingdom Now preachers shine as bright lights offering hope and meaning. Preterism, with its belief that the Tribulation is past, offers the hope that because of the "cultural mandate" to infiltrate society, Christians can have a positive impact on society. Rather than finding fault with so much of society, as dispensationalists are charged with doing, covenant theologians seek to transform it "all for the glory of God." This appeals to many in the Christian community who consider themselves born-again believers, but who claim that they are cut out of a different mold than their fundamentalist brethren.

Will Mankind Survive?

In the early, turbulent years of the twentieth century, pre-millennialism seemed to have the answers that people were looking for. Interest in prophecy usually soars during times of turmoil and confusion. The industrialization of society and the urbanization of America opened the door to mass immigration as many were needed in factories and shipyards. Many of these immigrants were of a different faith than those who had been raised in rural American Protestant churches. Roman Catholics, Eastern Orthodox and those of other faiths came to America's shores. Growing tension with minorities brought division and conflict in many areas. While the country was seeking to face these issues, World War I and the Great Depression produced more upheavals, followed by World War II.

The advent of weapons of mass destruction in general, and the use of the atomic bomb on Hiroshima and Nagasaki in particular, led prophecy teachers to see this as setting the stage for the literal fulfillment of many prophetic passages that speak of destruction by fire (2 Pet. 3:10), and a war of such unprecedented destruction that "their flesh shall consume away while they stand upon their feet" (Zech. 14:12). Yet, the same science that produced these weapons that could create the kinds of catastrophes described in Bible prophecy is also the science that made the God of the Bible look unnecessary.

Man was beginning to look like the creator and master of his own destiny. Rationalism, higher criticism, and evolutionary theory challenged the authority of Scripture and led many to believe that science had disproved Scripture. For an interest in prophecy to thrive, the calamities affecting mankind must defy explanation. But modern science was becoming increasingly more adept at giving a scientific reason for the problems mankind was facing. While premillennialism seemed to correctly interpret what was happening, and also allowed for Christ's immediate return without of necessity establishing a timetable, its emphasis on apostasy, tribulation, and the utter inability of human endeavor to establish any Utopia on earth was producing a growing disenchantment in many Christian circles. Health-and-wealth teachers who name-it-and-claim-it, along with covenant theologians and Christian reconstructionists who were teaching about the "cultural mandate," seemed to offer a positive alternative. The Moral Majority and similar conservative groups were staging mass rallies and seemed to be able to tie into large numbers of supporters. These "victories" had inflamed the aspirations of many who began preaching "you can make a difference." Pre-millennial beliefs seemed to be out of step with all this exuberance and was viewed as putting too much emphasis on the return of Jesus Christ. Teaching that there can be no kingdom victory until the King physically comes to establish His Kingdom seemed to encourage a defeatist attitude. Why wait for the King when we can produce a kingdom right now?

Moreover, many pre-millennialists are pre-tribulational. They believe that the church will be removed from the earth prior to the Great Tribulation. Pre-tribulationism has many enemies. "Rapture escapism" is criticized by reconstructionists. Moreover, pre-tribulationists also draw fire from those in the Christian Identity movement. The Identity movement, with its emphasis on active involvement in society to bring about change and preparedness for the coming world conflict, regards the pre-trib Rapture as a cowardly notion. Identity maintains that instead of looking forward to being taken away from the conflicts of the Tribulation, Christians "must participate in the final apocalyptic struggle between good and evil."

The Association of Pre-millennialism with Extremism

In a book that is highly critical of pre-millennialism, author Richard Abanes associates pre-millennialism with various extreme groups. Abanes concludes that there is some kind of a connection between date-setting and pre-millennialism, and writes: "Most of these doomsday deadlines have been set by persons subscribing to a view known as pre-millennialism, which is currently the most popular Christian eschatology ..."

He never supports this statement with the results of a survey. And just what does he mean by the statement? Does he mean that there is something about pre-millennialism itself that causes pre-millennialists to naturally believe that date-setting is a valid approach to end-time events? If he does, is Abanes willing to admit that the pre-millennialists who have set dates have only done so because they are inconsistent pre-millennialists and that they are date-setting not because of their pre-millennialism, but in spite of it?

The blanket charge that pre-millennialists are date-setters is surely overworked, but in order to make his point Abanes picks a notorious date-setter, the retired NASA engineer Edgar C. Whisenant, to totally discredit biblical prophecy and pre-millennialism.

In 1988, Whisenant came into the evangelical spotlight with two books: *88 Reasons Why the Rapture Could Be in 1988* and *On Borrowed Time*. Whisenant engaged in some dogmatic date-setting, something that led scoffers to multiply like rabbits. Whisenant postulated that somewhere around September 11, 1988—the Jewish New Year, or Rosh Hashanah—the Lord was going to Rapture His church. Calculating dates is always precarious, especially when using Jewish festivals and applying them to eschatological issues affecting the church instead of Israel. Significantly, but not mentioned by Abanes, this is something that consistent dispensationalists recognize as being a violation of basic dispensational principles. At any rate, Whisenant was dead wrong, but he was not willing to admit it, and Abanes picks up on this:

> Nothing cataclysmic happened on Rosh Hashanah 1988. This, however, did not deter Whisenant in the least. Immediately after the scheduled time of Christ's return the *Atlanta Journal and Constitution* reported that the Arkansas prophet had revised his prediction saying that the Rapture could possibly occur by 10:55 a.m., Wednesday [September 15]. As September drew to a close, Whisenant still had not lost confidence. He revised his date again; this time to October 3. Even when that date passed, Whisenant remained undaunted: "The evidence is all over the place that it is going to be in a few weeks anyway," he told *Christianity Today.*

I agree with Abanes on this one. Date-setting is idiotic. However, there is nothing intrinsic with pre-millennialism that requires date-setting. True, many date-setters are pre-millennial. But it is also true that many Americans are murderers.

Abanes is also against those who engage in "date-suggesting." What does he mean by this term? "Date-suggesting," writes Abanes, is something which is done "by attaching predictions to open-ended qualifiers such as 'near,' 'close to,' 'just beyond,' 'not long after,' 'possibly by,' or 'very soon.'" Date-suggesters suggest a date in order to avoid the condemnation of Deuteronomy 18:21. Abanes believes that date-suggesters are really date-setters at heart, but who want to leave an easy out just in case they are wrong. He particularly doesn't approve of prophecy teachers who write with a question mark and ask: "Could this possibly be what the Bible is referring to when it says … ?" Evidently, Abanes falls under his own condemnation. He has included a big question mark in the very title of his book—*End-Time Visions: The Road to Armageddon?*

While neither Jesus nor the prophets and apostles ever set dates, they did speak of signs, and they did speak of the nearness of the Lord's return. Abanes and other preterists may not like to speak of the Lord's coming as being "soon," but the Bible uses language that tells us that it is "soon." Our

Lord said that He would come at "such an hour as ye think not" (Matt. 24:44), which means "it may be later than you think." Jesus also said, "Watch therefore: for ye know not what hour your Lord doth come" (Matt. 24:42). Our Lord is warning His audience to be on the alert because His return may be shockingly soon.

Whatever view Abanes takes, he has serious doubts about the sanity of individuals who are interested in prophecy. It is as if the baser side of man leads to an interest in prophecy. In fact, Abanes states that "humanity's preoccupation with doomsday" is "a timeless obsession."

I checked the word "obsession" in the dictionary. *Webster's New World Dictionary,* second edition, defines it as:

> **Obsession**—1. Orig., the act of an evil spirit in possessing or ruling a person. 2. a) the fact or state of being obsessed with an idea, desire, emotion, etc. b) such a persistent idea, desire, emotion, etc., esp. one that cannot be got rid of by reasoning.

Evidently, if Abanes is using the word according to the dictionary definition, all who are interested in Bible prophecy are suffering from some uncontrollable passion that cannot be dealt with on a reasonable basis. An interest in prophecy is, according to Richard Abanes, some kind of a demonic fatal attraction that we need to repent of—and quickly!

In what is an extremely predictable approach, Richard Abanes associates the teachers of Bible prophecy with various heretics in the early church and sees an interest in prophecy as a purely social phenomena sparked by hard times.

> During the worst of Roman persecutions against Jesus' followers (c. 156–172), a number of other troubles affected not only Christians, but the entire Roman Empire. In the year 166, "havoc was wrought by plague,

flood, famine, and barbarian invasion from beyond the Danube frontier." The chaos and violence gave birth to a "new variety of Christian life and activity" known as Montanism. This social phenomenon was the first of many doomsday movements to emerge from within Christianity.

Abanes goes on to describe Montanism which, he believes, was "the first example of an earnest and well-meaning, but gloomy and fanatical hyper-Christianity." The devotees of Montanism "eschewed marital relations, fasted frequently ... and ate dried foods only." They were strict separatists who "forbade ornamental clothing for women, required virgins to be veiled, saw art as incompatible with Christian soberness" and had several other "hyper-Christian distinctions." On the basis of conclusions such as this, a young Christian will all too readily conclude that prophecy is something for strict separatists who want their virgins to wear veils.

One of the marks of this prophetical dementia is, according to Abanes, a preoccupation with the signs of the times. That Jesus spoke about the different phases in the development of figs and said, "So likewise ye, when ye see these things come to pass, know ye that the kingdom of God is nigh at hand" (Luke 21:31), doesn't seem to faze Abanes. "End-time visionaries," he writes, "are thoroughly convinced that our era is experiencing natural disasters, man-made catastrophes, social/political unrest, and devastating diseases in record numbers and severity," but throughout his book he disputes that anything bad is happening with any greater frequency or severity than before.

He applies this to earthquakes and says, "The *apparent* rise of earthquakes over the last several years is due to nothing more than the use of technologically advanced seismographs." He quotes Charles F. Richter, the inventor of the Richter scale, who "explained that modern seismographs can record minor quakes that previously would have gone unnoticed."

So, things are only *apparently* worse—no doubt, modern instruments are more sensitive than less sophisticated instruments, but a 9.0 earthquake does not require a sensitive instrument to record its effects. Simple instruments will do just as well, and toppled bridges will give ample testimony to the quake's severity. Of course, one thing that Abanes doesn't mention is that an earthquake with its epicenter under a nuclear reactor or chemical dump might have some very unusual collateral effects, the likes of which have never been experienced before.

It is simply not true, however, that all seismologists would agree that there is no increase in frequency or intensity of earthquakes. The U.S. Geological Survey National Earthquake Information Center has published a chart indicating the number of earthquakes worldwide for 1987 through 1999. In the period 1987 to 1992, there was only one earthquake in the 8.0–9.9 category, but in the years 1993 to 1999, there were nine earthquakes in the 8.0–9.9 category—surely a substantial increase. In the period 1987 to 1992, there were 11.8 earthquakes in the 7.0–7.9 category, but in the years 1993 to 1999, there were 19.5. Again, this was a substantial increase. The averages of the total number of earthquakes in all categories are revealing. In the years 1987 to 1992, there was an average of 15,210 earthquakes for all magnitudes, but in the years 1993 to 1999, the average was much higher—20,559. Assuming that the instruments in 1987 were capable of accurately recording earthquakes, the fact that there has been a substantial increase must not be ignored.

Abanes goes on to refer to the Babylonian *Epic of Gilgamesh* (c. 4000 B.C.) which bears some striking similarities to Noah's Flood as recorded in the Hebrew scriptures. Abanes observes that "this same story, including most of the aforementioned elements, can be found in the religious tradition of numerous cultures Most of these civilizations also preached about a *future* doomsday.

I must confess that I am hard-pressed to really understand the point of that statement. Does he mean to associate pre-millennialists with writers of a Babylonian epic? He says, "most of these civilizations also preached about a *future* doomsday." But so did Jesus preach about a future doomsday. Should

He be likewise associated with the writers of a Babylonian epic, too?

Abanes's vendetta is not just against pre-tribulationists, but also against those whom he labels "historic pre-millennialists." He observes that these differ from pre-tribulationists in that they believe that Christians will not be rescued from the Tribulation, and that there is no pre-tribulational Rapture. But, says Abanes, such a view has led "some people to form survivalist sects and retreat to isolated regions of America with large quantities of food and weapons."

It seems like pre-millennial dispensationalists just can't get anything right. They get connected with too many evil associations. But is guilt by association a valid approach to truth?

The following humorous analysis appears in a book on the Bible and health. The author, Michael Jacobson, uses this material to show how, if a problem is misstated and the data is wrongly interpreted, the investigator will end up with the wrong conclusions. Jacobson tells that a headline in a local newspaper read: "Smell of Baked Bread May Be Hazard to Health." He received a humorous analysis of the report on his e-mail. The anonymous writer states:

> I was horrified. When are we going to do something about bread induced global warming? Sure, we attack tobacco companies, but when is the government going to go after Big Bread? Well, I've done a little research, and what I've discovered should make anyone think twice ...
>
> » More than 98 percent of convicted felons are bread users.
> » Fully HALF of all children who grow up in bread-consuming households score below average on standardized tests.
> » More than 90 percent of violent crimes are committed within 24 hours of eating bread.
> » Bread is often a "gateway" food item, leading the user to "harder" items such as butter, jelly, peanut butter, and even cold cuts ...

At the hands of these scholars who are writing about prophecy, premillennialism receives the same harsh treatment as bread does in the preceding humorous presentation. But just as bread should not be outlawed on the basis of such reasoning, neither should pre-millennialism be criticized in the cavalier manner with which Abanes treats it.

Pre-millennialism and Conspiracy Theories

Gregory Camp, in his book *Selling Fear: Conspiracy Theories and End-times Paranoia*, comes down hard on pre-millennialism because it creates a sense of urgency leading to a high level of lunacy, which, according to Camp, is not true of other eschatological positions. I quote him on this lest I be charged with misrepresenting the views of an author:

> One may well disagree with the post-millennial or a-millennial positions from a theological point of view, but it is difficult to deny the many (and embarrassing) pronouncements that Christians have made concerning the coming of Jesus. Those holding to post-millennial or a-millennial beliefs, whether one agrees with them or not, have not engendered the lunacy and anticipation common to the pre-millennial view concerning the return of Jesus. Indeed, there is little sense of urgency in either of these views.

Camp's words, though not written to support pre-millennialism, actually do that. By his own admission he claims that post-millennial and a-millennial beliefs do not have the "sense of urgency" that the pre-mil view does. Did Jesus teach that we should not have a sense of urgency regarding last things?

Of course, it is not just the conservative pre-millennial preachers who talk of a conspiracy. As Jones points out, "According to the modern myth of feminism, there exists an oppressive, pervasive patriarchal conspiracy which demands vigilance, indeed radical suspicion." Once again, I must emphasize that there is nothing intrinsic to pre-millennialism that makes it more conspiracy-theory prone than other views dealing with other topics. Anyone who passionately holds to a particular position or view may find some conspiracies against that cherished view. Moreover, even those who write against conspiracy theorists do blame the government for some of our problems.

Richard Abanes, for example, is certainly not on our side, yet he writes: "Making the current situation even worse has been the government's refusal to ease justifiable fears and frustrations of patriots. In fact, on more than one occasion federal behavior has only increased tensions." He explains by referring to the 1992 incident involving Randy Weaver and also "the government's botched raid on the Branch Davidian compound in Waco, Texas." "These events," writes Abanes, "and a host of other government mishandlings have served to inflame an already smoldering anger in the hearts of many Americans who are sick and tired of being abused by big government."

Pre-millennialists are therefore not the only ones who are concerned about the growing government bureaucracy. "On this point," writes Abanes, "the patriots are not alone. An April 1995 Gallup Poll found that thirty-nine percent of Americans think the federal government 'poses an immediate threat to the rights and freedoms of ordinary Americans.'" Abanes asks,

> Why are flagrant attacks on constitutionally protected rights continuing to occur with alarming regularity? Why does it seem that law enforcement personnel are rarely punished for their "mistakes"? Much of the American public has had its fill of the standard answers given by officials—e.g., poor intelligence reports, bad planning, improper judgment and neglect of duty.

Abanes makes some significant statements here and asks some pressing questions. But why is it that when pre-millennialists make these statements and ask these questions that, somehow, they are showing an unreasonable paranoia? The fear of a multi-jurisdictional task force (MJTF) leading to an eventual national police force is not reasonable. Abanes writes, "There is no MJTF. There are, however, a number of ways local police and federal authorities work together." He observes that in a few cases local officers may be federalized, "but this is a far cry from having a national police force," argues Abanes. "Policy analyst Craig Hulet notes that for many years various law enforcement agencies have been joining forces in order to overcome jurisdictional impairments. These joint efforts, however, belie nothing sinister."

But have there really been no changes in law enforcement procedures and practices that should give us cause for alarm?

Some of my readers who were raised in the city can remember when the friendly "cop on the beat" walked down the street twirling his nightstick and whistling some bright and happy tune. Those who were raised in rural areas remember how the local sheriff would help grandpa dig his truck out of a snowbank, and then get invited to a big farm breakfast. Those days are long gone. Many have come to regard law enforcement officers with disdain, and perhaps with good reason. *The National Review* featured a report by David Kopel entitled "Smash-up Policing: When Law Enforcement Goes Military. " Using as a springboard the commando raid that snatched Elian Gonzalez from his uncle's home, Kopel details the growing trend to take the SWAT-team approach to local law enforcement. He reports that at present as many as twenty percent of U.S. police departments in municipalities with a population over fifty thousand have put their own paramilitary units into local enforcement work:

> When law enforcement agencies create SWAT teams, they often assure the public that the squads will be used for hostage rescue and similar activities. Fortunately, there are not enough actual hostage takings to keep the SWAT teams busy; as a result, the paramilitary units have a tendency to look for other tasks, ones in which there is no need for their special violent skills.

The SWAT-team approach was developed in the sixties to meet the need created by the growing drug problem. Future police chief Daryl Gates created the first Special Weapons and Tactics team. Initially, according to Kopel, Gates wanted it to be called the "Special Weapons Attack Team," but changed the name for public relations purposes.

There are various U.S. military organizations that are willing to train and equip law enforcement agencies for paramilitary work. The Navy SEALS, the Army's Delta Force, and other elite government attack troops provide extensive free training to police tactical teams. However, as Kopel states,

> Military training—which stresses absolute obedience and swift annihilation of the target—is not appropriate for good police behavior, which, after all, requires capturing suspected criminals (not killing them), minimizing the use of force, and acting with a scrupulous regard for the Constitution.

This militarization of the police may explain the recent rash of police actions, such as in New York City, where a single unarmed man was cut down in a hail of bullets.

Recent changes in law enforcement planning and strategies need to be regarded as a menace to the general population. Under the United States Constitution, law enforcement personnel serve as "peace officers." Under the new approach they function as "war officers."

Analysts like Abanes wish to ignore this. It's too troubling. Even the U.N., according to Abanes, has been demonized. It is not a real threat, he argues, and gives several reasons to back up his contention. These reasons reveal a fundamental misunderstanding and are instructive.

"First," says Abanes, "the U.N's ineptitude since its creation has been well documented. U.N. operations are still hampered by poor planning, incompetent forces and politics." As proof of this Abanes quotes a Marine Corps sergeant who wrote a letter to *Soldier of Fortune* stating that "the United Nations is a nutless bureaucracy."

The second reason Abanes advances to show that the U.N. really poses no threat to freedom and liberty is that "the U.N. is constantly on the brink of insolvency and chronically facing delays and logistical restraints." Abanes puts the blame on the United States: "This hindrance is due largely to America's failure to pay its portion of the world organization's operating costs."

The third reason Abanes ridicules the notion that the U.N. poses any threat to freedom is that "although it is true that the U.N. had increased its level of influence over U.S. foreign policy, it is not true that the U.N. has any control over *domestic* policy." Abanes scoffs at the patriot movement because it turns "a deaf ear to such explanations, convinced that the U.N is presently setting up a strike force in this country." Conspiracy theorists erroneously believe that "at some point in the near future, the president will declare martial law in response to a trumped-up national emergency."

Abanes' three reasons are totally invalid. While it is true, as he argues in points one and two, that the U.N. is often inept and facing financial insolvency, what happens if the U.N. cleans up its act and gets more money for its financial coffers? His reasoning is about as logical as those who said that the German National Socialist Party posed no threat to Europe and America in the thirties because it had neither the money nor the organizational structures to do any real harm. The day quickly came when all of that changed.

Abanes' third point is even more ludicrous. Only the uninitiated in current events and development of the new world order could say that the U.N. has control over foreign policy in the U.S. but not over domestic policy. The day has long gone when one can separate foreign policy from domestic policy. NAFTA, GATT, and WTO have repercussions both at home and abroad. Billions of dollars of American money have been invested overseas. A financial collapse in the Orient could have some drastic effects on the American economy.

Last Days Scoffers

The critics of pre-millennial teaching claim that pre-millennialists are alarmists and paint a gloomy picture of current events. Our critics scoff at the magnitude of world problems, the potential severity of future wars, and the prophetic significance of modern technology.

As if anticipating this, Peter writes about the end times and tells his readers that there is something of primary importance that he wants to share:

> Knowing this first, that there shall come in the last days scoffers, walking after their own lusts, And saying, Where is the promise of his coming? for since the fathers fell asleep, all things continue as they were from the beginning of the creation.
>
> —2 Peter 3:3–4

The nature of their scoffing was that they denied the possibility of Divine intervention in the affairs of men. This contention was based on their observation that "all things continue as they were from the beginning of creation."

There are scoffers in the present hour and many of them come from within the ranks of the Christian community. They discount the significance of the unique nature of current events and like to say that "things have always been this way."

In his book *End-Time Visions,* Richard Abanes totally discounts the destructive potential of modern warfare and the precarious position of the human race at the present hour. He quotes the book *The Wages of War, 1816–1965* to make his point:

> Is war on the increase, as many scholars as well as laymen of our generation have been inclined to believe? The answer would seem to be a very unambiguous negative. Whether we look at the number of wars, or their severity or magnitude, there is no significant trend upward or down over the past

150 years.

But is it true that "there is no significant trend upward in the number of wars, or their severity or magnitude"?

In an Associated Press report entitled "World got more dangerous in 1997 with rise in conflicts," Andy Messing Jr., executive director of the National Defense Council Foundation, an organization which tallies hostilities worldwide, stated: "We're not in a world of peace. We're in a world of conflict."

In recent years there has been widespread nuclear proliferation. Small countries, such as North Korea and Pakistan, have developed missiles that could reach Alaska, and even the continental United States. Rogue nations now possess the technology to make nuclear weapons, and to deliver them to targets in the U.S. Added to that is the fact that though many undeveloped nations do not possess the technology to make a nuclear warhead and to deliver that warhead, they can nevertheless make bio-weapons, the effects of which would also lead to the deaths of millions. Toxins can be sprayed from small aircraft and have an appeal to terrorist nations because such weapons have a delayed action. A lag period, or incubation period—sometimes several hours or even several days—must elapse between the time the victim is exposed to the infectious agent and the actual time symptoms begin to show themselves. This means that the perpetrators have ample time to escape and even, perhaps, to avoid detection. We live in a dangerous world, one that is far more dangerous than ever before.

Abanes persists in his line of reasoning when he takes Tim LaHaye to task for claiming that the twentieth century has seen more people killed "than all the wars of history put together." Abanes writes, "Contrary to what LaHaye and other end-time prophets may declare, the last one hundred years of warfare represent nothing more than the tail end of humanity's long and bloody history."

Debunkers Debunked

On May 12, 1951, newspapers around the world reported the following: "The explosive equivalent of several million tons of TNT was released here today on the tiny atoll of Eniwetok as scientists of the Atomic Energy Commission detonated the world's first thermonuclear device—the H-bomb." The report went on to state that while most of the technical details of the bomb's design are secret, "scientists have long known of the tremendous energy that could be released if the nuclei of heavy hydrogen, deuterinum, could be made to combine." This is the way the sun makes its heat. "But to make the nuclei react, temperatures of several million degrees would be required. The only way of achieving such heat on earth," the report stated, "is by nuclear fission, using an atomic bomb of the kind dropped on Hiroshima as a trigger for the fusion bomb."

Despite what debunkers and scoffers say, we have now progressed to the point where the bomb that was used to take out a city and snuff out seventy thousand lives in 1945 in one instant, is now simply the "trigger" for a much larger bomb.

Another news report—this one dated January 21, 1954—was headlined with these words: "U.S. launches Nautilus, first atomic sub." The report indicated that "because its high-speed turbine engines are powered by an atomic reactor that needs no air, the submarine is expected to be able to circumnavigate the globe without having to surface." Just a few years later, on May 10, 1960, the news reported: "Sub Triton circles globe under water." In just eighty-four days the Triton covered 41,500 miles. The report related the military significance of this event: "The feat also raises the nuclear stakes: missile-carrying Polaris subs will soon roam the seas."

We would all hope and pray that these weapons would never be used in conflict, but even apart from an actual conflict there is the distinct possibility of an accidental exchange. *The London Times* of July 13, 1998, reported:

"Russian Nukes: Five Minutes to Nuclear War." The article told of the sad state of the Russian early warning system and how a "false alarm" had almost triggered a nuclear exchange between the U.S. and Russia. The Russians had picked up a Norwegian weather research rocket which they thought was an approaching American Trident ballistic missile. As the burners of the Black Brent rocket fell to earth, the Russian military command mistook them for warheads homing in on Russian targets.

Pre-millennialists do not have to create doomsday scenarios. They already exist. Denials of the critical nature of our present situation will not make the danger go away.

Once again, I must affirm that pre-millennialism is really the only approach to the Scriptures that can give an adequate explanation of what is happening today. It is unfortunate that so many Christians are turning to approaches to Scripture that create more problems than they answer. Preterism has no explanation for current events other than that they are the general outworking of Divine providence and must support its contention by pretending that "all things continue as they were from the beginning of the creation.

Chapter 5

Preterism: Its Support of Replacement Theology

Those who are preterists not only have a unique view of when prophecy is fulfilled, but they also challenge widely accepted Christian beliefs about how it is fulfilled. Preterists claim that the Church is "the new Israel," and that God's ancient promises to Israel are received by the Church. Known as "replacement theology," this is the view that says that the Church has replaced Israel. Allegedly, if you really want to understand prophecy, substitute "Church" for "Israel" in the Old Testament Kingdom promises.

A-millennial preterist Jay Adams speaks about how many conservatives are "on the move, eschatologically." In fact, he believes that dissatisfaction with the pre-trib position has led many to embrace a post-trib position and then, being dissatisfied with that, many are making the full circle to a-millennialism. Adams shows how a replacement view of Israel is ultimately tied in with this search for a satisfying eschatology. He writes:

> In this transition from pre- to post-tribulationism, some have gone further, and are beginning to test the foundations of pre-millennialism itself. In the process, doubts about fundamental presuppositions have arisen. Having rejected the unbiblical principle of exclusively literal interpretation of Old

Testament prophecy, many no longer look upon so-called "national Israel" as God's chosen people. They cannot agree to a "Jewish" millennium, fully equipped with rebuilt temple and restored sacrificial system ...

Even a passage such as Romans 11 and its clear references to Israel means nothing to Adams. For him "all Israel" has nothing to do with Israel alone, but is a reference to the totality of the elect as found in the Church:

> Romans 11 indicates that both the "fulness" of the Gentiles and "all Israel" shall be completed either prior to or immediately at the coming of Christ. The "fulness" of the Gentiles and "all Israel" surely comprises the total number of that body which we call the *church*. In fact, it is impossible to see who is left to be saved during a future millennial period, in the light of Romans 11.

Predictably, this leads preterists to debunk the significance of present-day developments in the Middle East in general and Israel in particular:

> For years futurists, especially dispensationalists, have attached prophetic significance to the reestablishment of Israel as a nation in 1948. Many maintain that this event was prophesied in Matthew 24:32: "Now learn the parable of the fig tree: when its branch has already become tender, and puts forth its leaves, you know that the summer is near." This text has been made to read: "Now learn about restored nationhood for Israel. When Israel becomes a nation again, similar to the way a fig tree puts forth leaves to herald the coming of summer, then you will know that I am near to rapture the church."

For DeMar the cursing of the fig tree by Jesus is the focus of the fig tree comparison. The reason why Jesus cursed the fig tree, in his view, was not because that particular tree was guilty of some moral shortcoming. Rather, it was to be a lesson to the Jews that God had cast them aside and that they will never produce any fruit in the future. The judgment of A.D. 70 was God's final anathema on Israel.

Pre-millennialism Considered a "Heresy"

For replacement theologians, pre-millennialism, with its view of a future Antichrist and the literal, future restoration of Israel, is heresy. It is, they claim, a view which falls into the trap of unbiblical dualism and racial bigotry. Rushdoony represents this view when he writes:

> ... the expectation that history will culminate in the triumph of antichrist is not only a dualistic surrender of the material world to Satan, but also a direct offense against the announced power and supremacy of God in, through, and over all creation and history. Pre-millennial and a-millennial interpretations are tainted with the background of manichaean heresy, with its surrender of matter to darkness. A further heresy clouds pre-millennial interpretations of Scripture—their exaltation of racism into a divine principle. Every attempt to bring the Jew back into prophecy as a Jew is to give race and works (for racial descent is a human work) a priority over grace and Christ's work and is nothing more or less than paganism.

Rushdoony has misrepresented the pre-millennial position. We do not believe that "history will culminate in the triumph of antichrist" as he alleges. Though there will be a period in which Antichrist will set up his kingdom of world dominion, this is certainly not the culmination of history.

And the charge of racism is ludicrous. In the pre-millennial scheme God has a place for both the Jew and the gentile. The future exaltation of Israel in fulfillment of God's unconditional promises cannot be any more racist than the fact that God chose the people of Israel as the special bearers of His covenant mercies in the past could be considered racist. If pre-millennialism's belief in God's special love for Israel in the future is racist, then God must have been a racist in the past when He said, regarding Israel, "You only have I known of all the families of the earth ..." (Amos 3:2). The Scripture never allows us to hold to a meritorious election of Israel, for God's choice of Israel was a *grace* choice: "But because the LORD loved you, and because he would keep the oath which he had sworn unto your fathers, hath the LORD brought you out with a mighty hand" (Deut. 7:8). Rushdoony's erroneous notions need to be offset by a proper understanding of what the national election of Israel really means, as is articulated in the following statement by Fruchtenbaum:

> National election does not guarantee the salvation of every individual within the nation since only individual election can do that. Nor does national election guarantee the physical salvation of every member of the nation. What national election does guarantee is that God's purpose(s) for choosing the nation will be accomplished and that the elect nation will always survive as a distinct entity. It guarantees the physical salvation of the nation and in the case of Israel, even a national salvation. It is the national election of Israel that is the basis of Israel's status as the Chosen People.

There are many problems with replacement theology. God has made some very definite promises to Israel which He has never cancelled. Indeed, the very warp and woof of the New Testament is itself Jewish through and through. Messianic Jewish believer David H. Stern writes:

> ... the New Testament is in fact a Jewish book—by Jews, mostly about Jews and for Jews as well as Gentiles The central figure of the New Testament, Yeshua the Messiah, was a Jew who was born into a Jewish

family in Beit-Lechem, grew up among Jews in Galil, and died and rose from the grave in the Jewish capital, Yerushalayim—all in *Eretz-Yisra'el*, the land God gave the Jewish people. Moreover, Yeshua is still a Jew, since he is still alive: and nowhere does Scripture say or suggest that he has stopped being Jewish. His twelve closest followers were Jews. For years all his *talmidim* (disciples) were Jews, eventually numbering "tens of thousands" in Yerushalayim alone. The New Testament was written entirely by Jews (Luke being, in all likelihood, a proselyte to Judaism); and its message is directed "to the Jew especially, but equally to the Gentile." It was Jews who brought the Gospel to non-Jews, not the other way around. Sha'ul ("also known as Paul"), the chief emissary to the Gentiles, was a lifelong observant Jew, as is abundantly clear from evidence in the book of Acts. Indeed the main issue in the early Messianic Community—that is, the "Church"— was not whether a Jew could believe in Yeshua, but whether a Gentile could become Christian without converting to Judaism! The Messiah's vicarious Atonement is rooted in the Jewish sacrificial system. The Lord's Supper is rooted in the Jewish Passover. Immersion (baptism) is a Jewish practice. The New Covenant itself was promised by the Jewish prophet Yirmeyahu (Jeremiah). The very concept of Messiah is exclusively Jewish, and that Jewish Messiah taught that "salvation is from the Jews."

Jesus' Directives to Fulfill God's Plan

There are two very important scriptures that help us to ascertain the purpose of Jesus' ministry with reference to Israel. Matthew 10:5–6 speaks about the twelve apostles, our Lord's purpose for them, and His specific instructions to them: "These twelve Jesus sent forth, and commanded them, saying, Go not into the way of the gentiles, and into any city of the Samaritans enter ye not. But go rather to the lost sheep of the house of Israel."

Jesus' discussion with the Syrophoenician woman is similar. It will be remembered that a mother came to Jesus and related to him that "my daughter is grievously vexed with a devil" (Matt. 15:22). Jesus seemed not to heed her pleas; yet she continued crying out to Him, so much so that she was bothering the disciples. What was our Lord's initial response to her? "I am not sent," He said in Matthew 15:24, "but unto the lost sheep of the house of Israel."

These two passages from Matthew's gospel seem to contradict passages like John 3:16, Hebrews 2:9, and 1 John 2:2, but there is no contradiction. When Jesus first appeared at the commencement of His earthly ministry, He announced that the Kingdom was "at hand" (Mark 1:15). By putting Mark 1:15 and others like it with these two passages in Matthew it becomes clear that Jesus came to offer the Kingdom to Israel. His ministry was Israel-centered.

These considerations make it rather hard to believe that God is done with Israel. The Christian faith is so closely connected with Israel that anyone who teaches so radical a doctrine that is out of keeping with Scripture needs to have very good reason for doing so. Is it possible that replacement theologians have missed something?

Various arguments are used to support their position. Preterists, who hold to a replacement view, appeal to the stinging words of rebuke that Jesus had for the Jewish leaders, and then argue from the New Testament scriptures in which the church is described using Old Testament terminology to build their case. Also important to their argument are those Old Testament scriptures that seem to indicate that God's promises to Israel were all fulfilled in the conquest of the land and in the Solomonic Empire. Moreover, preterists find the actions of many Christians regarding Israel and the Jew to be ludicrous. DeMar quotes a statement made by futurist John Walvoord on Zechariah 13:8–9, where Scripture states that two-thirds of the children of Israel in the land will perish. DeMar writes:

> Israel's present population is around 4,500,000. If two-thirds of the Jews

living in Israel at the time of the "Great Tribulation" are to die, this will mean the death of nearly 3,000,000! In addition there is continued immigration from the former Soviet Union supported by Christian organizations. ... Financial support is raised by Christians to fund Jewish settlements in the occupied territories. ... Why aren't today's dispensationalists warning Jews about this coming holocaust by encouraging them to leave Israel until the conflagration is over? Instead, we find dispensationalists supporting and encouraging the relocation of Jews to the land of Israel. For what? A future holocaust?

DeMar, however, has missed something very important. We don't have to warn Jews "about the coming holocaust." Many of them already know about it! For Jews who read the Bible returning to the land is not an easy way out, but the way of faith and obedience to God.

The monthly magazine *Israel Today* features a "Torah Section." For July 2000 the devotional was entitled "Prosperity or Promise?" It relates the reports of the envoys of the tribes of Reuben and Gad. Moses responded to the report with anger (Numb. 32:14). The writer of the column asks:

> What was it that made Moses so angry? Were they involved in sexual orgies or murder? Did they set up foreign idols or profane the sacrifices? No, they only asked Moses, "Do not take us across the Jordan" (32:5), but let us stay here, in the land of Jazer and Gilead, "a place suitable for livestock" (32:1). In this request, Moses saw contempt for the Promised Land. Material benefits and prosperity were more important to the Reubenites and the Gadites than claiming God's promise. Moses was furious because they despised God's gift to Israel—the gift of the Land. Many Jews take God's promises regarding the land very seriously.

Again, reading from the devotional in the July 2000 issue of *Israel Today*:

There are still about 11 million Jews living in the Diaspora, some of them in totalitarian countries without freedom to emigrate to Israel. However, the majority of Jews who live outside the Land (5.8 million in the United States alone) could immigrate to Israel, but prefer to stay on "the other side of the Jordan," or the ocean, because the pastures are greener there. Their human reasoning is quite understandable, but it is natural and *not* based on *faith*.

DeMar can warn faithful Jews against returning to Israel if he wants. But they will regard such a warning as a word from an enemy, not a friend!

A Literal Approach to Prophecy or a Theological One?

Pre-millennial dispensationalism holds to a literal interpretation of prophecy rather than a theological one. I do not deny that prophecy uses symbolic language, or that the prophetic scriptures use figures of speech, as covenant writers often charge. Covenant theologians love to cite a passage in prophecy that is obviously figurative, and which is taken by dispensationalists in a non-literal manner, and then covenant writers will fault dispensationalists with inconsistency. The charge is that dispensationalists have a strict definition of "literal," but then apply it in such a fluid way that no one can quite tell what dispensationalists mean by the word "literal."

The charge is a straw tiger. Dispensationalists readily acknowledge the existence of symbols, figures of speech, and allegorical language in Scripture, as well as in the prophetic scriptures. However, when it comes to prophecies regarding God's Kingdom on earth and the nation of Israel, we believe that these prophecies are to be taken literally.

"Israel" means "Israel," not "church." God's promises to Israel literally dwelling safely in a land of abundant blessings are all to be taken literally. Though the Old Testament reveals the use of figures of speech and poetic language, those expressions are historically and prophetically descriptive of God's earthly people, Israel. Couch explains the dispensational understanding of the symbolic language in the Book of Revelation:

> A pre-millennialist will argue for a systematic, hermeneutical approach to unlocking Revelation. Signs, symbols, and figures of speech explain literal concepts. It is true that Revelation is very symbolic (though not totally), but there are still literal events embedded behind the figurative language. The typical a-millennialist approaches Revelation with a symbolic bias. The pre-millennialist understands that symbols are used to explain concepts that are difficult to comprehend. The pre-millennialist approach renders consistent patterns for understanding Revelation.

The Early Church and the Change in Focus

Though the apostolic church was made up, in large part, of Jews, by the second century A.D. this was quickly changing, and the church was becoming overwhelmingly gentile. Scripturally, the gentiles are a wild olive branch grafted into the believing family of Abraham (Rom. 11:16–17). The apostle Paul exhorted the saints, "Be not highminded, but fear" (Rom. 11:20), and warns them about boasting against the branches (Rom. 11:18). But as the church spread to gentile regions, a strange spirit of arrogance began to develop. In the early centuries of Christian history, the gentiles began to see themselves as the "new" Israel and came to believe that they had replaced physical Israel. The emergence of this "theology of replacement" became very pronounced in Justin Martyr's *Dialogue with Trypho, a Jew*. Justin (d. 166) emphasized that what was of old and had belonged to Israel was now the property of Christians. The Jewish scriptures were a central part of this transference. They are "not yours but ours," Justin stated emphatically to Trypho.

Covenant theology is one of the more popular forms that replacement theology takes. Various forms of replacement teaching are found in covenant writers. Some would argue that God's promises to Israel were originally intended for the church. A variant of this view is that Israel forfeited her promises through disobedience. Another shade of teaching claims that Israel's promises have already been completely fulfilled, either under Joshua or Solomon (Josh. 11–12; 1 Kings 4), and that no further fulfillment need be expected in the future. In discussing the various biblical texts to which replacement theologians appeal, Paul Benware reminds us that

> ... First Kings 4:21–24 and Joshua 11:23 and 21:43–45 do not teach the final fulfillment of the Palestinian covenant. In the Joshua passages it is obvious that when the statements were made Israel had not come close to possessing the land area that was promised to Abraham. Joshua had conquered thirty-one kings, and now the way was prepared for each individual tribe to conquer the Canaanites in their own designated land areas. Both of these passages are followed by statements that list large areas of the Promised Land that still needed to be taken (cf. Joshua 13:1–7 and 23:4–7). So the land was not yet conquered and, in fact, would not be conquered by Israel at that time in history (Judg. 1:21–36). The statement in Joshua reflects an Old Testament concept of fulfillment wherein the promise of God was being fulfilled and that generation was getting their share. But it was not the final or ultimate fulfillment of the promise.

It is most significant that many centuries after the statements in Joshua and elsewhere (that are wrongly understood by replacement theologians as indicating a total and complete fulfillment of God's promises to Israel) were given, that the later prophets were speaking of a *yet future* fulfillment of God's promises to Israel (Mic. 4:4–7; Zech. 8:3–8, et al). If God's promises to Israel had already been fulfilled, then why does God continue to tell Israel to hope in the future fulfillment of His promises?

Also compelling is the fact that the fulfillment of God's yet future promises to Israel rests on the highest motive possible, the glory of God, not the merit or wellbeing of the Jewish people. Hence, the standard replacement arguments that Israel has forfeited her promises through disobedience, or that somehow God has changed His mind, are totally without merit. In Ezekiel we read:

> Therefore say unto the house of Israel, Thus saith the Lord GOD; I do not this for your sakes, O house of Israel, but *for mine holy name's sake,* which ye have profaned among the heathen, whither ye went. And I *will sanctify my great name,* which was profaned among the heathen, which ye have profaned in the midst of them; *and the heathen shall know that I am the* 1LORD, saith the Lord GOD, when I shall be sanctified in you before their eyes.
>
> —Ezekiel 36:22–24

We must not miss the significance of this Scripture. Israel had profaned God's name by her wicked deeds, yet God would not forsake His people. His unconditional love for the people, and the land He had given them, will overcome their hard-heartedness. He will redeem them for the honor of His name, and He will do it openly and publicly. Covenant theology prides itself on being one of the few groups of Christians that emphasizes the glory and sovereignty of God, but in this respect, it has failed to live up to its calling.

Prophecies Concerning A.D. 70 Don't Match Prophecies of the Future

Is there any basis for claiming that prophecy regarding Israel was fulfilled in A.D. 70? The answer that I must give is an unequivocal "no." Interpreters can only fall into this trap when they read "church" for "Israel," something that always yields confused results. Walter Kaiser explains with reference to Zechariah:

> In no other chapter of the Bible is the interpretation of the name "Israel" more important than in Zechariah 14. To say that "Israel" means "church," as many have done, would lead to a most confusing picture in this chapter and in the end of chapter 13. For example, 13:8–9 affirms that two-thirds of the land (Israel) will die, but few would be willing to say that two-thirds of the church will be slaughtered in the final day. Clearly "Israel" refers to that geopolitical unit known today as the nation of Israel.

Moreover, though preterists affirm that Zechariah chapters twelve through fourteen refer to the events Of A.D. 70, a comparison of these chapters with Luke 21:20–24—a passage that both preterists and futurists agree refers to the events of A.D. 70—will readily show that what is described in Zechariah 14 is not what is predicted for A.D. 70. In Luke 21:20–24 we read:

> And when ye shall see Jerusalem compassed with armies, then know that the desolation thereof is nigh. Then let them which are in Judea flee to the mountains; and let them which are in the midst of it depart out; and let not them that are in the countries enter thereinto. For these be the days of vengeance, that all things which are written may be fulfilled. But woe unto them that are with child, and to them that give suck, in those days! for there shall be great distress in the land, and wrath upon this people. And they shall fall by the edge of the sword, and shall be led away captive into all nations: and Jerusalem shall be trodden down of the Gentiles, until the times of the Gentiles be fulfilled.

The Roman general Vespasian set siege against Jerusalem, but temporarily pulled back to return to Rome upon the death of Nero to become emperor.

Titus, Vespasian's son, subsequently returned to Jerusalem and razed the city and temple in A.D. 70.

The above-cited passage provides a prophecy of this event. It would be a time of Jerusalem's desolation (vs. 20), and also a time of vengeance and wrath against Jerusalem and the Jewish nation in fulfillment of prophecy (vss. 22–23). This came about as a result of the Romans exacting retribution against the Jews for their rebellion against Caesar, but the wrath was also from God for Israel's rejection of her Messiah and had been predicted both by Christ (Luke 13:9, 34–35; 19:41–44) and Moses and the prophets (Deut. 28:49–68; 32:35; Jer. 6:1–8; 26:1–9; Hos. 9:7). The passage in Luke 21 predicts that there would be great distress in the land (vs. 23) and that the nations would bring a sword to Jerusalem (vs. 24). This condition of desolation is given a time limit—"until the times of the Gentiles be fulfilled" (vs. 24).

I have given the prophetic picture of the destruction of Jerusalem and the temple at the hands of the Romans in A.D. 70 in some detail because I want to contrast it with Zechariah chapters twelve through fourteen to show that the two cannot reasonably be considered as describing the same event. There are too many conflicting details. Therefore, it would be far more in keeping with the Scriptures to conclude that while Luke 21 describes an event that is past from our perspective, Zechariah, chapters twelve through fourteen, describes something which is yet future. By comparing the two passages we discern that:

1. *There are differences in the time of fulfillment.* While Luke 21 describes a past fulfillment, Zechariah uses words descriptive of eschatological fulfillment: "Behold, the day of the LORD cometh " (14:1). "And it shall come to pass in that day, that the light shall not be clear, nor dark" (14:6).
2. *There are differences in God's relationship to the Jewish people.* God is now the defender of Jerusalem instead of her enemy: "In that day shall the LORD defend the inhabitants of Jerusalem … And it shall come to pass

in that day, that I will seek to destroy all the nations that come against Jerusalem" (12:8–9).

3. *There are differences in the relationship of the Jewish people to God.* There is confession of sin and a looking to the Messiah in repentance and expectation instead of continued hard-heartedness: "And I will pour upon the house of David, and upon the inhabitants of Jerusalem, the spirit of grace and supplications: and they shall look upon me whom they have pierced" (12:10). "In that day there shall be a fountain opened to the house of David and to the inhabitants of Jerusalem for sin and for uncleanness" (13:1).

4. *There are differences in Israel's promises.* Israel will be judged, as in A.D. 70, but this eschatological judgment will produce spiritual renewal: "And I will bring the third part through the fire, and will refine them as silver is refined, and will try them as gold is tried: they shall call on my name, and I will hear them: I will say, It is my people: and they shall say, the LORD is my God" (13:9).

5. *There are differences in Israel's religious condition.* After A.D. 70 Israel was in spiritual decline, but in the future the idols will be removed from the land: "And it shall come to pass in that day, saith the LORD of hosts, that I will cut off the names of the idols out of the land, and they shall no more be remembered" (13:2).

6. *There are differences in Israel's relationship to the nations.* The nations shall bring their wealth to Jerusalem instead of destroying the city: and the wealth of all the heathen round about shall be gathered together, gold, and silver, and apparel, in great abundance" (14:14) The nations shall come and worship Israel's God. "And it shall come to pass, that every one that is left of all the nations which came against Jerusalem shall even go up from year to year to worship the King, the LORD of hosts, and to keep the feast of tabernacles (14:16).

7. *There are differences in Israel's relationship to "the times of the Gentiles."* They

are now fulfilled, and the redemption prophesied in Luke 21:28 is now a reality. "And it shall be in that day, that living waters shall go out from Jerusalem ... And the Lord shall be king over all the earth: in that day shall there be one Lord, and his name one" (14:8–9).

Testimony from the New Testament

It would be wrong to conclude that God's future plans for Israel are revealed only in the Old Testament scriptures. Though the New Testament scriptures are mainly written to and for the church they, nevertheless, give abundant testimony to God's plans for the people and nation of Israel. It is to these scriptures that we will now turn.

Paul's epistle to the Romans is carefully organized. It has several discernible sections in which the apostle deals with a number of key issues. In chapter eight Paul presents the truth of the security of the believer in Christ, and the unshakable purposes of God in grace and mercy toward His people. Indeed, chapter eight is very encouraging. This encouragement is rooted in the immutable character of God and His unchanging purpose. "What shall we then say to these things? If God be for us, who can be against us?" (Rom. 8:31).

With such a statement as this, we might assume that nothing else of a doctrinal nature can be said. Surely, Romans 8 says it all! It is the apotheosis of all chapters setting forth the glory of God and our security in His Son. Why then doesn't the apostle just move on to chapter twelve and deal with the so-called "practical" and "applied" truths of Scripture? The answer: Because there is some "unfinished business" that needs to be addressed. It is of such a nature that, if left unresolved, might seem to even contradict what Paul has set forth in Romans 8. An objector might raise a hand and ask: "Well, if God is faithful, how come He hasn't been faithful to Israel?"

Chapters nine through eleven deal with this issue. Paul knew that if God could not be trusted to be faithful to His ancient covenant people, how could He be trusted to be faithful to Christians in Rome in the first century A.D.?

In these chapters the apostle takes the "long look" at Israel. Chapter nine treats Israel's election in the *past;* chapter ten treats Israel's hardness in the *present;* chapter eleven treats Israel's restoration in the *future.*

When I first began to seriously study Romans, chapter eleven, I began to see how the preceding two chapters form a very important line of reasoning in the apostle's train of thought. I had to conclude that a-millennialism is wrong. It seemed quite clear to me at that time, as at the present time, that God is not yet through with the Jew. There is much that will happen in the future regarding Israel. If this is true, then there is something terribly wrong with any eschatology that holds to preterism or a replacement view.

As a young Christian growing in an a-millennial church, I was puzzled by Israel. It appeared to be a "fossil nation" that still, for some reason that escaped me, continued to exist. Significantly, I realized that the apostle Paul was himself a key to prophetically understanding this issue. In Romans 11:1 he asks a question and provides the answer: "Hath God cast away his people? God forbid. *For I also am an Israelite."* Paul is challenging his detractor: "If you believe that God has cast away His people, how then do you explain MY conversion to Christ?"

The student of Scripture will notice that Paul's conversion is presented three times in the Book of Acts (chapters nine, twenty-two, and twenty-six). It must have been an important matter. But why did Luke, the human author of Acts, give Paul's conversion account three times?

We must dismiss the idea that Paul's conversion is a model for all future conversions because it is not. There is much in Paul's conversion experience that bears no resemblance to the conversion experience of most Christians today. How many of us have been blinded by a light from heaven and thrown to the ground by the manifest presence of the Lord?

Romans 9—The Real Jew Is Not a Gentile

As Paul opens chapter nine, he expresses great sorrow for his *Jewish* brothers. "I have great heaviness and continual sorrow in my heart. For I could wish that myself were accursed from Christ for *my brethren,* my kinsmen *according to the flesh*" (Rom. 9:2–3). There can be no doubt about it. Paul is not speaking about the gentiles, nor about people in general. He is speaking about his physical and ethnic "relatives"—Jews, the descendants of Abraham.

But is the apostle being carnal and selfish about this familial concern? Is this concern just a personal preference on Paul's part? No, because Paul knew of God's past election of Israel:

> Who are Israelites; to whom pertaineth the adoption, and the glory, and the covenants, and the giving of the law, and the service of God, and the promises; Whose are the fathers, and of whom as concerning the flesh Christ came ..."
>
> —Romans 9:4–5

The apostle, however, interjects an important word of clarification:

> Not as though the word of God hath taken none effect. For they are not all Israel, which are of Israel: Neither, because they are the seed of Abraham, are they all children: but, in Isaac shall thy seed be called. That is, They which are the children of the flesh, these are not the children of God.
>
> —Romans 9:6–8

The apostle effortlessly strips away an argument that preterists and replacement theologians would raise in the future. Paul, the Jew, did not teach that one is saved by automatically being a Jew. So much for Rushdoony's charge that pre-millennialism elevates a principle of racism! "The children of the flesh are not the children of God."

Abraham had two sons: Ishmael (with Hagar) and Isaac (with Sarah). Not all the descendants of Abraham receive God's special covenantal promises, but only those who are in the line of Isaac. This is the point of Romans 9:7. It is not "because they are the seed of Abraham, are they all children." Even the racial and national promises made to Abraham did not include every physical descendant of Abraham.

We can begin to see how the apostle is dealing with an objector. He emphatically states: "Not as though the word of God hath taken none effect" (vs. 6). It all has to do with God's sovereign decision in election. What Paul has to say about Israel has to do with God's choice. Since Ishmael was Abraham's firstborn, he, according to the laws and practices of primogeniture, should have been the one to be the bearer of the Divine promise. But he wasn't. Abraham's son, Isaac, likewise had two sons, Jacob and Esau. Esau was the firstborn and should have been chosen, but he too was not. More startling is the way the electing grace of God becomes even more apparent in the case of Jacob and Esau. They both had the same parents, Isaac and Rebecca.

No doubt, in this passage the apostle is not speaking of an individual election—as though God loves one individual and hates another. Jacob and Esau were two individuals, and God's choice of Jacob over Esau took place before the children were born or had done anything good or bad (Rom. 9:11), but the Lord indicated a national election when he said to Rebecca, "two *nations* are in thy womb, and two manner of *people* shall be separated from thy bowels" (Gen. 25:23).

God's faithfulness, therefore, should not be in question. It never was His purpose to save every single descendant of Abraham. That was the error of the Jewish leaders of the first century A.D. They were deeply offended when Jesus taught that they were not all Abraham's children: "I know that ye are Abraham's seed; but ye seek to kill me, because my word hath no place in you. If ye were Abraham's children, ye would do the works of Abraham" (John

8:37, 39). Jesus acknowledged that the religious leaders of his day were "Abraham's seed," but they really weren't behaving like his "children."

These considerations are vitally important in dealing with the objections raised by replacement theologians. The fact that God has turned away from certain groups of Jews in the New Testament does not mean that He has rejected Israel. He did the same thing during the Old Testament era, when He was working uniquely and distinctly with Israel. If God's rebuke of *some* Jews in the Old Testament did not mean that Israel was not God's elect nation, why should His rebuke of *some* Jews in the New Testament era be taken as an indication that He has now turned away from Israel?

Romans 10

In Romans 10 the apostle leaves his discussion regarding the true meaning of Israel's *past* election and moves on to discuss Israel's *present* rejection of Christ. No doubt, there were some in Israel who welcomed Christ, such as Simeon and Anna (Luke 2:25–38), but they were in the minority. By and large, Israel has rejected her Messiah. "He came unto his own," we read in John 1:11, "and his own received him not." Why did that happen?

In Romans 10 Paul addresses this issue. He points out that the Jews were very religious and very zealous, something that was especially true of the Pharisees. The word "Pharisee" is most likely derived from the word *perushim,* meaning "separated ones." They were strong objectors to the Hellenization of Jewish culture. In order to avoid being "tainted" by those around them, the Pharisees developed a comprehensive system of rules and regulations that were guaranteed to keep them from being defiled. Gundry notes:

> Some rabbis of the Pharisees forbade spitting on the bare ground during the Sabbath lest the action by disturbing the dirt constitute plowing and therefore Sabbath-breaking. A woman could not look in the mirror on the

Sabbath lest she see a gray hair, be tempted to pluck it out, yield to the temptation and thereby work on the Sabbath. The Pharisees devised legal loopholes for their convenience. Although one could not carry his clothes in his arms out of a burning house on the Sabbath, he could put on several layers of clothing and bring them out by wearing them. A Pharisee was not supposed to travel on the Sabbath more than three-fifths of a mile from the town or city where he lived. But if he wished to go farther, on Friday he deposited food for two meals three-fifths of a mile from his home in the direction he wished to travel. The deposit of food made that place his home away from home, so that on the Sabbath he could travel yet another three-fifths of a mile.

This kind of behavior is probably what Paul was referring to when he wrote:

> For I bear them record that they have a zeal of God, but not according to knowledge. For they being ignorant of God's righteousness, and going about to establish their own righteousness, have not submitted themselves unto the righteousness of God.
>
> —Romans 10:2–3

This was, perhaps, precipitated by the Babylonian captivity, which was a traumatic and devastating experience for Israel. A foreign invader had come into the land, desecrated the Jewish temple, and carried away many captives. Large numbers of Jews came to believe that God had brought this judgment upon the Jewish people and nation because they had failed to preserve their Jewish distinctiveness. They therefore resolved that this would never again happen. The sufferings of the captivity left a lasting impression and "cured" them of their idolatry. However, their zeal went too far. It produced a haughty self-righteousness that finds no place for God.

Though they tried to follow their own Scriptures, they were woefully ignorant of their true intent, so Paul quotes Isaiah 28:16 to show that salvation is not by works, but by faith: "Whosoever believeth on him shall not be ashamed" (Rom. 10:11). And Paul writes that this way of salvation is true for all:

> For there is no difference between the Jew and the Greek: for the same Lord over all is rich unto all that call upon Him. For whosoever shall call upon the name of the Lord shall be saved.
> —Romans 10:12–13, quoting Joel 2:32

Romans 10:14–17 advances Paul's argument. The apostle writes:

> How then shall they call on him in whom they have not believed? and how shall they believe in him of whom they have not heard? and how shall they hear without a preacher? And how shall they preach, except they be sent? as it is written, How beautiful are the feet of them that preach the gospel of peace, and bring glad tidings of good things! But they have not all obeyed the gospel. For Esaias saith, Lord, who hath believed our report? So then faith cometh by hearing, and hearing by the word of God.

A Mission to Jews

This is an oft-quoted passage used to bolster the church's missionary program. The context, however, shows that this missionary program needs to have some focus on Israel. The context is a treatment of Israel's spiritual blindness. Paul writes, "Brethren, my heart's desire and prayer to God for Israel is, that they might be saved" (Rom. 10:1).

No doubt, the church's missionary activity to gentiles is also included. In verses twenty and twenty-one of chapter ten, the apostle quotes from Isaiah 65:1. Paul writes:

> But Esaias is very bold, and saith, I was found of them that sought me not; I was made manifest unto them that asked not after me. But to Israel he saith, All day long I have stretched forth my hands unto a disobedient and gainsaying people.

During this present period of Israel's hardness, God is bringing salvation to the gentiles. Nevertheless, the Lord's heart is still with Israel.

In Romans 10:19–20 the apostle brings up a subject he will develop later, namely God's plan to provoke Israel to jealousy with gentile conversions:

> But I say, Did not Israel know? First Moses saith, I will provoke you to jealousy by them that are no people, and by a foolish nation I will anger you. But Esaias is very bold, and saith, I was found of them that sought me not; I was made manifest unto them that asked not after me.

Again, Paul quotes Deuteronomy 32:21. Earlier he referenced this truth in Romans 9:22–26. God's grace is never frustrated. In Israel's case it was redirected, but only temporarily. God is now sending the gospel to the gentiles, but He has, as it were, another motive than that which immediately meets the eye. He is provoking Israel to jealousy. It was grace for gentiles, but it was also how God would demonstrate His grace to the Jew.

This helps us gain insight into the statement found in Romans 1:16: "to the Jew first, and also to the Greek." Preterists and replacement writers act as if Paul simply said, "to the Greek." But the text states, "to the Jew *first*," and then to the Greek.

"First" does not mean "first in time," as though the apostle were merely saying that God chronologically worked among Jews first, but after that, his plan now is to the Greek. Covenant theologian John Murray explains:

> It does not appear sufficient to regard this priority as that merely of time.

... The implication appears to be rather that the power of God unto salvation through faith has primary relevance to the Jews.

It is in this way that Paul is preparing his readers for the truths which follow in chapter eleven. Great numbers of Jews will be saved in the future because the gospel of Christ is for them. He is saying, in effect, "There is nothing unusual about large numbers of Jews coming to Christ because the gospel is to the Jew *first*."

This principle is evident on the pages of the New Testament. When Jesus commissioned His disciples, He forbade them to preach to the gentiles or Samaritans but sent them to Israel (Matt. 10:1–6). Following His resurrection, Jesus commanded His disciples to wait in Jerusalem and to start their preaching from there (Luke 24:46–49; Acts 1:8). In keeping with this it is to be observed that the first seven chapters of the Book of Acts were about Jews. Gentiles who were brought into the sphere of grace were Jewish proselytes. However, because of the stoning of Stephen, which was a dramatic display of Israel's persistent rejection of her Messiah, the gospel was sent to the Samaritans (Acts 8:1–8) and then to other gentiles (Acts 10).

Romans 11—God's People

The question Paul asks in Romans 11:1, and the way he phrases it, is significant: "I say then, Hath God cast away his people?" Notice, the question is not: "Has God cast away the Jews?" If it had been presented in that language, we may rightly infer that a negative answer would imply that Jews, along with gentiles, are objects of God's love. Paul, however, calls the Jews "his people." They are God's and they are God's people, indicating ethnic Israel as being in a unique and privileged position.

The words "his people" are used in a similar fashion in the Old Testament. "For the LORD will not forsake his people for his great name's sake" (1 Sam.

12:22; see also Ps. 94:14; Jer. 31:37). And this certainly implies a unique national identity. Murray, dean of Reformed Presbyterian commentators and certainly no dispensationalist, nevertheless writes:

> There should be no difficulty in recognizing the appropriateness of calling Israel the people whom God foreknew. Israel had been elected and peculiarly loved and thus distinguished from all other nations.

This conclusion is certainly justified by the answer to the question of verse one that Paul gives in the first part of verse two: "God hath not cast away His people *which he foreknew.*" It is doubtful if "foreknowledge" simply means "to know about beforehand." In Amos 3:2 God says, with reference to Israel: "You only have I *known* of all the families of the earth: therefore I will punish you for all your iniquities." God is not saying that He only knew about the Jews, and knew nothing about the other people of the world. Rather, He is saying: "You only have I *loved* [and therefore showered you with my special blessings] of all the families of the earth." That's why He would punish them. He loves them too much to allow them to continue in their sin.

How the Gentiles Fit In

Israel's future conversion is connected with the bringing in of the gentiles. After giving those wonderful promises of worldwide peace and the removal of the enmity between man and the wild beasts, Isaiah states: "And in *that* day there shall be a root of Jesse, which shall stand for an ensign of the people; to it shall *the Gentiles* seek" (Isa. 11:10). This is described in conjunction with Israel's regathering "the dispersed of Judah from the four corners of the earth" (Isa. 11:12). Another passage in Isaiah speaks about this unique time of blessing upon Israel and the gentiles:

> Arise, shine; for thy light is come, and the glory of the LORD is risen upon thee. For, behold, the darkness shall cover the earth, and gross darkness the people: but the LORD shall arise upon thee, and his glory shall be seen upon thee [Israel]. And the Gentiles shall come to thy [Israel's] light, and kings to the brightness of thy rising. Lift up thine eyes round about, and see: all they gather themselves together, they come to thee: thy sons shall come from far, and thy daughters shall be nursed at thy side. Then thou shalt see, and flow together, and thine heart shall fear, and be enlarged; because the abundance of the sea shall be converted unto thee, the forces of the Gentiles shall come unto thee.
>
> —Isaiah 60:1–5

The problem, however, in this present age, is that instead of Israel's rise, we see Israel's fall. The gentiles are to come to Israel's light, but in the present age there is nothing but darkness in Israel. And the same was true in Paul's day. Jewish unbelief was rampant. Paul knew about it firsthand because he had been persecuted by Jews who regarded him as an apostate Jew and a traitor of Judaism. As I have pointed out, this did not really frustrate the grace of God, but it did reveal some features in God's program for Israel that had not been heretofore revealed. In this period of Israel's hardness God is working in and through the church. The Church Age is unique in that it reveals: (1) a new people; (2) a new program; (3) a new plan. Of course, "new" doesn't mean that God changed His mind or had second thoughts about the whole matter. It was "new" to God's people because God had not yet revealed the details of the Church Age.

The Church Age Not the Fulfillment of God's Promises

While the Church Age is "new" in the above-mentioned ways, the Church Age is not the fulfillment of God's promises to Israel. In Isaiah 11, and also in Isaiah 60, gentiles are seen as the recipients of God's grace during the time of Israel's renewal. Therefore, since we are not living in the time of Israel's renewal, the present Church Age cannot be the time of the fulfillment of these Old Testament promises. God prophesied that large numbers of gentiles would be saved, but it would be in a time of a great spiritual awakening in Israel, not during a period of spiritual blindness and hard-heartedness.

These scriptural considerations are important because they tie ethnic Israel's restoration with her *national* restoration. Isaiah was not speaking about a future time of blessing upon ethnic Jews "wherever they may find themselves." He was speaking about a future time of blessing upon Jews who have been renewed by the Spirit of God and who have been miraculously brought to their land from afar.

Some replacement theologians reluctantly admit that some degree of blessing is anticipated for Israel in the future, but they see the fulfillment in connection with the church. Adams gives the standard replacement view of Romans 11:25–26 when he writes, "The 'fulness' of the gentiles and 'all Israel' surely comprises the total numbers of that body which we call the *church*." Adams admits that "it is possible that during this period, there will be a large turning of Hebrews to faith in Christ, as Romans 11 may indicate." But is it true that large numbers of Jews "may" be saved in the future and brought into the church? It seems to me that the Bible is quite clear that large numbers of Jews *will* be saved in the future. They won't be brought into the church, however, but they will be brought into their own land:

> But ye, O mountains of Israel, ye shall shoot forth your branches, and yield your fruit to my people of Israel; for they are at hand to come. For, behold, I am for you, and I will turn unto you, and ye shall be tilled and sown: And I will multiply men upon you, all the house of Israel, even all of it: and the cities shall be inhabited, and the wastes shall be builded ...
>
> —Ezekiel 36:8–10

> For I will take you from among the heathen, and gather you out of all countries, and will bring you into your own land. Then will I sprinkle clean water upon you, and ye shall be clean: from all your filthiness, and from all your idols, will I cleanse you.
>
> —Ezekiel 36:24–25

> Thus saith the Lord GOD', In the day that I have cleansed you from all your iniquities I will also cause you to dwell in the cities, and the wastes shall be builded. And the desolate land shall be tilled, whereas it lay desolate in the sight of all that passed by. And they shall say, This land that was desolate is become like the garden of Eden; and the waste and desolate and ruined cities are become fenced, and are inhabited. Then the heathen that are left round about you shall know that I the LORD build the ruined places, and plant that that was desolate: I the LORD have spoken it, and I will do it.
>
> —Ezekiel 36:33–36

If God doesn't do what He has promised, His name will be dishonored. The Bertrand Russells of the world will laugh.

Preterists and replacement theologians like to respond to passages like this by saying that they are all from the Old Testament, and that not one is from the New Testament. My answer: Why should New Testament books and letters, written primarily to Christians in the Church Age, present God's promises of a land to Jews? The church has a heavenly inheritance, not an earthly one (1 Pet. 1:4).

In addition, I would have to ask if these promises have (1) ever been fulfilled; (2) ever been cancelled? It simply will not do to claim that these promises were fulfilled in times past. God promised to bring a tremendous outpouring of His Holy Spirit upon Israel. This revival among the Jews will be accompanied with changes in the topography of the land, abundant blessings being poured upon the land, and the Jewish people being in the land.

Nothing like this has happened in Israel in the past or present. Though many Jews are returning to their land at the present time, the world yet awaits the fulfillment of God's spiritual promises to Israel. If we believe that God can be trusted to bring His promises to pass, we must believe that these promises will be literally fulfilled. To try to explain a future conversion of large numbers of Jews in the future apart from the land-promises given to Israel will not do. Scripture does not envision the church as taking any part in this prophetic fulfillment. Expositors of Scripture only arrive at such a conclusion by bringing to Scripture the presuppositions of Reformation theology. Should we get our eschatology from John Calvin and his disciples, or is there a better course to follow?

Two Illustrations: The Lump and the Olive Tree

In Romans 11:16–24 Paul uses two illustrations to show that even though Israel is in a condition of apostasy at the present time, God is not yet done with Israel. The first illustration is the lump of dough. Paul writes: "For if the firstfruit be holy, the lump is also holy" (Rom. 11:16a). This illustration is taken from Numbers 15:17–21, which reads:

> And the LORD spake unto Moses, saying, Speak unto the children of Israel, and say unto them, When ye come into the land whither I bring you, Then it shall be, that, when ye eat of the bread of the land, ye shall offer up an heave offering unto the LORD. Ye shall offer up a cake of the first of your dough for an heave offering: as ye do the heave offering of the threshingfloor, so shall ye heave it. Of the first of your dough ye shall give unto the Lord an heave offering in your generations.

A heave offering was a symbolical act of the priest in which he would lift the right shoulder of an animal up and down (Lev. 7:32). This symbolically set aside the animal as an item to be used by the priests and meant that the animal had been consecrated for a special purpose. In Romans 11:16a, the reference to the first of the dough means that the entire lump was set aside for a special purpose.

The second illustration is that of an olive tree, first referenced in this passage in Romans 11:16b: "... and if the root be holy, so are the branches." "The firstfruit and lump are parallel to the root and the branches," writes Murray. "The root is surely the patriarchs. Furthermore, in verse 28 Israel are said to be 'beloved for the fathers' sake'" It is the root that supports the tree and is a fitting symbol of the Old Testament patriarchs. God entered into a covenantal relationship with Abraham, Isaac, and Jacob. Thus, it is God's covenantal relationship which sustains Israel even to this day.

But what about the large number of Jews in Paul's day who had rejected Christ? Paul pictures them as branches that were broken off (Rom. 11:19–20), but quickly adds that "branches" of "a wild olive tree" were grafted into the olive tree to share in the life of the tree (vs. 17). In verse twenty-four Paul says that the gentiles were grafted in "contrary to nature," meaning that it is more natural for Israel to be a part of the tree then for the gentiles to be grafted in. The fact that the gentiles have been grafted in, therefore, implies Divine agency.

These illustrations used by the apostle are made more powerful when we realize the difference between apostasy in Israel and apostasy in the church. The Scriptures lead us to think that prior to the Rapture of the church there will be great apostasy in the professing church. People will want entertainment and stories rather than the truth of God's Word. Yet, as Wiersbe observes,

> There is no hope for the apostate church, but there is hope for apostate Israel! Why? Because of the roots of the olive tree. God will keep his promises to the patriarchs, but God will break off the Gentiles because of their unbelief.

No matter how far Israel falls, the root is still living, and the fall will not be final nor irremediable.

This is supported by the words of Romans 11:26: "And so all Israel shall be saved." Replacement writers seek to evade the force of these words by stating that "all Israel" means "all the elect of God," allegedly "the true Israel." However, covenant theologian John Murray observes that

> ... it is exegetically impossible to give to "Israel" in this verse any other denotation than that which belongs to the term through this chapter. There is the sustained contrast between Israel and the Gentiles. It is of ethnic Israel Paul is speaking and Israel could not possibly include Gentiles.

Once again, I have quoted John Murray because he is in the covenant camp. However, it is most significant that despite his covenant position, his integrity as a careful expounder of the Word of God necessitates that he be honest with the sacred text.

"All Israel" is to be contrasted with "blindness in part" (Rom. 11:25) to avoid a common misconception. "All Israel will be saved" no more means "all Jews without exception will be saved" than "blindness in part" means "all Jews without exception are currently hardened against Christ." Once again, to quote Murray:

> The salvation of Israel must be conceived of on a scale commensurate with their trespass, their loss, their casting away, their breaking off, and their hardening, commensurate, of course, in the opposite direction In a word, it is the salvation of the mass of Israel that the apostle affirms.

Romans 11:27 brings all of this into the sphere of God's covenantal promise: "For this is my covenant unto them, when I shall take away their sins." The apostle's reference to God's covenant, in a context of Israel's hardness and unbelief, demonstrates that the future restoration of Israel is not something that God does on the basis of Israel's merit. Indeed, Paul has argued that Israel has no merit. Verse twenty-seven, when taken in conjunction with the statement in verse twenty-eight, that the Jews are beloved for the "fathers' sakes," makes it indisputable that Israel's future restoration is all a work of grace.

Replacement Theology Deletes an Earthly Millennium

By now it should be no surprise to my readers that replacement theology not only sees no future for Israel but does the same with the promises of an earthly millennium: There is no earthly millennium. They claim that there is no room in God's prophetic scenario for such a millennium. When Christ returns there is a resurrection of both the just and the unjust immediately followed by the end of the universe as we know it. The answer to Question 87 of the *Westminster Larger Catechism* states:

> We are to believe that, at the last day, there shall be a general resurrection of the dead, both of the just and unjust; when they that are then found alive shall in a moment be changed; and the self-same bodies of the dead which are laid in the grave, being then again united to their souls forever, shall be raised up by the power of Christ.

By allegorizing the Old Testament Kingdom promises and missing some of the details of the New Testament eschatological passages, Reformed theologians end up with a truncated eschatology. A-millennialist Adams explains his view from 2 Peter 3:

> ... Second Peter 3 is conclusive evidence that no partially-golden millennial age on this earth can follow the second coming. Peter does not say that

at Christ's coming things will be improved merely by partial changes, but that they will be so completely transformed that they can only be called a brand new heavens and earth. For this we are to look [he says], for this new heavens and earth "wherein dwelleth righteousness" not for a millennial age … In addition, there could not possibly be any flesh and blood mortals left to populate a millennium, even if there were such a future age. Peter assures us that it is at Christ's coming (not 1,000 years later) that the judgment will occur and the eternal destiny of unsaved men will be determined. Where could they even find a place to stand when the heavens and earth are exploding about them and melting beneath their feet?

The author of this statement contends that when Jesus Christ returns a second time, the universe is burned up. Hence, there is no room allowed in God's scenario for a millennial reign following Christ's return. However, while it may appear that when the Lord returns everything is immediately destroyed in a cosmic conflagration, a closer reading of the text will reveal that there is plenty of room for an earthly millennium. Second Peter 3:10 does not say that the eschatological conflagration takes place at the beginning of the Day of the Lord. Rather it states: "But the day of the Lord will come as a thief in the night; *in the which* the heavens shall pass away with a great noise, and the elements shall melt with fervent heat, the earth also and the works that are therein shall be burned up." According to this Scripture cosmic dissolution occurs somewhere *within* this time period known as "the Day of the Lord." A-millennialists erroneously assume that the Day of the Lord is a very short time—maybe an instant—in which the Lord comes, and everything is over, but that is not a necessary conclusion. In Scripture "day" can certainly refer to a twenty-four–hour period and, as when the word appears in Genesis with "first day," "second day," and so on. But "day" can also refer to a longer period of time. It certainly doesn't mean "a fraction of a second." The Day of the Lord will come suddenly, according to Peter. We are living in man's day, but it will be God's day. Somewhere in that period of time the physical universe will be radically transformed. There is nothing in 2 Peter that militates against an earthly millennium.

Other a-millennialists will argue that because millennial promises are absent from the New Testament there are no longer any such promises. W. J. Grier states: "The New Testament has nothing to say about a return of the Jews to their own land, with Christ reigning on a throne at Jerusalem over a kingdom in which the Jews will have a national preeminence." Oswald T. Allis makes a similar comment:

> It is significant that practically all the texts upon which the claim is based that the Jews are to return to their own land and enjoy special privileges, are taken from the Old Testament. Even more significant is the fact that while Paul devotes a considerable part of Romans (chaps. ix–xi) to the discussion of the future of the Jews, he has nothing to say about their restoration to their own land or of their enjoying special rights and privileges. He longs most intensely for their conversion, for their re-engrafting into the olive tree. But he does not connect this with restoration to the land of Canaan.

I addressed this argument earlier in this chapter, but there are a few more things that need to be said. In Matthew 19:28 Jesus said:

> Verily I say unto you, that ye which have followed me, in the regeneration when the Son of man shall sit in the throne of His glory, ye also shall sit upon twelve thrones, judging the twelve tribes of Israel.

"Twelve tribes" clearly means "the twelve tribes of Israel." Our Lord's original audience would never have understood "the regeneration" as referring to a celestial kingdom. The fact that a-millennialists must fudge on this passage is further proof that Jesus is speaking of a future, earthly kingdom. Though generally a highly reliable commentator, a-millennialist William Hendriksen sidesteps the real import of Matthew 19:28 when he writes:

> Turning to the first of these promises, it is to be noted that it pertains to the position of the Twelve in "the regeneration," that is, in what we would call "the restored (or: renewed) universe," "the new heaven and earth" described in such passages as Isa. 65:17; 66:22; II Pet. 3:13; Rev. 21:1–5 ... What is meant by these "twelve tribes of Israel"? In all probability the term refers to the restored new Israel. Whether, as such, it indicates the total number of the elect gathered out of the twelve tribes of the Jews from the beginning to the end of the world's history (cf. Rom. 11:26), or even the chosen ones of both the Jews and the Gentiles (Cf. Gal. 6:16), in either case it must refer to those who have been regenerated, for into the reborn universe to which 19:28 refers nothing unclean will ever enter (Rev. 21:27).

This is certainly not the meaning of the phrase "the twelve tribes" that would have been understood by Jesus and the apostles. "The regeneration" the Jews were anticipating was an earthly one. Jesus did not come to offer a heavenly paradise to the Jews. Faithful Jews desired what God's Word, through the ancient prophets, had instructed them to desire. They spoke about an earthly kingdom centered in Jerusalem.

Though Hendriksen is generally a reliable commentator, it is my opinion that he takes a flight of fancy in explaining Matthew 19:28. In the above statement he equates the eternal state brought in by the conflagration of 2 Peter 3 and described in Revelation 21:1–5 with Isaiah 65:17 and Isaiah 66:22. Yet that can only be done by "Christianizing" the Old Testament pretty much in the same way that covenant theologians Judaize the New. Isaiah 65:17–20 speaks about God creating "new heavens and a new earth," but this is applied by the prophet to 'Jerusalem" and her future joyous people. Verse twenty indicates that in that period "there shall be no more thence an infant of days, nor an old man that hath not filled his days: for the child shall die an hundred years old; but the sinner being an hundred years old shall be accursed." It is hard to see how this could possibly refer to the eternal state. The same objections can be made about Hendriksen's understanding of Isaiah 66:22–24, which he equates with eternity future.

Hence, I must believe that Matthew 19:28 is referring to Israel restored to the land. The statements by Grier and Allis to the effect that the New Testament does not speak about Israel restored to the land, do not stand the test of Scripture. This is reinforced by our Lord's words in a parallel passage, Luke 22:29–30:

> And I appoint unto you a kingdom, as my Father hath appointed unto me; That ye may eat and drink at my table in my kingdom, and sit on thrones judging the twelve tribes of Israel.

This is clearly an imperfect, earthly arrangement, though one that is better than any existing kingdom at the present day. It is a kingdom promised to overcomers:

> And he that overcometh, and keepeth my works unto the end, to him will I give power over *the nations:* And he shall rule them with a rod of iron; as the vessels of a potter shall they be broken to shivers: even as I received of my Father.
>
> —Revelation 2:26–27

I must believe that, on several occasions, the New Testament presents, though not with the kind of detail found in the Old Testament, a future earthly kingdom with Israel occupying a position of preeminence. This was what the apostles were expecting. As can be seen from Acts 1:6, Jesus never contradicted this expectation.

So What Texts Do Replacement Theologians Use to Support Their Position?

Every aberrant teaching has its "proof texts." Replacement theology is no exception. Claiming biblical support for their views, replacement teachers appeal to Jesus' words of rebuke to the Jewish leaders of his day. Matthew 21:43 is one of those texts: "Therefore say I unto you, the kingdom of God shall be taken from you, and given to a nation bringing forth the fruits thereof." Replacement theologians understand this to mean: "Therefore I say unto *the Jewish people of all times,* the kingdom of God shall be taken from you and given to a spiritual nation bringing forth the fruits thereof."

In determining the validity of this understanding of our Lord's statement, we must note both the context of the statement and the people to whom it was addressed. Jesus has just told the parable of the landowner (Matt. 21:33–41). It relates the story of a landowner who planted a vineyard, fertilized the soil, and did what was necessary for a good crop. The landowner leased the vineyard out to vinedressers, and then went to a distant land. In scripture, the vineyard is a commonly-used emblem for Israel (Isaiah 5). The vine-dressers represent the Jewish religious leaders of the first century A.D. It is important that we take note of the fact that in this parable there is not the slightest word of condemnation for the vineyard itself. Verse thirty-four simply indicates that harvest time had come, but there is no hint that the vineyard had produced poorly, or that there was anything wrong with the grapes. The problem was with the vinedressers. The landowner sent his personal servants to receive the crop but it was the vinedressers who beat one, killed one, and stoned another. So the landowner sent more servants, but they were likewise abused and mistreated. Finally, the landowner sent his son, whom the vine-dressers murdered. Verses thirty-eight and thirty-nine state: "But when the husbandman saw the son, they said among themselves, This is the heir; come, let us kill him, and let us seize on his inheritance. And they caught him, and cast him out of the vineyard, and slew him." Once again, the problem was with the husbandmen (the "vine-dressers"), and therefore the landowner's anger is directed at them: "When the Lord therefore of the vineyard cometh, what will he do unto those husbandmen?" (vs. 40).

The specific setting of these words proves conclusively that Jesus was speaking to the rulers of the Jewish nation who, *at that time,* had rejected their Messiah, Jesus Christ. The Kingdom promises, therefore, would be taken from *them* because of *their* hard-heartedness. There is not even the slightest hint that Israel is being permanently rejected and God no longer has a plan and purpose for either the nation or the people. When Jesus stated, "the kingdom of God shall be taken from you," He meant, "you apostate Jews of my day." Our Lord's indictment of the leaders of that particular generation, and the responsibility that they bore for their sin of rejecting Him, is clearly presented in Luke 11:50–51:

> That the blood of all the prophets, which was shed from the foundation of the world, may be required of this generation; From the blood of Abel unto the blood of Zacharias, which perished between the altar and the temple: verily I say unto you, It shall be required of *this generation.*

But what did Jesus mean when He said that the Kingdom shall be "given to a nation bringing forth the fruits thereof"? What "nation" is being referenced?

There are two distinct possible interpretations, neither of which supports the tenets of replacement theology. One possibility is that "nation" refers to the church, the people of God during that period of Israel's temporary hardening (Rom. 11:25). Or "nation" could mean the nation of Israel in the future millennial Kingdom. In this case Jesus is saying that the Kingdom is being postponed until a future time, the time of Israel's restoration.

At the eighth annual (December 1999) meeting of the Pre-Trib Research Group, Michael J. Vlach presented an excellent paper on the topic

"Has the Church Replaced Israel in God's Plan." He presented a convincing case that "nation" refers to a future generation of Jews. I will summarize his arguments.

First, the contrast is not between two different groups of people—Israel and the church—but between Israel at two different periods of time. Jesus is rebuking the religious leaders of Israel *at that time*. The contrast, therefore, does not seem to be ethnic or racial, but spiritual and moral. Israel *at that time* was spiritually and morally insensitive, but that would not be true of Israel in the future.

Second, the term "nation" implies race, government, and territory, something that could not be said of the church. The church is never restricted to one ethnic group, nor does it occupy one specific territory. While there are a few occasions in which "nation" (*ethnos*) is sometimes used of gentiles, in the great preponderance of cases it is used with reference to Israel or to the Jewish people (Luke 7:5; 23:2; John 11:48, 50, 52; 18:35). While some believe that "nation" is used of the church, the references are disputed, as we shall see when we discuss 1 Peter 2:9–10.

Third, the context suggests a future generation of Jews. In Matthew, chapter twenty-three, Jesus addresses His disciples and utters sharp words of rebuke to the religious leaders of his day, promising "woe" upon them and calling them "hypocrites" and "fools" (vss. 13–17, 19, 23–27, et al); but despite that He still speaks of *future blessings* on Israel. In verse thirty-nine Jesus says, "For I say unto you, Ye shall not see me henceforth, till ye shall say, Blessed is he that cometh in the name of the Lord." They haven't said it yet, but one day they will. Vlach writes:

> It makes good contextual sense to conclude, then, that the nation to whom the kingdom would be given, as mentioned in Matthew 21:43, would be the future generation of Jews that Jesus spoke about in Matthew 23:39 [see page 15 of Vlach's paper].

Replacement theologians also find their replacement doctrine in New Testament passages that apply Old Testament designations for Israel to the church. They take this to be an indication that the church is the "new Israel" that has taken the place of the nation of Israel in God's plan. First Peter 2:9–10 is one of the passages replacement theologians use for this purpose:

> But ye are a chosen generation, a royal priesthood, an holy nation, a peculiar people; that ye should shew forth the praises of him who nath called you out of darkness into his marvellous light: Which in time past were not a people, but are now the people of God: which had not obtained mercy, but now have obtained mercy.

In this passage Peter uses four titles—"a chosen generation," "a royal priesthood," "an holy nation," "a peculiar people"—taken from Isaiah 43:20 and Exodus 19:5–6 to describe New Testament believers, i.e., supposedly Jews and gentiles in the Church Age. Hence, the church, the body of Christ consisting of both Jew and gentiles, is the "New Israel," or so the argument goes.

This argument, however, is based on the false assumption that similarity equals identity. No doubt, there are many similarities between the New Testament church and the nation of Israel. Those who are a part of the body of Christ are to be a separate and holy people, as was true of Israel. In 1 Peter 1:16 Peter writes: "Be ye holy, for I am holy." This is a quotation from Leviticus 11:44–45. Likewise, those who are a part of the body of Christ are to seek to do good, and if they do so they can be assured of God's blessings (1 Pet. 3:10–13). Peter backs this promise up with a quotation from Psalm 34:13–17, a promise that was given to Old Testament Israel. It is indisputable that there are similarities between the Old Testament people of God and the New Testament people of God. But does this mean that the church has replaced Israel? I don't believe so. To conclude that from such similarities is to conclude more than the evidence warrants.

The parallels, and the correspondence, between Israel and the church do not mean that the latter is to be identified with the former, or that the latter has now taken over the promises given to the former. Peter is simply using similar terms to underscore similar truths. To reason otherwise is foolhardy. Just because my automobile has four wheels and a trunk and may resemble your automobile, does not mean that it is my automobile, and I am justified in driving your car without your permission. Similarity is not identity.

While it is true that Peter uses Old Testament terminology to refer to the church, one can argue that Peter was writing primarily to Jewish Christians and not to Jewish and gentile Christians. He was writing literally to those who are "sojourners of dispersion" (1 Pet. 1:1) which was a technical designation for Jews living outside of the land of Israel (Acts 8:4; 11:19). Moreover, Peter's ministry was primarily to Jews (Gal. 2:7). This would explain why Peter uses Old Testament quotations and references some twenty-nine times in 1 Peter. Replacement theology simply has no argument from 1 Peter.

Galatians 3:28 may also seem to endorse replacement theology: "There is neither Jew nor Greek, there is neither bond nor free, there is neither male nor female: for ye are all one in Christ Jesus."

Allegedly this indicates that all ethnic distinctions are removed in the New Testament. In a sense, this is true. Dispensationalists readily admit this and support such a contention with a scripture like Ephesians 3:5 where we are told that the gentiles are "fellow heirs" with the Jew. Galatians 3:28 teaches that regarding access to the redemptive blessings of the Gospel, all are equal—Jews, gentiles, men, women, slaves, freemen, boys, and girls. However, there are still certain distinctions that remain. Just as there are still men, there are still women. Putting one's faith in Christ does not obliterate these distinctions, nor does it obliterate the various roles that God has assigned.

Though Paul wrote Galatians 3:28, he also wrote 1 Timothy 2:12: "But I suffer not a woman to teach, nor to usurp authority over the man." Was Paul contradicting what he wrote in Galatians 3:28? Of course not. In Galatians he is speaking about redemptive privileges. In Timothy, he is speaking about role and function. I must affirm that the New Testament never denies that Jews are still Jews, nor does it deny that God still has a special place for them in His plan.

Periods of Apostasy
Do Not Cancel Unconditional Promises

Replacement theologians are fond of citing periods of great apostasy in Israel's history, as though such were an indication that God has cast off His people.

No doubt, there have been periods in Israel's history when the nation and people fell into great apostasy and were severely judged by God. There were many such periods during the Old Testament era. Later, during both the ministry of Jesus and during the apostolic period, the Jews harshly persecuted the church and resisted the testimony of the apostles, and the miraculous signs God gave to authenticate that testimony (2 Cor. 12:12; Heb. 2:4). The destruction of Jerusalem was undoubtedly God's judgment on that hardhearted and evil generation. That judgment, however, in no way cancelled God's unconditional covenant with Abraham and his physical descendants.

Several scriptures show that an unconditional covenant in no way denies the possibility of judgment. For example, God's covenant with Noah was unconditional. It involved the commitment of God to both man and the creation. God promises never again to curse the ground or destroy all living creatures as He did in the Flood, and He gave a rainbow as a sign and seal of that covenant (Gen. 9:11–17). And yet that promise did not exclude local exceptions. There existed times of famine (Gen. 26) as well as severe judgments in response to flagrant and heinous sin, as in the case of Sodom and Gomorrah (Gen. 19). However, these periodic displays of retributive justice in no way cancel God's covenant, nor His promises. While there still are floods from time to time in various parts of the world, the exceptions do not invalidate the rule. The same is true with the Abrahamic covenant and the various judgments that fall on Israel. The Lord revealed to Abraham that he would have a great number of descendants, as multitudinous as the stars in the sky (Gen. 15:4–5). The Lord also confirmed this covenant with a solemn ritual signifying the certainty of God's promises to Abraham (Gen. 15:8–21; Heb. 6:13–19). Judging from various statements in Scripture (e.g. Jer. 34:18–20) and the parallels in the ancient Near Eastern treaties, as the Lord passed among the remains of the slaughtered animals he affirmed His oath to Abraham in the most emphatic of terms, in effect stating: "May it be done to me as it has been done to these animals if I do not fulfill my promise."

Nevertheless, despite these statements of God's gracious purpose toward Abraham and his descendants, God commands Abraham, "Walk before me, and be thou perfect" (Gen. 17:1). Furthermore, Abraham's willingness to sacrifice the son whom he so dearly loved is given as the reason why God will bless Abraham (Gen. 22:16–17). Later, with the passing of time, the Hebrew prophets utilize the metaphor of God "divorcing" Israel when she proves unfaithful (Hos. 2:2–13; Jer. 3:1–3). However, the prophets also hearken back to God's promises to Abraham and never really envision a time when God will permanently sever his relationship with Israel, or that the "divorce" would be permanent, and He would never take her back (Isa. 50:1–3; Isa. 49:14–26; Mic. 7:18–20). It is in this way that God commits himself to fulfill His promises, but not without Israel's cooperation; yet He Himself will provide the inner dynamic whereby this will become a reality (Jer. 32:40).

These are important considerations. The words of rebuke and censure addressed by Jesus to His generation should be taken in this light. They are expressive of God's sporadic and partial judgment of Israel, but they do not indicate that He will cast Isr3ael off. In Romans 11:2 the apostle affirms, "God hath not cast away his people which he foreknew."

Part Two

The Response

Chapter 6

The Question of the "Time Texts"

Gary DeMar writes:

... The discerning reader will recognize that these verses are found in Matthew 24:19–21, verses that dispensationalists and other futurists say are yet to be fulfilled. But Eusebius tells us that "these things took place in this manner in the second year of the reign of Vespasian, in accordance with the prophecies of our Lord and Saviour Jesus Christ, who by divine power saw them beforehand as if they were already present, and wept and mourned according to the statement of the holy evangelists." Vespasian began his reign in A.D. 69.

What statement of the holy evangelists? Eusebius quotes verses from Luke's description of the destruction of Jerusalem: Luke 19:42–44; 21:20, 23–24. The passages in Luke 21 parallel those in Matthew 24:1–34.

Of course, a first-century fulfillment, in contrast to a yet-future fulfillment, changes the entire prophetic landscape cultivated by numerous contemporary date-setters. Last days madness would be eliminated if Christians could be convinced, through a thorough study of Scripture, that the Olivet Discourse is a prophecy that was fulfilled by A.D. 70 ...

The Main Weapon of Preterism

There is no question but that the so-called "time texts" of the Bible form the main weapon of preterism. Statements indicating that these things are to happen "shortly," or that "the time is at hand," or that "this generation shall see all these things," are statements that are used to ridicule and mock futurism.

It is with these "near-to-now" texts, especially found in the New Testament, that preterists seek to prove that all (for extreme preterists) or nearly all (for moderate preterists) prophecy was fulfilled within the lifetimes of the original writers of the New Testament, meaning a first-century fulfillment. When these "time texts" are combined with an allegorical interpretation of biblical prophecy, preterists feel scripturally justified in concluding that nothing more than a first-century disaster upon Jerusalem is needed to satisfy the requirements of these predictions. On the basis of this, preterists look to the history books to find individuals and events that fit the prophetic descriptions of a first-century A.D. disaster. Predictably they conclude that the judgments of the Great Tribulation and the coming of Jesus Christ in the clouds of glory occurred in A.D. 70—more than nineteen hundred years ago.

In no aspect of their approach to "the future" are preterists more adept at using the Bible against the Bible than in their attempt to limit both the time and extent of biblical prophecy. If they are to successfully make their point, they must show that the biblical prophecies are not universal, but limited and local. They must, for example, demonstrate that the Roman invasion of Jerusalem, the destruction of the city and the Jewish temple, are really all that are implied by the Tribulation passages of prophecy. Passages that speak of Divine wrath coming upon the whole world are taken to mean "the ancient Roman world," or "the known world of the first century." How do preterists do this, and what scriptures do they use? This is the issue to which we now turn.

A favorite preterist verse for localizing prophecy is Colossians 1:23

which speaks of "the hope of the gospel, which ye have heard, and which was preached to every creature which is under heaven." Preterists argue that though Paul wrote about the gospel as being "preached to every creature which is under heaven," it is evident that such a statement did not refer to the entire planet—from North America to South America, from China to Europe, from the North Pacific islands to the Falklands—for Paul lived in the first century A.D., and neither Paul nor the other early Christians had compassed the entire world. Obviously, so the argument goes, when Paul spoke about the gospel being preached everywhere, he really meant "everywhere in the ancient Roman Empire."

Another proof text for this assertion is Colossians 1:6 where Paul writes that the gospel has "come unto you, as it is in all the world." Once again, they argue that "all the world" means "all the Roman world." Here we see preterists seeking to appeal to the language and authority of the apostle Paul to validate their argument that there had been, in some sense, a universal spread of the gospel in the first century.

Reformed preterists are Five Point Calvinists and believe in a "limited atonement," or in "particular redemption," that is that Christ did not really die for all, but really for "all of the elect." How do they know? Their answer: Words like "world," "all," and "all men" are not universal terms. "All," they argue, means "all classes of men"— rich and poor, free and bond—or men from "all ethnic groups"—Jew and gentile, Roman and Greek. Regarding the extent of the atonement—that is, for whom did Christ die? —Reformed preterists reason that:

1. if Christ died for all men and only *some* are saved, then this means that Christ failed in His purpose; or
2. if Christ died for all men and only *some* are saved, then this means that the ones who are saved "cast the deciding vote" and owe their salvation not to the work of God but to their personal decision.

Regarding the fulfillment of prophecy, they argue in this way to avoid having a fulfillment that takes place far in the future. To this end Reformed preterists apply this kind of an approach to Matthew 24:14: "And this gospel of the kingdom shall be preached in *all the world* for a witness unto *all nations;* and then shall the end come." Another verse that they use to make the same point is Luke 2:1: "And it came to pass in those days, that there went out a decree from Caesar Augustus, that *all the world* should be taxed."

DeMar, who holds to limited atonement, carefully argues his case from these verses, and then quotes Romans 10:18 which, in the New American Version reads: "But I say, surely they have never heard, have they? Indeed they have: *'Their voice has gone out into an the earth, and their words to the ends of the world'* [oikumene]." He then writes the following:

> The Greek word translated "world" in Matthew 24:14 is *oikumene*, "the inhabited earth." The same Greek word is used in Luke 2:1: "Now it came about in those days that a decree went out from Caesar Augustus, that a census be taken of all the inhabited earth." In the New American Standard Version, the marginal reading is "the Roman Empire.' ... The marginal reading of Luke 21:26—a verse parallel to Matthew 24:14 in terms of word choice and geography— is also "inhabited earth."

It is with this kind of reasoning that preterists seek to prove that all the conditions for "the end" were met in the first century. In Matthew 24:14 the gospel would be preached in the entire world and would be a witness to all nations, and then the end would come. If "all the world" means the "entire planet" and "the end" refers to some yet future cataclysm, preterists would have no argument. But they object:

> Since the Bible clearly states that the gospel "was proclaimed in *all* creation under heaven" (Col. 1:23), then the end spoken of by Jesus is a past event

for us. Earlier in Colossians, Paul describes how the gospel was "constantly bearing fruit and increasing in *all* the world [*kosmos*]" (Romans 1:8). These statements by Paul reveal a fulfillment of what Jesus told His disciples would be to the destruction of Jerusalem.

For preterists, then, the conditions for "the end" were already met in the first century. The gospel has been preached "everywhere" by Pauline standards. The people in the Mediterranean basin and environs had been given an opportunity to hear. Therefore the "end" spoken of in prophecy is already behind us. But is this sound reasoning and is the "end" a past-tense event?

There are several problems that immediately rise from a preterist understanding of Scripture. To be sure, the problems are not with the Bible in general, or with the prophetic scriptures in particular. These are problems that preterists have created with their own peculiar approach to prophecy.

First: There is the problem of inconsistency

If prophecy has already been fulfilled then Jesus Christ must have already returned. Moderate preterists would not argue in this way, but if they are consistent, they must.

Both Jesus, Paul, and the other human authors of the New Testament speak of the return of Christ as being very near. They never write as though it were something in the very far distant future. No one reading the New Testament would get the impression that Christ would not return for at least two thousand years. In fact, when writing of being caught up in the air, the apostle included himself as one of the participants. He wrote, "Then *we* which are alive and remain shall be caught up together with them in the clouds, to meet the Lord in the air: and so shall we ever be with the Lord" (1 Thess. 4:17). If the eschatological destruction of Jerusalem took place in the first century, then so did the eschatological return of the Lord. One cannot argue from their so-called "time texts" as preterists do and *not* come up with a first-century return of Christ.

As pointed out, moderate preterists don't argue that Christ physically returned in the first century. But they do so not *because* of their understanding of prophecy, but in *spite* of it.

Second: there is the problem of ignoring the plain meaning of the biblical text.

The only way that preterists can claim that the Tribulation judgments—stars falling, the sun and moon becoming dark—occurred in the first century is by taking them in a non-literal manner. Jesus said, "Immediately after the tribulation of those days shall the sun be darkened, and the moon shall not give her light, and the stars shall fall from heaven, and the powers of the heavens shall be shaken" (Matt. 24:29). How do preterists "get around" such plain statements? J. Marcellus Kik gives his figurative explanation:

> The above portion of Scripture employs such strong and vivid language that many think it can be descriptive of nothing else than the end of the world and the second coming of Christ. These descriptive terms would seem to indicate a catastrophic end of the earth. And yet when this passage is studied in the light of prophetic language and pronouncements, it can readily be that it is descriptive of the passing of Judaism.

Preterists are notorious for such a blatant wresting of Scripture. If they are correct, we must conclude that God gave prophecy to confuse, not to reveal. For them, prophecy is evidently little more than a collage of word colors scrambled together in some haphazard fashion just waiting for someone with a creative bent to edit. Post-millennialist David Chilton takes a similar approach with the two witnesses of Revelation 11:

> A preliminary conclusion about the two Witnesses, therefore, is that they represent the line of prophets, culminating in John the Baptizer, who bore witness against Jerusalem during the history of Israel. ... That these

Witnesses are members of the Old Covenant rather than the New is shown, among other indications, by their wearing of sackcloth—the dress characteristic of Old Covenant privation rather than New Covenant fullness.

Thirdly: there is the problem of minimizing Scripture.

If God's declarations of judgment on the world must be limited to the ancient Mediterranean world of the first century, what about God's commands to evangelize the world? In Acts 1:8 Jesus states: "... and ye shall be witnesses unto me both in Jerusalem, and in all Judea, and in Samaria, and unto the uttermost part of the earth." Did Jesus mean what He said, or did He simply mean "uttermost part of the Roman Empire in the first century?"

Preterists, especially those of the reconstructionist variety, generally regard the Great Commission as a mandate to world evangelism. They often point out that it is an educational mandate to disciple all nations. This fits in nicely with a post-millennial eschatology. Yet if one were to apply preterist principles to Matthew 28:19 it must mean: "Go ye therefore, and teach all nations of the ancient Roman Empire." Or what about preterism applied to Revelation 5:9. God's mercy then comes to be merely local in extent—"Thou art worthy to take the book, and to open the seals thereof: for thou wast slain, and hast redeemed us to God by thy blood out of every kindred, and tongue, and people, and *nation of the ancient Roman world.*" If preterists are right, the God of Scripture is only a tribal deity which, as we shall see, is what they make of Revelation 1:7.

Did Paul Evangelize the Whole World?

The reader will remember that one of the reasons preterists limit prophecy is their claim that universal designations have only a local reference. When Paul wrote to the Roman Church and said, "I thank my God through Jesus Christ for you all, that your faith is spoken of throughout *the whole world*" (Rom.

1:8), "whole world" doesn't really mean that. Allegedly, neither did Jesus when He said that the gospel would be proclaimed throughout the entire world before the end would come.

The statements in Romans 1:8 and Colossians 1:23 must be understood from the perspective of the human author. From Paul's perspective, the ancient Roman world was the *entire* world. Scripture bears the marks of the culture in which it was given. The New Testament was not written in contemporary English, and one does not find references to automobiles and airplanes. Scripture is not the Word of God given in some esoteric language. The Bible is the Word of God given in the words of men. This can be readily demonstrated from the personal notations and comments that one often finds in the New Testament letters. In 2 Timothy 4:13 Paul wrote to Timothy and states: "The cloke that I left at Troas with Carpus, when thou comest, bring with thee, and the books, but especially the parchments." He didn't write, "and especially the floppy discs." The humanity of the author, who was writing from his point of view, clearly comes through.

This does not mean that it has errors, because it doesn't. Scripture does, however, bear marks of the culture and thought processes of the human author. Paul, in his travels, had left a cloak somewhere with a particular individual. The apostle had been in Troas and had given the cloak to Carpus. Now, as Paul writes, he wants the cloak, and therefore instructs Timothy to bring it when he comes.

The first lesson that must be taught and caught in biblical hermeneutics—the science of interpreting the Scriptures—is that the interpreter must first know what a scripture meant to the original audience before we can know what it means to us. Paul's instructions about meat offered to idols, for example, are couched in the first century imagery of a practice that is no longer common in our modern world.

Both the author and purpose of a passage must be borne in mind. A particular word used by Matthew in speaking about last things may have a different meaning than the same word used by Paul in another context. At one time, certain residents of the British Isles used the word "homely" as a commendation. If they wanted to speak about a man's wife as being a faithful woman who was a good homemaker, they would praise the man and say that his wife was "homely." In contemporary American English, however, to say to your friend that his wife is "homely" might cause a rift to develop in your friendship!

Both the intent of the author, and the purpose of a text, must be a factor in understanding the meaning of that text. I mentioned Luke 2:1 earlier. That is where we read that "all" the world was to be taxed. Those who hold to a limited atonement argue that since "all" here cannot mean "everybody," therefore passages that state that Jesus Christ died for "all" likewise cannot mean "everybody." Geisler observes:

> In light of John's explicit use of the word "world" in salvation passages to mean all fallen human beings, it is painful to watch the contorted logic of extreme Calvinists in response, claiming "that often the Bible uses the words *world* and *all* in a restricted, limited sense," adding 'it is clear that *all* is not *all*' [quoting 5 Point Calvinist Edwin Palmer]. Then, in support they cite passages (like Luke 2:1–2) from another book, in another context, used in a geographical (not redemptive) sense in a futile attempt to prove their point. If "all" does not mean "all" fallen human beings, then what does it mean in Romans 3:23: *"All* have sinned, and come short of the glory of God?"

Preterists have created a communication problem. They have so drastically infused their own meaning into biblical language that God can no longer mean what He says. If universal terms don't have universal meanings, how could the biblical writers ever indicate events of universal proportions? This is a significant objection. By saying that universal terms only have limited local meanings we are forced to the conclusion that the biblical writers had no way of relating universal events.

Supposing God really wanted to speak about an event affecting *the entire planet Earth*? Preterists would miss the message. God could not even tell them what He meant. In fact, on the basis of preterism, 2 Peter 3 and its description of the passing away of the heavens, and the elements burning up, must really refer to something like the burning of Rome, or maybe even the destruction of the Jewish temple in the first century. Yet even most preterists don't understand 2 Peter 3 in this way. They look at it as an end-time conflagration that brings in the eternal state. I said "most."

Believe it or not, a few understand 2 Peter 3 as referring to A.D. 70! DeMar quotes the Puritan divine John Owen (1616–1683). Owen wrote the standard treatise on limited atonement, entitled *The Death of Death in the Death of Christ*. Owen wrote that 2 Peter 3:5–7 refers "not to the last and final judgment of the world, but to that utter desolation and destruction that was to be made of the Judaical church and state." Likewise, the Scottish Reformed Presbyterian exegete John Brown (1784–1858) believed the same thing:

> "Heaven and earth passing away," understood literally, is the dissolution of the present system of the universe; and the period when that is to take place, is called the "end of the world." But a person at all familiar with the phraseology of the Old Testament Scriptures, knows that the dissolution of the Mosaic economy, and the establishment of the Christian, is often spoken of as the removing of the old earth and heavens, and the creation of a new earth and new heavens.

For readers who are just being exposed to these issues for the first time, perhaps the most unbelievable aspect of preterism is their characteristic manner of treating certain words portending the most stupendous of cataclysmic judgments—falling stars and various heavenly disturbances— and then claiming that such occurred in A.D. 70. Since the stars didn't literally fall in A.D. 70 how do they "explain" their position?

When Did the Stars Fall?

Once again, as we have seen earlier, preterists appeal to Scripture. Kik well realizes that Matthew 24:29–31 appears to teach the end of the world and the physical return of Christ, but he believes that people conclude this because they are ignorant of the nature of apocalyptic language.

Kik's explanation of this passage is twofold. First, he argues that such language is not to be taken literally. Such language simply indicates the downfall of an empire, or kingdom. His "proof" is Isaiah 13:9–10, which describes the fall of Babylon: "Behold, the day of the LORD cometh, cruel both with wrath and fierce anger, to lay the land desolate: and he shall destroy the sinners thereof out of it. For the stars of heaven and the constellations thereof shall not give their light: the sun shall be darkened in his going forth, and the moon shall not cause her light to shine." Kik explains:

> The entire chapter is related to the destruction of that mighty and glorious city. We may compare the fame and glory of Babylon to New York, London, and Moscow combined. In the days of Isaiah, the glory of Babylon shone as the sun, the moon, and the stars. This glory, Isaiah prophesies, was to be darkened. Babylon in all its shining beauty and marvelous glory was to be totally eclipsed; hence the prophet uses highly figurative language.

Secondly, Kik argues that if the fall of a pagan nation was significant and far-reaching in its implications, and its fall properly indicated by apocalyptic language descriptive of fake heavenly signs, how much more significant would be the fall of God's own nation Israel?

This particular aspect of our study—the nature of apocalyptic language and whether or not it is used simply of the downfall of kingdoms, rather than the end of all things as when the words are literally understood—is a pivotal issue. If apocalyptic language is nothing more than gross exaggerations, then the preterists are right. Based on this, the Olivet Discourse describes a regional event occurring in the past, not something universal that will happen in the future. But is this all that can be said, or is there something else, like "the rest of the story"?

While it is true, as Kik asserts, that Isaiah 13 speaks about the fall of Babylon, it is not at all true that the passage can be limited to the fall of Babylon in 539 B.C. Isaiah 13:19–20 states:

> And Babylon, the glory of kingdoms, the beauty of the Chaldees' excellency, shall be as when God overthrew Sodom and Gomorrah. It shall never be inhabited, neither shall it be dwelt in from generation to generation.

This was definitely not fulfilled in 539 B.C. Babylon was not destroyed "as when God overthrew Sodom and Gomorrah." The historical fall of Babylon simply does not match all the particulars given in the prophecy of Isaiah 13. Babylon was not destroyed as was Sodom and Gomorrah. What happened in 539 B.C.? Babylon fell without a struggle to the Achaemenid Persian, Cyrus the Great. It was not destroyed and there was no battle.

> ... The Persian army entered the city without a battle. This appears to have been effected by the strategem of diverting the river Euphrates, thus drying up the moat defenses and enabling the enemy to enter the city by marching up the dried-up river bed, This may also imply some collaboration with sympathizers inside the walls. That night Belshazzar was killed (Dan. 5:30). For the remainder of the month Persian troops occupied Esagila, though without bearing arms or interrupting the religious ceremonies. On the 3rd of Arah-samnu (Oct. 29, 539 B.C.), sixteen days after the capitula-

tion, Cyrus himself entered he city amid much public acclaim, ending the Chaldean dynasty ... Cyrus treated the city with great respect, returning their own shrines and statues of the deities brought in from other cities. The Jews were sent home with compensatory assistance. He appointed new governors, so enduring to peace and stable conditions essential to the proper maintenance of the religious centers.

Ancient Babylon capitulated without a struggle. The site and city have continued to be occupied into modern times, its most recent and notorious leader being Saddam Hussein. Clearly, Isaiah 13 was not completely fulfilled in 539 B.C., but still awaits future fulfillment. Other Old Testament passages lead us to the same conclusion and do further damage to the preterist position. Jeremiah 50:1–5 is especially revealing:

> The word that the LORD spake against Babylon and against the land of the Chaldeans by Jeremiah the prophet. Declare ye among the nations, and publish, and set up a standard; publish and conceal not: say, Babylon is taken, Bel is confounded, Merodach is broken in pieces; her idols are confounded, her images are broken in pieces. For out of the north there cometh up a nation against her, which shall make her land desolate, and none shall dwell therein; they shall remove, they shall depart, both man and beast. In those days, and at that time, saith the LORD, the children of Israel shall come, they and the children of Judah together, going and weeping: they shall go, and seek the LORD their God. They shall ask the way to Zion with their faces thitherward, saying, Come, and let us join ourselves to the LORD in a perpetual covenant that shall not be forgotten.

There are several features of this prophecy that show it still awaits a future fulfillment. For one thing, the Medes and the Persians came from the east, not from the north, as the prophecy indicates in verse three. Furthermore,

Cyrus did not render the land desolate nor did the population flee. Jeremiah 50:3 was therefore not fulfilled in 539 B.C. And neither was verse four fulfilled in the past. The prophecy that Israel and Judah would unite and seek the Lord (Jer. 50:5) has certainly not yet occurred.

Many other Old Testament prophecies concerning Babylon clearly show that the preterist contention of a past fulfillment does not stand the test of careful examination in the light of the Scripture. I hate to belabor the point, but erroneous notions die hard, so I will add just one more Scripture.

In Jeremiah 30:7 we read: "Alas! for that day is great, so that none is like it: it is even the time of Jacob's trouble; but he shall be saved out of it." Premillennial scholars agree that "the time of Jacob's trouble" refers to the future Tribulation period. But is it possible that the reference is really to something that happened in Jeremiah's day?

I believe the answer to that is an emphatic "no." If Jeremiah were speaking about some contemporaneous event, such as the Babylonian invasion, he most likely would have said, "Alas! For this day is great, so that none is like it ..." But rather he speaks of "that day," and calls "that day" "the time of Jacob's trouble."

Verses eight and nine continue to speak of "that day," in terms that show the reference could not possibly be to "this day":

> For it shall come to pass in that day, saith the LORD of hosts, that I will break his yoke from off thy neck, and will burst thy bonds, and strangers shall no more serve themselves of him: But they shall serve the LORD their God, and David their king, whom I will raise up unto them.

This is all set in the context of a future return of the people of Israel to the land.

> Therefore fear thou not, O my servant Jacob, saith the LORD; neither be dismayed, O Israel: for, 10, I will save thee from afar, and thy seed from the land of their captivity; and Jacob shall return, and shall be in rest, and be

quiet, and none shall make him afraid. For I am with thee, saith the LORD, to save thee: though I make a full end of all nations whither I have scattered thee, yet will I not make a full end of thee ...

—Jeremiah 30:10–11

Kik and others who try to explain away the plain meaning of Matthew 24:29–31 by an appeal to the historical fall of Babylon have failed to make their case. This is not highly figurative apocalyptic language that referred to the invasion of Cyrus in the past. Matthew 24:29–31 is to be taken literally of future cataclysmic events. This language cannot be referred to A.D. 70 because there are no examples in Scripture of such phenomena being used exclusively of the end of an earthly kingdom. The claim that Isaiah used such language for the historical fall of Babylon does not bear the test of careful exegesis.

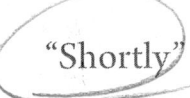 "Shortly"

In the opening verse of the Book of Revelation we read: "The Revelation of Jesus Christ, which God gave unto him, to shew unto his servants things which must shortly come to pass ..."

Preterists find this to be one of the supreme indicators that most, if not all, of the Book of Revelation was fulfilled in the past. They understand "shortly" as a reference to the immediate future. John was writing about things that would take place "in the immediate future," according to preterists. Hence, the Book of Revelation is not a book of Bible prophecy, but a book of church history recording what took place in the last half of the first century A.D.

It does not take much thinking, however, to realize that there is something wrong with that statement. The Book of Revelation addresses issues that find fulfillment at different times. For example, in Revelation 1:19 we read: "Write the things *which thou hast seen*, and the things *which are*, and the things *which shall be hereafter.*"

John is writing about what he saw in his vision of the resurrected Christ (chap. 1), that which was happening in the first century (the seven churches, chaps. 2–3), and the things "which shall be hereafter." One could agree with preterists that "shortly" means "in the immediate future" without affirming that the *whole book* of Revelation has to do with the immediate future. "Shortly" could be a reference to the power of Jesus Christ, the Lord of His church, bringing judgment and blessing upon the churches of the first century A.D. After all, Jesus Christ is in the midst of the seven golden candlesticks (Rev. 1:13), and He has in His right hand the seven stars (Rev. 1:16) which are "the angels ["messengers," "pastors"] of the seven churches (Rev. 1:20). "Shortly" could very well refer to the Lord removing the candlestick of the church at Ephesus (2:5), and not to all of the eschatological events of the succeeding chapters.

Without controversy, the word "shortly" [*en tachei*] often means "in the immediate future," or "in the near future." Preterists try to argue that this is the *only* meaning that it has. As proof, they show how "shortly" is used with reference to *human* affairs:

» *1 Corinthians 4:19:* "But I will come to you shortly, if the Lord will."
» *Philippians 2:19:* "But I trust in the Lord Jesus to send Timotheus shortly unto you."
» *Philippians 2:24:* "But I trust in the Lord that I also myself shall come shortly."
» *1 Timothy 3:14:* "These things write I unto thee, hoping to come unto thee shortly."
» *2 Timothy 4:9:* "Do thy diligence to come shortly unto me."
» *Hebrews 13:23:* "Know ye that our brother Timothy is set at liberty; with whom, if he come shortly; I will see you."
» *2 Peter 1:14:* "Knowing that shortly I must put off this my tabernacle, even as our Lord Jesus Christ hath shewed me."

» *3 John 14:* "But I trust I shall shortly see thee, and we shall speak face to face."

No one doubts that "shortly" in these passages has reference to events contemporary with the writer. The writers were speaking about a personal visit they would make "shortly," or about a visit that someone whom they knew would make "shortly." Paul is coming to minister at the church at Colossae "shortly." In a little while he will be in their midst.

These passages, however, refer to human affairs. Man has a different sense of time than God. "One day is with the Lord as a thousand years, and a thousand years as one day" (2 Pet. 3:8). Because God is eternal and has no beginning or end, a thousand years are nothing to Him. That which is a thousand years off is but as a day in the future. Preterists need to reckon with this. They try to show that "shortly" means "in the near future," but they fail to notice that what is "shortly" for man may not refer to the same length of time for God. In fact, 2 Peter 3:8 affirms that it is not.

It should be no surprise, then, that the word "shortly" is used at the end of the Book of Revelation to refer to something that is, from the standpoint of the original human author, far in the future. "And he said unto me, These sayings are faithful and true: and the Lord God of the holy prophets sent his angel to shew unto his servants the things which must *shortly* [*en tachei*] be done." What "things" are being referred to? To answer I quote the preceding verses:

> And there shall be no more curse: but the throne of God and of the Lamb shall be in it; and his servants shall serve him: And they shall see his face; and his name shall be in their foreheads. And there shall be no night there; and they need no candle, neither light of the sun; for the Lord God giveth them light: and they shall reign for ever and ever.
>
> —Revelation 22:3–5

This is a reference to the new order. In Revelation 21:1 John writes: "And I saw a new heaven and a new earth: for the first heaven and the first earth were passed away; and there was no more sea." Revelation 22:6 says that these are "things which must *shortly* be done."

Evidently "shortly" for man is not the same thing as "shortly" for God. No doubt, extreme preterists argue that "shortly" in Revelation 22:6 means "in the immediate future." They see *all* prophecy as having already been fulfilled. Though the preterists I have cited are moderate preterists and do not hold to such a position, moderate preterists would be extreme preterists if they really believed what they teach. Moderate preterists are looking for the Lord's return in spite of, and *not* because of, their theology.

What Does "Shortly" Really Mean?

The word "shortly" is a translation of two Greek words, *en tachei,* which literally means "with speed," or "quickly." Both ancient and modern lexicographers give information that supports the futurist interpretation of *tachos* in its various forms. G. H. Lang's observation is noteworthy, especially as it bears on Revelation 1:1:

> ... *tachy* does not mean soon but swiftly. It indicates rapidity of action, as is well seen in its accurate use in the medical compound *tachycardia* (*tachy* and *kardia*=heart), which does not mean that the heart will beat soon, but that it is beating *rapidly*. Of course, the swift action may take place at the very same time, as in Mt. 28:7–8: "Go *quickly* and tell His disciples ... and they departed *quickly* from the tomb"; but the thought is not that they did not loiter, but that their movement was swift. Thus here also. If the Lord be regarded as speaking in the day when John lived, then He did not mean that He was returning soon, but swiftly and suddenly whenever the time should have arrived ... it is the swiftness of His movement that the word emphasizes.

In a paper entitled "Has Bible Prophecy Already Been Fulfilled," p. 22, delivered at the December 1999 meeting of the Pre-trib Research Group, Thomas Ice shows how *tachos* can mean both "soon" and "quickly." First Timothy 3:14 is an example of the former meaning: "These things write I unto thee, hoping to come unto thee shortly [*tachos*]." Paul knew that he was coming to see Timothy shortly and therefore he is writing these things. However, the same word *tachos* is used in Acts 22:18 to indicate manner: "And saw him [the Lord] saying unto me, Make haste, and get thee quickly [*tachos*] out of Jerusalem: for they will not receive thy testimony concerning me." The Lord was telling Paul to hurry up because he was in grave danger. We don't want to fail to notice that "quickly" is presented in the same construction that appears in Revelation 1:1—"things which must shortly ["quickly"] come to pass"—and in both cases can mean "with speed" or "with haste."

"The Time Is at Hand"

Preterists confidently move from Revelation 1:1 and their explanation of "shortly," to Revelation 1:3 where they find more cannon fodder to lob at pre-millennialists: "Blessed is he that readeth, and they that hear the words of this prophecy, and keep those things which are written therein: *For the time is at hand.*" Preterists understand this to mean that the time of the fulfillment of the events mentioned in the Book of Revelation is "at hand."

As pointed out in our examination of "shortly" in Revelation 1:1, "at hand," like "shortly," could very well be a reference to a portion of the Book of Revelation without necessarily implying that everything is "at hand." Even futurists do not claim that the whole book has a future fulfillment. Likewise moderate preterists don't claim that everything has a past fulfillment either. What, then is "at hand"? Quite possibly the events of chapters two and three, things such as the removal of the "candlestick" of the church at Ephesus (2:5) and judgment upon Jezebel spoken of in connection with the church at Thyatira (2:22). However, more can be said about Revelation 1:3. What is meant by the phrase "the time is at hand?"

The word translated "time" is *kairos*. In New Testament Greek there are two basic words that are used to translate "time." One is *aion*, which is descriptive of long periods of time. It means "age" or "era. Eternal life" is a translation of *zoe aionios*. It is descriptive of salvation and indicates an unending period of time.

Another word for time is *chronos,* the word referring to chronological or historical time. It denotes the quantitative, linear aspect of time, and can be used to designate a point of time in an individual's life span, as in Acts 13:18 where we read: "And about the time [*chronos*] of forty years suffered he their manners in the wilderness."

The word used in Revelation 1:3, however, is *kairos*. It does not speak of an era or time span, but signifies "the right time," "the right moment," "the opportune time." It is used in Galatians 4:4 where in the Bible states, "But when the fulness of the time [*kairos*] was come, God sent forth His Son …" Christ came at just the right moment. The time was "ripe" for the coming of God's Son. Some scholars think that it was the opportune time in the sense that the ancient world could pretty much converse in one language: *koine* Greek. Others think it refers to the sense of emptiness that the world experienced because of the failure of Greek philosophy to meet man's deepest needs. Still others would argue that it refers to a combination of these factors. At any rate, Christ came at the best possible time because God always does things in the best of possible ways.

An important question must be asked: Does any event in the first century meet the demands of such language? Is there any sense in which the events of A.D. 70 can be said to be the reference? Was A.D. 70 "a time of destiny?" Is it worthy of being described with the word *kairos*?

Before we can intelligently answer that, we must look at another important word in Revelation 1:3, "at hand." This is the English translation of one

Greek word, *engus*. In some passages *engus* has a geographical reference in the sense that they were "near" Jerusalem (John 19:20; Acts 1:12). It can also indicate that a particular season of the year is near, such as the Passover (Matt. 24:32; John 2:13). As used in these passages *engus* is speaking about proximity. The place so described is "near at hand."

Yet, as is true with many biblical words, it can have other deeper meanings and can refer to an event predicted by the prophets, as when Mark indicates that "the time [*kairos*] is fulfilled, and the kingdom of God is at hand [*engus*]" (1:15). Something was "at hand" that has to do with *kairos* time. It was the Kingdom hope and aspiration of every Old Testament Jew who knew the writings of the Hebrew prophets. Jesus said that it was "at hand." Since the Kingdom spoken of in the Old Testament did not become a reality at the First Advent of Christ, in what sense was it "at hand?"

I would like to answer that with another scripture. In Luke 21:20ff we are told of a series of events that are catastrophic. As pointed out earlier, both preterists and futurists hold that Luke 21:20–24 is a reference to the destruction of Jerusalem in A.D. 70. There must be another fulfillment, however, because Jesus speaks about heavenly signs and the appearance of the "Son of man coming in a cloud with power and great glory." This is a sign that something wonderful is about to happen: "And when these things begin to come to pass, then look up, and lift up your heads; *for your redemption draweth nigh.*" In its normal New Testament usage, the word "redemption" speaks of the consummation of the work of God in the behalf of His believing people. "Redemption" is something enjoyed by "the redeemed." It is not punishment for apostasy, or for unbelief.

The events associated with Israel's judgment in A.D. 70 were not works of redemption but works of judgment. And yet in speaking to a first-century audience Jesus related all these events to the Kingdom. "So likewise ye, when ye see these things come to pass, know ye that the kingdom of God is *nigh at hand*" (Luke 21:31). If the destruction of Jerusalem and the slaughter of over a million Jews is being referenced in these passages, as preterists argue, it is difficult to see how this could be described as "your redemption" or the coming of the Kingdom of God.

"This Generation"

These considerations must be kept in mind as we deal with another preterist time text, Matthew 24:34: "Verily I say unto you, This generation shall not pass, till all these things be fulfilled." Much needs to be said about this as it is an important matter. Chapter eight, dealing with multiple references in biblical prophecy, bears much light on this and other so-called "time texts." At this point, however, we will look at these words in their immediate context to ascertain their meaning.

Preterists make much of the words "this generation," but they have the wrong generation. Luke 21:32 is the parallel of Matthew 24:34. Luke 21:31 tells us something about the "generation" to which reference is made: "So likewise ye, when ye *see these things come to pass,* know ye that the kingdom of God is nigh at hand." Preterists claim that by affirming a first century fulfillment, preterism will convince non-believers like Bertrand Russell, who objects to Christianity on the basis that nothing of what Jesus prophesied has yet come to pass. But I'm afraid that neither will preterism convince people who argue like Russell. Jesus spoke about *seeing* some things. They must be obvious to the sight, like the signs that He mentions in Luke 21. Nothing happened in the first century that even vaguely matches these signs.

There are several indicators in Luke 21 that verify for the reader what generation Jesus was speaking about:

» *verse 25:* "And there shall be *signs* ... "
» *verse 27:* And then shall *they see* the Son of man coming in a cloud ..."
» *verse 28:* "And when *these things begin to come to pass,* then look up ..."

> *verses 29–30:* "Behold the fig tree, and all the trees; When they now shoot forth, *ye see and know* ... that summer is now nigh at hand."

The things Jesus spoke about are to be visible and open. He calls them "signs." A "sign" is something that points to something else, but the sign is of no value if it cannot be seen. A hidden sign cannot function as a sign. Preterism changes the meaning of the words of Scripture because it cannot accommodate to its system what Scripture teaches. It speaks about a "coming" that is hidden and signs that no one can really see.

Jesus was sincerely offering the Kingdom to Israel. If Israel had accepted the offer, all these things would have literally taken place. It was based on the sincerity of His promise to Israel that He uttered these prophetic words. Though the Kingdom has been postponed, the signs are still valid *for the generation that sees them.*

The words of verse twenty-eight, that the disciples lift up their heads at the seeing of these signs, is a command, but it is also a promise for those living in that future generation. The generation that is living on earth at that time and that sees these signs can take courage. They will be preserved to the end. That generation will enjoy its "redemption." He promises that the generation that sees these signs "shall not pass away, *till all be fulfilled"* (Luke 21:32). After speaking about such horrifying things that will come upon the earth, Jesus is seeking to encourage them not to be disheartened. That generation will endure to the end. His words are absolutely certain. In fact, He states: "Heaven and earth shall pass away, but my words shall not pass away" (Luke 21:33). If He were referring to A.D. 70, what encouragement could He possibly offer?

"The End of the World"

In Matthew 24 we are told that Jesus pointed His disciples toward the temple complex and said to them, "I say unto you, There shall not be left here one stone upon another, that shall not be thrown down" (vs. 2). In verse three we are told that while Jesus was sitting on the Mount of Olives His disciples came and asked, "Tell us, when shall these things be? And what shall be the sign of thy coming, and of the end of the world [*aion*]?"

Preterists do not believe that Matthew 24, or any of the other passages recorded in the Olivet Discourse, speaks about a catastrophic end of the world, but simply about the end of the Old Testament sacrificial system. In explaining the disciples' question, DeMar asserts that "the numerous New Testament time indicators demonstrate that Jesus did not have a distant 'end' in mind when He spoke of 'the end of the age.'" Moreover, DeMar seeks to show that when Jesus spoke about "the age to come," He was not referring to some far distant age, but the New Testament era. An important question, then, that bears on whether the Olivet Discourse deals with the last days or the past days, is: What is the meaning of the word *aion*? Does it describe something that is still future from our modern perspective, or can it be limited to something that occurred in the first century, such as the destruction of the temple and the end of the Old Testament sacrificial system?

In answering this, it should be pointed out that *aion* is a word that is used in different constructions to indicate concepts of great duration, such as "a very long time," or "eternity." In Romans 1:25, the apostle writes of "the Creator, who is blessed for ever" (*eis tous aionas*). The word is used this way in several other passages, such as Romans 16:27, Philippians 4:20, and many others.

Furthermore, the word *aion* can be used of eternity future. Jesus spoke about the danger of sinning against the Holy Spirit and said: "And whosoever speaketh a word against the Son of man, it shall be forgiven him: but whosoever speaketh against the Holy Ghost, it shall not be forgiven him, neither in this world ["age," *aion*], neither in the world to come" (Matt. 12:32). Jesus speaks of two ages—this one and the one to come. In Mark 3:29 this is explained: "But he that shall blaspheme against the Holy Ghost hath never forgiveness, but is in danger of eternal damnation (*aioniou kriseos*)."

The New Testament speaks about two ages, "this age" and "the age to come," the latter being eschatological and associated with the separation of the righteous from the unrighteous. The Parable of the Dragnet is a picture of eschatological separation and cannot be understood as teaching a judgment at the time of the Roman invasion of Jerusalem: "So shall it be at the end of the world [*aion*]: the angels shall come forth, and sever the wicked from among the just, And shall cast them into the furnace of fire ..." (Matt. 13:49–50). It is at the end of the *aion* that an unprecedented separation shall take place. Do preterists wish to link this with A.D. 70?

It is based on these considerations that the preterist understanding of Matthew 24:3 doesn't stand the test of careful exegesis. In asking about the Lord's "coming" and the "end of the *aion*" (Matt. 24:3) the disciples had in mind future events of cosmic proportions. The language certainly requires something more than a first century fulfillment. Luke 19:11 records that the disciples believed that the Old Testament messianic Kingdom would appear immediately. They thought that Jesus was going to do something dramatic, like drive the Romans out of Judea and establish the messianic Kingdom. They did not perceive that He had to die on the cross first. The disciples were not given to modern theological niceties and distinctions and they were not thinking of "the end of the Christian dispensation." They were not looking for a "Christian dispensation" at all, but the inbreaking of the Kingdom promised in the Old Testament.

Luke 19:11 reads: "And as they heard these things, he added and spake a parable, because he was nigh to Jerusalem, and because they thought that the kingdom of God *should immediately appear.*" This was their hope. The appearance of the Kingdom meant deliverance for Israel, not the destruction of Israel. Their anticipation was Israel's exaltation, not her defilement at the hands of the Romans. When the disciples asked, "What shall be the sign of thy coming [*parousia*, "appearing, presence"], and of the end of the world," they were thinking of a dramatic destruction of the old order.

The Question of the "Time Texts"

But weren't the disciples wrong in their expectation? Partly, but only in their timing of what would happen. They were right in expecting the Kingdom, but it would not come in their lifetimes. In Acts 1:6 they asked, "Lord, wilt thou at this time restore again the kingdom to Israel?" Their kingdom aspirations were not rebuffed by Jesus. Rather He said, "It is not for you to know the times or the seasons, which the Father hath put in his own power."

Preterists give A.D. 70 far more weight than it really deserves. The destruction of the Jewish temple did not bring the Jewish dispensation to an end. It had already ended at Pentecost. The temple was simply the remaining skeleton of that old order. The coming of the Holy Spirit as a universal donation on the church ushered in something new and marvelous, but preterists must focus on A.D. 70 because their replacement theology forces them to do so. They make it the end of the age and consequently allegorize the prophetic references that can only be fulfilled in the future. This faulty approach by which they arrive at this conclusion is clearly indicated in the following quote from preterist Marcellus Kik:

> One of the chief reasons why many commentators reject the idea that the first section [of Matthew 24] refers only to the destruction of Jerusalem is that they think the language of the section is too striking and bold for a description of such a local event. Such vivid language, they believe, can refer only to the events just previous to the second coming of the Lord. They forget that the destruction of Jerusalem, which resulted in the excision of the Jewish nation from the Kingdom, was one of the most important events that has ever occurred on earth, and that it had tremendous consequences.

Kik believes that the destruction of Jerusalem "resulted in the excision of the Jewish nation from the Kingdom." This is an utterly incredible statement coming from someone who claims to believe in the sovereignty of God. What? An invasion by the Romans—a pagan power—removed the Jewish nation from the Kingdom? God never gave any human army *that* power. It is not within the scope of human power to remove nations from God's Kingdom. Didn't God say, "Jerusalem shall be trodden down of the Gentiles, *until* the times of the Gentiles be fulfilled" (Luke 21:24)?

Preterism makes much of its so-called "time texts." I have dealt with some of these texts in this chapter, but yet need to address a few more issues related to "time texts."

Chapter 7

A.D. 70 and Other "Preterist Texts"

Did the End of Something Occur in A.D. 70?

By now the reader has gathered that preterists place a great deal of weight on the Roman invasion of Jerusalem and subsequent destruction of the temple in A.D. 70. Almost all prophecy looks to this event. Was it really an event of such importance that virtually all prophecy was fulfilled in its occurrence?

Of course, preterists say "yes." For them the destruction of the temple along with its system of worship—the Jewish priesthood and the Old Testament sacrificial system—ushered in the new era in which the blood of Christ, and not the blood of animals, cleanses the conscience from dead works to serve the living God (Heb. 9:14). Preterists argue that "the end of the age" means "the end of the Jewish age."

Investing the destruction of the temple with such epoch-making significance, however, is another one of the many root errors of preterism. According to Scripture, the new era began with the outpouring of the Holy Spirit as a universal donation, not with the destruction of the temple. In the

Old Testament era the Holy Spirit was with certain individuals at key times in their lives and ministries, but with the outpouring of the Spirit, He became the motivating power for all believers (John 14:17). When the Holy Spirit was poured forth, things changed dramatically. Peter, who was somewhat timid and vacillating, addressed a crowd of Jews and a great multitude of people were saved (Acts 2:41–42). Nothing of this sort happened with the destruction of the Jewish temple. The Jewish dispensation had been terminated many years earlier. God had left the temple and cancelled the sacrificial system many years before. His destruction of the temple was simply an outward demonstration of something that had already happened.

If A.D. 70 were such an epoch-making date you would think that the Bible would at least say a few words about something of such significance. Contrary to the emphasis of preterism, there is a decided nonemphasis in Scripture concerning the destruction of the temple. Though the event is prophesied in Scripture as an historical event, the Bible never treats the destruction of the temple as ushering in a dispensational change.

To see the utter folly of the preterist position just imagine that you wanted to write a book on missions. In your book you want to stress the church's missionary obligation as well as the Divine empowerment that God has provided for missionaries. What title would you give the book? Would you entitle it *The Destruction of the Jewish Temple and Missions,* or would you call it *Pentecost and Missions?*

The distinctive ministries of the Holy Spirit during the Church Age can be traced to the book of Acts. To say that the Holy Spirit's sealing, filling, and baptizing ministry began in A.D. 70 is ludicrous. To be sure, preterists don't teach that it did. They know that the Old Covenant system of worship came to an end with the death, resurrection, and ascension of Jesus Christ, not with the destruction of the temple some forty years later.

Jewish exclusivism was one of the hallmarks of the old era. Even some of the earliest Christians were confused on how God regarded gentiles. Was the issue cleared up in A.D. 70 and did the inclusion of gentiles receive acceptance at that date? Not at all. It was the conversion of Cornelius and his family that was a most dramatic statement from God.

Luke begins to unfold the story in Acts 9:32–43 where he describes Peter's visits to Lydia and Joppa. This passage serves as an introduction to Peter's housetop experience and his subsequent visit to Caesarea, the conversion of Cornelius, and the reaction of the church to Peter's telling of it (10:1–11:18). Jewish exclusivism was so entrenched that even Peter struggled with God's message. "Not so, Lord; for I have never eaten any thing that is common or unclean" (Acts 10:14). Peter finally realized what was happening, but it took three repetitions of the command to "eat."

This was a radical and startling departure from the old order: salvation had come to the gentiles. Through the outpouring of the Holy Spirit, Jews and gentiles were now on an equal footing before God. The gospel was intended for gentiles no less than for Jews. When the church heard Peter's amazing story, they all responded, "Then hath God also to the gentiles granted repentance unto life" (Acts 11:18). "It is not stated that God had given repentance to gentiles who had become proselytes," writes Boer, "or to gentiles who really ceased to be gentiles, or to gentiles who would not have to become Jews first, but it is stated that God had granted repentance to gentiles without qualification." The Book of Acts records something of monumental significance. Clearly, this change did not occur in A.D. 70.

A study of the Acts of the Apostles makes it clear that the passing of the old era, and the ushering in of the new, preceded A.D. 70 by many years. In *A Bible Handbook of the Acts of the Apostles,* pages 18–20, Mal Couch discusses seven transitions found in the Book of Acts.

First, there is the historical transition. Acts not only gives the historical origin of the church, but it also provides the historical background for the Pauline letters. It is in Acts that we find out about the founding of churches in Rome, Corinth, Galatia, Ephesus, Colossae, Philippi, and Thessalonica.

Secondly, there is the transition from synagogue to church. In the Gospels the faithful met in the temple and in synagogues. While the temple and synagogue continue in Acts, there is a new corporate entity that appears: the church. While Paul met with various groups in the synagogues, his purpose there was not to establish the synagogue, but rather he had an evangelistic end in view.

A third transition mentioned by Couch is the cessation of God's dealing with Israel nationally, except in judgment, and his turning to the gentiles. Cornelius, Lydia, and the Philippian jailer, to mention a few, are reached by the grace of God. In Acts 10:34–35 Peter boldly declares, "Of a truth I perceive that God is no respecter of persons: But in every nation he that feareth him, and worketh righteousness, is accepted with him."

Fourthly, Acts marks the transition from the physical presence of Christ with His select inner circle, to the indwelling presence of the Holy Spirit in every believer. When Christ ascended into heaven, He sent the Comforter.

Fifthly, there is the transition from the Holy Spirit being with believers, to His being *in* believers. This now makes it possible for the Holy Spirit to have an internal inner relationship with believers so that their character would become more like Christ's character. It is because of this inner dynamic that the apostle Paul could speak of "the fruit of the Spirit" (Gal. 5:22–23).

Sixthly, there is a national transition. With the opening of the Book of Acts, virtually every believer is from Israel. The few gentiles were Jewish proselytes. As we move through the book, however, it becomes clear that this is rapidly changing. With the preaching of Peter to the household of Cornelius, the gospel goes to uncircumcised gentiles and they, even though they had not first been Jewish proselytes, became a part of the church.

Seventhly, there is an ethical shift. No longer is the Mosaic Law the ethical "yardstick" for godly behavior, but the apostolic witness to the Person of Christ. Though the Sabbath command was preeminent in Jewish life, gentiles who are evangelized in the Book of Acts are never told to "keep the Sabbath."

Preterists must insist on the significance of A.D. 70 because it is supportive of their view. If the "time texts" speak of a first century disaster, the only one they can find that resembles Tribulation judgments is the destruction of the temple. Investing A.D. 70 with epoch-making significance is the only way that preterists can explain—or should I say—explain away the heavenly signs that they claim happened in the past. Jesus said: "And there shall be signs in the sun, and in the moon, and in the stars; and upon the earth distress of nations, with perplexity" (Luke 21:25). Preterists characteristically link this with the end of the Jewish dispensation in A.D. 70 and claim that this is the standard language for the end of a kingdom. DeMar voices this view when he writes:

> The language that Jesus uses is typical of Old Testament imagery where stellar phenomena represent kings and kingdoms. The first coming of Jesus was marked by a star (Matthew 2:2). The people of Israel were represented as stars (Genesis 22:17; 26:4; Deuteronomy 1:10). The flags of many nations include the use of multiple stars (United States, Australia, Brazil, China, Honduras, Iraq, New Zealand, Panama, Papua, New Guinea, Venezuela), a single star (Cameroon, Cuba, Israel, Senegal, Suriname, Vietnam, Yemen, Jordan, North Korea, Liberia), the moon and star (Algeria, Comoros, Mauritania, Pakistan, Singapore, Tunisia, Turkey), the moon and sun (Malaysia), and the sun (Japan, Malawi) ... We describe a person on the way up as a "rising star." When a well-known person is found to have done wrong, we say, "his star is tarnished," or "his star is fallen."

I find these to be poor explanations of the eschatological stellar phenomena. Most of them are pagan symbols on national flags. The star leading the wise men did just that—it led them, and directed their course to the Christ-child. It was visible to the travelers from the East and served a useful purpose. It's doubtful if it represented anything. DeMar says "the people of Israel were represented as stars," but eschatological passages speaking of the heavenly phenomena speak about fear, perplexity, and terror due to these phenomena and do more than represent people of nations. If stars falling out of heaven represent the demise of the Jewish nation, why would that produce fear on earth? The Olivet Discourse is not only about Israel's destruction, but about her victory and restoration (Matt. 24:31). I believe that such explanations are devices of convenience that are used to make A.D. 70 "the end."

Reformed theologians are notorious for taking liberties with prophetic texts. Perhaps no passage of scripture is treated more in this manner than Revelation 20 and its description of the binding of Satan. B. B. Warfield, a conservative Presbyterian scholar of an earlier generation, does some very strange things with this passage as the following quote shows:

> ... The element of time and chronological succession belongs to the symbol, not to the thing symbolized. The "binding of Satan" is, therefore, in reality, not for a season, but with reference to a sphere; and his "loosing" again is not after a period but in another sphere; it is not subsequence but exteriority that is suggested. There is, indeed, *no literal "binding of Satan" to be thought of at all:* what happens, happens not to Satan but to the saints, and is only represented as happening to Satan for the purpose of the symbolical picture. What actually happens is that the saints described are removed from the sphere of Satan's assaults. The saints described are free from all access of Satan—he is bound with respect to them; *outside of their charmed circle his horrid work goes on.*

Warfield was generally an able commentator who held a high view of Scripture, but from this quote we quickly see how he took liberties with the text of Scripture. The passage he is trying to explain gives no indication whatsoever that "what happens, happens not to Satan, but to the saints." Warfield is reading into this passage all kinds of things that are not there! One can understand how a rank liberal could do that. Warfield, however, was no liberal, but a staunch defender of the faith. Why he was so blind in eschatology is somewhat perplexing, although it is shared by almost all Reformed commentators. Stanton's comments are well-taken: "The statement by Warfield is most significant, for it illustrates the power of the spiritualizing method even in the hands of an outstanding conservative theologian, to alter if not to reverse the plain teaching of the Word of God."

Revelation 1:7

This scripture provides a wonderful hope for believers: "Behold, he cometh with clouds; and every eye shall see him, and they also which pierced him: and all kindreds of the earth shall wail because of him."

There have been many sermons delivered from this text to encourage persecuted and afflicted believers. They have been reminded that though there is much suffering in the present life (Acts 14:22) that nevertheless God's Word assures them of Christ's return. Even the Jews who took part in the crucifixion of Christ will see His glory. Not surprisingly, however, preterists insist that what is described in this verse has already taken place!

While moderate preterists claim that Jesus came in judgment upon Israel in A.D. 70, this does not mean that they deny a literal, physical, bodily return of Christ at the end of history. I want to make this clear lest moderate preterists be misrepresented. Gentry seeks to clear up the confusion and makes some revealing statements:

> Here is where a good deal of unnecessary confusion arises. Actually there are a number of ways in which Christ "comes." It is true that He will come at the end of history, bringing about the resurrection and the judgment (Acts 1:11; 1 Thess. 4:13ff; 1 Cor. 15:20–26). But Scripture also teaches that Christ comes to His people in other ways. He comes to us personally

in the Holy Spirit (John 16:16, 18, 28), in fellowship by His presence in the church (Matt. 18:20), to believers at death (John 14:1–3), to God in heaven to receive His kingdom (Dan. 7:13), and in judicial judgment upon men in history (Matt. 21:40, 41; Rev. 2:5). But to which sort of "coming" do these verses mentioned above from Revelation refer?

To making a point I will quote the above Scriptures that Gentry offers to show that Christ "comes … in other ways":

3. *John 16:16:* "A little while, and ye shall not see me: and again, a little while, and ye shall see me, because I go to the Father."
4. *John 16:18:* "They said therefore, What is this that he saith, A little while? we cannot tell what he saith."
5. *John 16:28:* "I came forth from the Father, and am come into the world: again, I leave the world, and go to the Father."
6. *Matthew 18:20:* "For where two or three are gathered together in my name, there am I in the midst of them."
7. *John 14:1–3:* "Let not your heart be troubled: ye believe in God, believe also in me. In my Father's house are many mansions: if it were not so, I would have told you. I go to prepare a place for you. And if I go and prepare a place for you, I will come again, and receive you unto myself; that where I am, there ye may be also."
8. *Daniel 7:13:* "I saw in the night visions, and, behold, one like the Son of man came with the clouds of heaven, and came to the Ancient of days, and they brought him near before him."
9. *Matthew 21:40:* "When the lord therefore of the vineyard cometh, what will he do unto those husbandmen?"
10. *Matthew 21:41:* "They say unto him, He will miserably destroy those wicked men, and will let out his vineyard unto other husbandmen, which shall render him the fruits of in their seasons."

11. *Revelation 2:5:* "Remember therefore from whence thou art fallen, and repent, and do the first works; or else I will come unto thee quickly, and will remove thy candlestick out of his place, except thou repent."

Points 1 and 2 prove nothing because they don't even speak about any "coming" of Christ. Neither does point 6. In that scripture "one like the Son of man" comes to "the Ancient of days," not to earth or to the people of God.

Point 5 is obviously eschatological and doesn't prove that Christ "comes" in some mysterious way other than dramatically and openly. Points 7 and 8 also can be applied to eschatological judgment on Israel in the future. Only point 4 possibly speaks of some other kind of "coming," yet it is so different in tone and descriptive detail from Revelation 1:7 that there is no sound reason to equate it with Revelation 1:7, which says that "every eye shall *see him.*"

Gentry does not believe that Revelation 1:7 describes the literal Second Coming of Christ. He believes that

> the references in Revelation to His coming have to do with His coming in judgment, *particularly on Israel.* This is evident in the theme verse of Revelation found in Revelation 1:7: "Behold, He is coming with the clouds, and every eye will see Him, even those who pierced Him; and all the tribes of the earth will mourn over Him. Even so. Amen." This cloud-coming of Christ in judgment is reminiscent of Old Testament cloud-comings of God in judgment upon ancient historical people and nations (PSS. 18:7–15; 104:3; Isa. 19:1; Joel 2:1,2; Hab. 1:2ff; Zeph. 1:14, 15).

When Jesus ascended into heaven from the Mount of Olives, "a cloud received him out of their sight" (Acts 1:9). Since He is returning in the same way that He left (Acts 1:11), His coming with "clouds" (Rev. 1:7) must be a physical coming. Old Testament "cloud" passages such as the above ones are either Tribulational passages or, as in the case of Psalm 97:2–5 and Isaiah 19:1ff, describe the Lord as riding on a cloud, not coming with the clouds. But even more important is the fact that in those "cloudy comings" He comes to bring judgment on Israel's *enemies, not upon Israel,* as preterists claim happens in Revelation 1:7. In Psalm 104:3 there is no mention of a "cloudy coming" of the Lord in judgment, but rather that the Lord rides the clouds as a chariot as King over the universe by virtue of His power to create (vss.1–2, 5–7).

In addition to these important considerations showing that Revelation 1:7 is not speaking about some non-corporeal "cloud coming" of Christ in A.D. 70, we must speak about the verse itself. The following is a brief analysis of Revelation 1:7.

» *"Behold, he ... him"*—These are clear references to Christ. He is the subject of verses one and five.
» *"Eye"*—A translation of the word *opthalmos*, the physical organ of sight. The word is used of our physical eyes in the Greek New Testament (Matt. 20:33; John 4:35; 6:5•, 9:6; Gal. 4:15).
» *"See"*—The word *horao* can be used to indicate perception, i.e., "to be aware of something" and, if this is the sense, then it could be used to support a non-physical coming. However, the word is also used in the sense of seeing something physical and visible to the eye. In John 16:16 Jesus spoke about His ascension and that the disciples would no longer "see" Him. The fact that this verb appears in Revelation 1:7 with the word describing the physical organ of sight lends support to the idea of a visible seeing. Indeed, the word *horao*, with its possible double meaning, is ideally suited to this text. Though every eye will "see" Christ, this produces a perception of distress: there is "wailing."
» *"Kindreds"*—The word *phylai* is understood by preterists as referring to "tribes," i.e., "the tribes of Israel in the first century A.D." However, in Revelation 7:9 the word has a universal application: "After this I beheld, and, lo, a great multitude, which no man could number, of all nations,

and kindreds [*phylai*]." The contrast with the 144,000 Jews in the previous verses demonstrates that "kindreds" must not be limited to "tribes of Israel."

» **"Earth"**—The word in the Greek text is *ge*. Preterists like to translate it as "land," meaning "the land of Israel." Sometimes ge denotes "land" in contrast with the sea or with a large body of water (Mark 4:1; 6:47; Luke 5:3; John 6:21). While ge can sometimes reference a land or region, it frequently indicates the earth in contrast with heaven. Jesus said, "For verily I say unto you, Till heaven and earth [*ge*] pass, one jot or one tittle shall in no wise pass from the law" (Matt. 5:18). John uses the word to mean "planet earth": "And I saw a new heaven and a new earth [*ge*]; for the first heaven and the first earth [*ge*] were passed away" (Rev. 21:1).

Preterists limit the applicability of Revelation 1:7 to the ancient Roman world. This is in keeping with their practice of limiting and restricting Scripture. I dealt with this in chapter six. I must add to those considerations by pointing out that the Book of Revelation cannot be limited to first century events and first century nations. For example, in Revelation 12:5 we read that the woman "brought forth a man child, who was to rule all nations with a rod of iron." Whatever one's eschatological position, all agree that Christ's rule is to extend to all nations *of the world.*" Moreover, Revelation 12:9 speaks about "that old serpent, called the Devil, and Satan, which deceiveth the whole world." By applying preterist standards, Satan only deceives the ancient Roman world which, of course, is a position that even preterists do not hold.

The Book of Revelation must not be limited in time or extent. Revelation abounds in universal statements that suggest fulfillments beyond the confines of the ancient Roman world. "Who shall not fear thee, O Lord, and glorify thy name?" ask the angels in Revelation 15:4, " ... for *all nations* shall come and worship before thee ..." We are called to worship God who is described in universal terms in Revelation 14:7 as the one who "made heaven, and earth, and the sea, and the fountains of waters." Based on these considerations, I firmly believe that Christians can still find encouragement and comfort in Revelation 1:7, and that this precious verse describes something that will happen in the future.

Matthew 10:23

This verse reads: "But when they persecute you in this city, flee ye into another: for verily I say unto you, Ye shall not have gone over the cities of Israel, till the Son of man be come." Preterists take note of the fact that Jesus is addressing His disciples with "ye"; and He says, "Ye shall not have gone over the cities of Israel, till the Son of man be come."

Interestingly, even some commentators in the Presbyterian-Reformed community do not believe that this verse has an exclusive first century reference. William Hendriksen, a Reformed commentator of a-millennial persuasion, discounts various alternate views, along with the view that it is a reference "to the terrible judgment upon the Jews in the years 66–70," and writes:

> These explanations ignore the fact that in the other Matthew passages in which the coming of the Son of man is mentioned and described the reference is linked with the second coming. It is a coming "in the glory of his Father," "with his angels, to render to every man according to his deeds" (16:27, 28); a coming when Christ shall "sit on the throne of his glory" (19:28); a coming that would be "visible" (24:27); "sudden and unexpected" (24:37, 39, 44); a coming "on clouds of heaven with power and great glory" (24:30; cf. 25:31; 26:64). It would be strange therefore if from 10:23 any reference to Christ's exaltation which attains its climax in the second coming would be wholly excluded.

Hendriksen understands our Lord's words to be words of comfort to both the disciples and the Jews, a point that I have argued in another context. Hendriksen adds that Matthew 10:23 "is a comforting assurance, and this not only for the missionaries themselves, whether the Twelve or their successors, but even for the Jews." For the disciples these words mean "'Do not be afraid, I will return to you.' For Israel it would signify, 'I am not through with you; your remnant, too, will be saved.'"

Hendriksen correctly believes that Matthew 24 is a key for understanding Matthew 10:23.

> If it be granted that according to Matt. 24 Jesus makes use of prophetic foreshortening when in vivid colors borrowed from the destruction of Jerusalem by the Romans he paints his coming at the close of history, why can we not have something of a similar nature here in 10:23?

It is interesting that Hendriksen finds some similarity between the destruction of Jerusalem in A.D. 70, with the return of Jesus Christ in the future, and says that Jesus uses the "vivid colors borrowed from the destruction of Jerusalem by the Romans," and "paints his coming at the close of history." Preterist R. C. Sproul, who serves as the general editor for the *New Geneva Study Bible,* likewise finds some similarity between the return of Christ and the destruction of the temple. In the note on Matthew 10:23 he writes:

> The other references to the coming of the Son of man view it as a great and terrible display of God's judgment. Although these cannot be limited to the destruction of Jerusalem, that event was terrible in intensity and fell on what had been the central visible symbol of God's presence, the temple.

Evidently, even non-pre-millennialists are not totally willing to limit Jesus' eschatological statements to the destruction of Jerusalem. They see the events of A.D. 70 as a type of something that will yet occur in the future. Lutheran commentator R. C. H. Lenski does not want to limit Matthew 10:23 to something that occurred in the past.

> In this section (vs. 16—23), as in the following, Jesus reaches out into the future, far beyond the lifetime of the Twelve, and yet he reverts also to the Twelve and to what shall occur during their lives.

Keeping all this in mind, we are led to see Matthew 10:23 as referring to Israel's future with the encouraging reminder added that Israel will not be abandoned by the Lord in the future. The tenor of the verse, which is a word of encouragement, militates against a first century fulfillment. "Ye shall not have gone over the cities of Israel, till the Son of man be come," Jesus says. This doesn't mean "till the Son of man comes to destroy Israel and punish the nation." Jesus is not speaking to Jewish apostates who have rejected Him and are therefore in need of a frightening word of judgment. Rather, He is speaking to His disciples who are in need of a word of encouragement.

Matthew 16:27–28

These two verses are also cited by preterists as supporting their position. Jesus says:

> For the Son of man shall come in the glory of his Father with his angels; and then he shall reward every man according to his works. Verily I say unto you, There be some standing here, which shall not taste of death, till they see the Son of man coming in his kingdom.

Verse twenty-seven reveals that when the Son of man comes, He is going to "reward every man according to his works." In Scripture, the giving of rewards is associated with the future. It is sometimes associated with the bodily resurrection, as in Luke 14:14, where Jesus says: "for thou shalt be recompensed [rewarded] at the resurrection of the just." Other passages likewise associate the giving of rewards with the return of Christ. "And, behold, I come quickly; and *my reward* is with me, to give every man according as his work shall be" (Rev. 22:12; see also 1 Cor. 4:5; 2 Cor. 5:8–10). When Matthew 16:27 states, "For the son of man shall come in the glory of his Father with his angels; and then *he shall reward* every man according to his works," it is highly doubtful that this is referring to a first century event.

Some interpreters try to relate these verses to the transfiguration of Christ. They argue that the transfiguration was, in some sense, a demonstration of Christ's Kingdom glory. The statement found in Matthew 16:27–28 appears in all the synoptic gospels, and in each case the account of the transfiguration immediately follows. Their argument is that there must be some connection between these words and the transfiguration.

No doubt, the transfiguration made such an impression on both Peter and John that both relate it to the glorified Christ (2 Pet. 1:16–21; Rev. 1:12–20). The transfiguration was a concrete historical event that took place during the earthly ministry of Jesus, but Peter regards it as being typical of Christ's return in glory and power. Peter writes:

> For we have not followed cunningly devised fables, when we made known unto you the power and coming of our Lord Jesus Christ, but were eyewitnesses of his majesty. For he received from God the Father honour and glory, when there came such a voice to him from the excellent glory, This is my beloved Son, in whom I am well pleased. And this voice which came from heaven we heard, when we were with him in the holy mount. We have also a more sure word of prophecy, whereunto ye do well that ye take heed, as unto a light that shineth in a dark place, until the day dawn, and the day star arise in your hearts.
>
> —2 Peter 1:16–19

Peter speaks about making known the coming of the Lord, and then says that he, along with the others, were eyewitnesses of the Lord's *majesty*. What coming of Christ could have anything to do with His majesty? Certainly not the first coming. He came as a babe, lived as a poor man, ministered to the multitudes, and died as a criminal. The first coming is not normally explained as a witness to the Lord's majesty.

We must conclude, therefore, that in some way the transfiguration of Christ pointed to His future return in glory. In a real sense, the transfiguration was a preview of the Second Coming.

It seems to me that if we do not recognize the typical significance of the transfiguration, we will miss the intent of the Matthew 16 passage by either claiming

1. that the passage was completely fulfilled at the transfiguration, and thereby be coerced into giving a forced interpretation to the words, "and then shall he reward every man according to his works" (Matt. 16:27), words that have a future reference; or we will miss the intent of the passage by claiming
2. that the passage refers to the physical return of the Lord and thereby be coerced into giving a forced interpretation to the words, "There be some standing here which shall not taste of death, till they see the Son of man coming in His kingdom" (Matt. 16:28), which clearly refers to something that would happen shortly.

Both numbers 1 and 2 have problems and must be rejected. Yes, the transfiguration was, in some sense, referenced by Jesus in Matthew 16:27—28. It happened in the past but was a picture of something that would happen in the future. The transfiguration is like the destruction of Jerusalem in A.D. 70 in that it was a first century picture of Jerusalem's future woes during the Tribulation.

There are many types and pictures in the Scripture. The "rest" in Canaan is a type of the church's rest in glory. In the same way the spiritual rest which God gives His people is based upon the finished work of Christ and is like the rest of God after the completion of His creative work (Heb. 4:3–4). The type is not the anti-type, but there is a sufficient correspondence between the type and the anti-type to make the comparison meaningful. Jesus said, "There be some standing here, which shall not taste of death, till they see the Son of man coming in *his kingdom*" (Matt. 16:28). "Coming in His kingdom" means "coming in his kingly glory." The transfiguration was a "coming in Jesus' kingly glory" and was a demonstration of His glory as King. This surely did happen at the transfiguration. Though the two greatest figures in Israel's history appeared with Jesus on the Mount of Transfiguration—Moses and Elijah— yet the voice of the Father gave preeminence to His Son when He said "hear ye *him*" (Matt. 17:5), thereby implying that Jesus' authority was over and above that of either Moses or Elijah.

The transfiguration occurred when Jesus was still offering the Kingdom to Israel. He speaks from the perspective of someone living before the revelation of the mystery, the church. Jesus fully believed that the Kingdom prophesied by the Old Testament prophets would be shortly upon them. He did not envision the Church Age. It was a parenthetical period of time not yet revealed through Paul. When Jesus taught the disciples to pray, "Thy kingdom come. Thy will be done in earth, as it is in heaven" (Matt. 6:10), Jesus was not thinking of the church. Jesus was a dispensationalist. In Matthew 10:5—6 He sent forth the twelve and said, "Go not into the way of the Gentiles, and into any city of the Samaritans enter ye not. *But go rather to the lost sheep of the house of Israel.*" With the same emphasis in mind, Jesus said, in the fifteenth chapter of Matthew, "I am not sent but unto the lost sheep of the house of Israel" (vs. 24). In the time frame of God's revealed plan to have Christ minister to "the lost sheep of the house of Israel" for the purpose of establishing the promised Kingdom, Jesus' disciples would "see the Son of man coming in His Kingdom."

This is a pivotal point that must be stressed. Jesus was speaking in the time frame revealed by God. God had not yet revealed the mystery, so all time considerations must be reckoned without the Church Age. If Israel accepted her Messiah, the Kingdom would have been established and the disciples would "see the Son of man coming in his kingdom."

The prophet Malachi predicted that Elijah would come before the establishment of the millennial Kingdom. Malachi 4:5–6 states:

> Behold, I will send you Elijah the prophet before the coming of the great and dreadful day of the LORD: And he shall turn the heart of the fathers to the children, and the heart of the children to their fathers, lest I come and smite the earth with a curse.

John the Baptist was a type of Elijah. In fact, we are told that John ministered "in the spirit and power of Elias [Elijah]" (Luke 1:17); yet John's coming did not change the hearts of the fathers and the children. In fact, the very opposite occurred at Christ's first coming (Matt. 10:34–36). What then, of this promise concerning the coming of Elijah? Some believe this promise will be literally fulfilled by the return of Elijah, by one of the two witnesses during the Tribulation (Rev. 11:3), or at some yet future time.

We know that John came with the pronouncement, "Repent ye: for the kingdom of heaven is at hand" (Mark 3:2), referring to the rule and reign of the Messiah in fulfillment of the Old Testament messianic prophesies. We also know that Jesus referred to John and said:

> Elias truly shall first come, and restore all things. But I say unto you, That Elias is come already, and they knew him not Then the disciples understood that he spake unto them of John the Baptist.
> —Matthew 17:11–13

From this scriptural data we must conclude that there is a sense in which John was Elijah, but we must also conclude that there is a sense in which he was not. Though this may seem like double-talk, the issue hinges on Israel's response to the proclamation of the inbreaking of the Kingdom. Jesus said, "And if ye will receive it, this is Elias, which was for to come" (Matt. 11:14). From the human perspective, it all depended on their reception of Divine truth. Matthew 16:27–28 cannot be divorced from this insight. If the Jews had received their Messiah, those living in that day would:

1. see the Messiah coming in His glory;
11. would see the Son of man rewarding every man according to his works.

While I would certainly admit that Matthew 10:23 and Matthew 16:27–28 are often cited as providing *major* problems for futurism, what is often ignored, and perhaps deliberately, is that they present major problems for preterists. In Matthew 16:27, for example, Jesus says: "For the Son of man shall come in the glory of his Father with his angels; and then he shall reward every man according to his works." Do preterists wish to claim that these rewards were given out in the first century? As we have seen earlier in this chapter, this is futuristic language. While preterists like to underscore verse twenty-eight—"There be some standing here, which shall not taste of death, till they see the Son of man coming in his kingdom"—they need to give an adequate interpretation of the promise of reward in verse twenty-seven.

I believe that understanding these passages in their historical and dispensational setting provides adequate answers.

Chapter 8

Prophetic Multiple References

The prophecies of the Bible are written in a unique and special way so that they often refer to more than one event. It is in this way that they have initial references that all bear some similarity to the most distant fulfillment prophesied by the ancient prophet. Because of this prophetic phenomenon of multiple references, the events described in the Olivet Discourse have a typical fulfillment in the Roman destruction of the temple in A.D. 70 which was a "mini-tribulation" that predates the eschatological Tribulation of the future.

Scripture shows that there may be an immediate reference to something that occurred in the prophet's lifetime, but also subsequent references to events occurring after the prophet's lifetime. The same prophecy may reference something that occurred in the Old Testament era, and then something in the Church Age, and yet still have a final and complete fulfillment to something prophesied for the future Tribulation period.

Multiple references are seen in Second Samuel 7:11–16, where there is a reference both to Solomon, and to Jesus Christ, David's greater son. In verse fourteen, the reference cannot be to Christ because the prophecy states: "I will be his father, and he shall be my son. If he commit iniquity, I will chasten him with the rod of men, and with the stripes of the children of men." However, in verse sixteen the prophet speaks to David and says, "And thine house and thy kingdom shall be established for ever before thee: thy throne shall be established for ever," words that can only find their ultimate reality in Jesus Christ.

Isaiah 6

In this chapter the prophet sees a vision of "the Lord sitting upon a throne, high and lifted up" (vs. 1). After the prophet voices his willingness to be God's faithful messenger, the Lord addresses him and says: "Go, and tell *this people* ... " (vs. 9). Isaiah's ministry is to "this people," the people who were contemporaries of Isaiah and who were living in rebellion against God.

Their rebellion is a constant theme in the early chapters of Isaiah. "Ah sinful nation, a people laden with iniquity, a seed of evildoers, children that are corrupters: they have forsaken the Lord, they have provoked the Holy One of Israel unto anger, they are gone away backward" (Isa. 1:4).

There are other references to the sins of Isaiah's generation. In Isaiah 5:1–30 we are presented with the parable of the vineyard. In this parable Israel is the vineyard. The Lord fenced it in, took stones out of the ground so that the vines would grow well. And, almost with a tinge of frustration, the Lord asks: "What could have been done more to my vineyard, that I have not done in it? wherefore, when I looked that it should bring forth grapes, brought it forth wild grapes?" Clearly, when Isaiah was commanded to "Go and tell *this people*," Isaiah was commanded to go to his generation, his contemporaries.

However, Isaiah's ministry did not exhaust the prophecy. It also referenced something that came to pass some seven hundred years later. At a time when Jesus Christ was experiencing growing opposition to His ministry He began to teach in parables. The disciples asked Him, "Why speakest thou unto them in parables?" (Matt. 13:10). The Lord answered them by speaking of the hard—heartedness of His hearers, and then added, "And *in them* is fulfilled the prophecy of Esaias …" (Matt. 13:13—15). Jesus quotes from Isaiah 6, words that were initially addressed to Isaiah's contemporaries. But Jesus says, "in them [Jesus' contemporaries] is fulfilled the prophecy of Esaias."

And yet, this does not exhaust the applications of Isaiah 6. Some two and a half decades after Christ ascended, the apostle Paul was in Rome under house arrest. Many Jews came to his quarters to hear him expound the Scriptures, something that Paul did from morning until evening (Acts 28:23). Scripture states that some believed, but others became hostile. Acts 28:25–27 tells us: "And when they agreed not among themselves, they departed, after that Paul had spoken one word, *Well spoke the Holy Ghost by Esaias the prophet unto the fathers …* " and then follows the words of Isaiah 6.

Isaiah 14

Multiple references can also take the form of typological references. In Isaiah 14, for example, the prophet is speaking against the king of Babylon. God addresses Isaiah and says, "Thou shalt take up this proverb against the king of Babylon, and say, How hath the oppressor ceased! The golden city ceased!" (vs. 4). However, as we proceed in the chapter it becomes obvious that the individual in view could not be the king of Babylon: "How art thou fallen from heaven, O Lucifer, son of the morning! … For thou hast said in thine heart, I will ascend into heaven, I will exalt my throne above the stars of God" (vss. 12–13). Similarly, Ezekiel 28:2 speaks of "the prince of Tyrus," but goes on to say, "Thou hast been in Eden the garden of God" (vs. 13).

Typological reference is a feature of the prophetic scriptures that has important implications for the understanding of biblical prophecy, especially those passages that deal with the oppression of Israel. This, of course, makes typological reference a key in understanding the Olivet Discourse because the passage deals with the oppression of Israel. Individuals and nations that oppress Israel are often anti-types of the eschatological Antichrist and the future Tribulation judgments against Israel. Oppression against Israel by gentiles—whether from Pharaoh, Haman, the Assyrians, the Babylonians, or the Romans—are Divine judgments for Israel's violations of God's covenant. It is in this way that Israel's past judgments (see Lev. 26; Deut. 28; Jer. 7–8:3; Ezek. 6:1–14; 8:1–18) are types that find their anti-type in the eschatological Tribulation period. The "this generation" of Matthew 24:34 is a type-generation. The antitype is the generation of Jews on earth at the time the Lord unleashes Tribulational judgments upon Israel prior to the return of the Lord to deliver Israel.

Israel's Deliverance

The concept of Israel's deliverance is fundamental to a proper understanding of the focus of the Olivet Discourse. One of the problems with the preterist understanding of the Olivet Discourse is that contrary to the words of Jesus in the discourse, there is no deliverance for Israel. If the Roman invasion Of A.D. 70 is the real and only fulfillment of the Olivet Discourse, then Israel's "hope" is invasion by a foreign oppressor, which, of course, is no hope at all. Luke 21:27–32 covers some of the material in Matthew 24, but with some significant additions. In this Lucan passage we read:

> And then shall they see the Son of man coming in a cloud with power and great glory. And when these things begin to come to pass, then look up, and lift up your heads, for your redemption draweth nigh. And he spake to them a parable; Behold the fig tree, and all the trees; When they now shoot forth, ye see and know of your own selves that summer is now nigh at hand. So likewise ye, when ye see these things come to pass, know ye that the kingdom of God is nigh at hand. Verily I say unto you, This generation shall not pass away, till all be fulfilled.

In Luke's account of the Olivet Discourse, there are several statements added that are not found in Matthew 24 or in Mark 13. In Matthew 24:33, which is parallel to Luke 21:31, Jesus is simply recorded as saying, "So likewise ye, when ye shall see all these things, know that it is near, even at the doors," but Luke explains what "it" is— "know ye that the kingdom of God is nigh at hand." The Olivet Discourse is not speaking about Israel's defeat and final doom, but about Israel's exaltation in the Kingdom. Luke 21:28 calls it "your redemption." We must ask preterists, "How can the destruction of Jerusalem in A.D. 70 be anyone's redemption?"

Other indicators in Luke 21 are also relevant. In verse twenty-four Jesus says: "Jerusalem shall be trodden down of the gentiles, until the times of the Gentiles be fulfilled." Jerusalem's desolation is not permanent but temporary. It is only "until the times of the Gentiles be fulfilled." Though the emphasis on Israel's deliverance is not as strong as in Luke 21, Matthew 24 does, nevertheless, show that this is an important theme in the discourse. In Matthew 24:15–21 Jesus speaks about "the abomination of desolation," and about the necessity of those in Judea fleeing into the mountains. In verse twenty-two, however, there is an encouraging note sounded: "And except those days should be shortened, there should no flesh be saved: but for the elect's sake *those days shall be shortened.*" God is going to do something special for the Jewish remnant. He is going to shorten that period of Tribulation.

Matthew 24:31 sounds an additional note of encouragement: "And he shall send his angels with a great sound of a trumpet, and they shall gather together his elect from the four winds, from one end of heaven to the other." Notice, this is a gathering of the "elect." It is not a gathering to judgment nor is it a scattering. Preterists have trouble with these plain words of scripture. The extent to which they will go to avoid admitting the obvious meaning of the text proves the weakness of their argument. Preterist Marcellus Kik explains "angels" in the following allegorical manner:

Actually the context determines the meaning of the Greek word *aggelos* and one does not have to translate it "angel." The word does not always mean a heavenly spirit. As the word *aggelos* is used to describe a minister of Christ in other portions of the New Testament, so it may be translated in this particular passage. We know that Christ gave the function of preaching the Gospel and gather in the elect to his disciples and through them to the church. They were to go to the uttermost ends of the earth and proclaim the glad tidings of salvation, and by baptism receive the elect into the church. From the day of the Great Commission unto this day his ministers have been fulfilling the function of messengers or angels in gathering the elect from all nations.

One only has to realize that "the elect" in Matthew 24 does not refer to "the elect from all nations" to see the utter desperation of this argument. Matthew 24 is *Jewish* to the core. Jesus speaks of "the abomination of desolation, spoken of by Daniel the prophet" (vs. 15) and those in Judea fleeing to the mountains (vs. 16). He also speaks about "the sabbath day" (vs. 20). To apply this to the preaching of the gospel to all nations and to make "elect" mean "the elect from all over the world" shows that preterists got started on the wrong track and always arrive at the wrong destination. If they were careful to rightly divide the Word they would have discerned much of their confusion and avoided the conclusions that they have reached.

As we seek to deal with the so-called "time texts" of Scripture upon which preterists base so much of their argumentation, all these considerations are extremely important. Sometimes prophetic passages have several references. The interpreter must avoid dogmatically insisting that it was all fulfilled in some past-time event. Preterists accomplish this by taking words and phrases that beg to be interpreted futuristically, and by twisting them against every rule of language and hermeneutics, force them into some preconceived preterist mold.

Jeremiah chapters twenty-nine and thirty are most instructive in this regard. They show how past events are often mixed with things prophesied for the far distant future. Jeremiah 29 speaks about the Babylonian captivity. The Jews are told that instead of hoping for a quick solution to the problems associated with their captivity, life is to go on as usual. "Build ye houses, and dwell in them; and plant gardens, and eat the fruit of them" (Jer. 29:5). And yet in the next chapter we read: "Alas! for that day is great, so that none is like it: it is even the time of Jacob's trouble; but he shall be saved out of it" (Jer. 30:7).

Predictably, preterists see this verse as having a past fulfillment in the Babylonian captivity. However, if Jeremiah had said "this day" instead of "that day" we would rightfully conclude that he was referencing the Babylonian captivity. We are led to believe, however, that something else is in view by the words of verse four: "And these are the words that the LORD spake concerning Israel and concerning Judah." This suggests a fulfillment at the time when the northern and southern kingdoms have been united. Verses eight and nine are conclusive, for they speak of Israel's future deliverance: "For it shall come to pass in that day, saith the LORD of hosts, that I will break his yoke from off thy neck, and will burst thy bonds, and strangers shall no more serve themselves of him. But they shall serve the LORD their God, and David their king, whom I will raise up unto them."

The Meaning of "Fulfill"

Multiple references and typological references indicate that events that are similar to the event prophesied may not indicate the fulfillment of that event. As Charles H. Dyer has explained, there are a number of biblical examples showing that the verb "to fulfill" (*pleroo*) is used for events that are not literal fulfillments of Old Testament prophecies. Matthew 2:13–15 is a case in point:

And when they were departed, behold, the angel of the Lord appeareth to Joseph in a dream, saying, Arise, and take the young child and his mother, and flee into Egypt, and be thou there until I bring thee word: for Herod will seek the young child to destroy him. When he arose, he took the young child and his mother by night, and departed into Egypt: And was there until the death of Herod: that it might be fulfilled [*pleroo*] which was spoken of the Lord by the prophet, saying, Out of Egypt have I called my son.

"The prophet" here is the prophet Hosea, and the reference is to Hosea 1:11. Hosea is speaking of Israel being delivered from Egyptian bondage. Matthew, on the other hand, applies Hosea's words to the return of Jesus from Egypt some fifteen hundred years after Israel's return from Egypt. Clearly, these are widely different events. The only similarity is the return from Egypt.

We are not justified in thinking that Matthew had discerned some veiled and "deeper" meaning to Hosea's statement. Matthew does not use Hosea 1:11 in that manner but uses it as a point of contrast. Matthew was writing to a Jewish audience, and he was seeking to show that while Israel failed to measure up as God's "son," that Jesus Christ completely "fulfilled" God's design and purpose for Israel. Here we find a contrast between Israel as a disobedient child and the obedience of Christ. Hosea 11:1—2 describes Israel's waywardness: "When Israel was a child, then I loved him, and called my son out of Egypt. As they called them, so they went from them: they sacrificed unto Baalim, and burned incense to graven images. ..."

Another example of this fluid application of "to fulfill" is found in Matthew 2:16–18:

Then Herod, when he saw that he was mocked of the wise men, was exceeding wroth, and sent forth, and slew all the children that were in Bethlehem, and in all the coasts thereof, from two years old and under, according to the time which he had diligently enquired of the wise men. Then was fulfilled [*pleroo*] that which was spoken by Jeremy the prophet, saying, In Rama was there a voice heard, lamentation, and weeping, and great mourning, Rachel weeping for her children, and would not be comforted, because they are not.

Jeremiah 31:15 is the Old Testament reference. It depicts Israel's crying out with grief at the time of her exile. Was Herod's merciless slaughter of the infants the fulfillment of a predictive prophecy found in Jeremiah? The answer is "no." What proof is there for such a categorical statement?

For one thing, Jeremiah 31:15 doesn't purport to predict anything. It is not even a prophecy. The closest prophetic words are found twelve verses later, in verse twenty-seven, and is expanded in verse thirty-one: "Behold, the days come, saith the LORD, that I will make a new covenant with the house of Israel, and with the house of Judah."

The reference to "Ramah" and "Rahel" in Jeremiah 31:15 has to do with a place (Ramah) and a person (Rahel). Ramah was a point of assembly for the captives taken to Babylon. Jeremiah personifies the older women of Judah who were left behind because they were too old to be taken into captivity (Jer. 40:7) with the name "Rachel." It wasn't Rachel who was weeping; it was the older women who were lamenting the loss of their sons as they were carried off by the Babylonians. In Matthew's citation of the Old Testament passage, he means neither Rachel nor the older women of Judah, but rather the women living in Bethlehem at the time of the birth of Jesus whose infants were slaughtered by Herod. Matthew is focusing on one point of comparison: the grief of these mothers at the loss of their children. Jeremiah 31:15 is a type of the slaughter of the infants recorded in the second chapter of Matthew.

Genesis 3:15 provides another example of how an Old Testament text may be fulfilled typically in several events without there being a specific literal fulfillment specified by any text of Scripture. Genesis 3:15 has been called "the first prophecy of the Bible." It is addressed by the Lord to the serpent: "And I will put enmity between thee and the woman, and between thy seed and her seed; it shall bruise thy head, and thou shalt bruise his heel." This verse is never said to be fulfilled in any future event, though there are several possibilities based on certain similarities and comparisons with future events that could very well "fit" this prophecy.

It could, for example, indicate the general fear that most people have of snakes. Since Eve is the predecessor of all women, the enmity between the serpent and Eve is typical of the enmity between Satan and all of Eve's descendants. Though this interpretation seems to miss the spiritual import of the verse, it is a possible indirect reference.

More likely it speaks of Mary's Child, Jesus Christ. At the cross Jesus Christ would "bruise" Satan's head and render a fatal blow. Satan's "seed"—his spiritual descendants—however, would cause Christ to suffer. Dyer observes: "The prophecy of Genesis 3:15 seems clearly to have its ultimate fulfillment in this conflict between Christ and Satan. Yet no New Testament passage uses *pleroo* [to fulfill] to say that it was (or will be) its fulfillment."

It is because of prophetic principles such as has been shared in this chapter that we can conclude that there are a sufficient number of similarities between first century events, and far-distant future events, to allow Jesus and the writers of the New Testament to address prophetic issues as they did.

It would be erroneous to conclude that all the Olivet Discourse was fulfilled in the first century, but it would also be wrong to conclude that all of it is purely eschatological. It is the nature of prophetic revelation in the Scriptures that allows us to understand Jesus' reference to His contemporaries, while at the same time indicating fulfillment in the future. When the disciples saw Jerusalem besieged by Roman armies in A.D. 70, they could take heart in that they knew that this would not mark the full and final destruction of Israel.

Chapter 9

Was A.D. 70 Really "The End?"

A Singing Antichrist?

Preterists believe that the Beast of Revelation 13, the Antichrist, has already appeared on the scene. "The view to be presented in this work," writes preterist Kenneth Gentry, "is that the Emperor Nero Caesar is the Beast of Revelation specifically considered and that Rome is the Beast generically considered." With such an "honor" given him, one would think that Nero was a very dynamic leader who would inspire a tremendous following. After all, Revelation 13 tells us that authority was given him over all nations (vs. 7) and that the entire population honors him with worship (vs. 12). This, however, is not at all the picture that we get of Nero from history. Regarding the circumstances of his death Gentry writes:

> Disgusted with his absence from Rome, his excesses in life, and enormous political abuses, a revolt against Nero began in Gaul. But it was quickly put down. Shortly thereafter the revolt broke out anew under Galba in Spain in A.D. 68. Torn with indecision as to what to do in such pressing circum-

stances, Nero hesitated in acting against Galba. When the revolt had gathered too much strength he talked of suicide, but he was too cowardly and again hesitated. As he considered his dire circumstances and the approach of certain death, he is recorded to have lamented: "What an artist the world is losing!" Finally, when he learned that the Senate had voted to put him to death by cruel and shameful means, he secured the assistance of his secretary Epaphroditus to run a sword through his throat. His suicide occurred at the age of 31 on June 9, A.D. 68.

Nero has been called "the singing emperor," hence his lament, "What an artist the world is losing!" Nero considered himself such a superlative performer in the theater that he forbade anyone in the audience from leaving while he was performing. Because of this decree, pregnant women sometimes had to give birth in the theater, and men who were overwhelmed with a boring performance had to quietly escape over the back wall.

Nero was hated. Consequently, there were many plots by senators, knights, and philosophers, to take his life. One of the conspirators, Subrius Flavus, after his plot was discovered, was asked by Nero to explain his treachery. Subrius explained: "Because I hated you. For as long as you deserved my respect, I was as loyal as any of your soldiers. I started to hate you after you murdered your mother and your wife and became charioteer, an actor, and an arsonist."

In March of A.D. 68 Nero heard that Spain's provincial governor, Servius Sulpicius Galba, had withdrawn his allegiance to him and declared himself to be the emperor of Rome. Nero's plight became more precarious when he heard that there was unrest among Rome's troops in the East. The senate decided that time had come to act and ordered that Nero be killed in the manner of the ancients, meaning that Nero would be stripped naked, have his head placed in a wooden yoke, and then whipped. Nero refused such an ignominious death and chose suicide instead.

Emperor Nero was a poor antichrist. I don't believe he fits the picture. It is hard to believe that a man who was too cowardly to cut his own throat would inspire personal worship and devotion. The Beast of Revelation 13 is far more successful in his endeavors than Emperor Nero ever was.

But what about Revelation 13:3, where we read: "And I saw one of his heads as it were wounded to death; and his deadly wound was healed: and all the world wondered after the beast." How does that fit Nero? Gentry gives several parallels which he believes establishes the identification between Nero and the Beast of Revelation:

1. Gentry cites Sulpicius Severus (A.D. 360–420) who wrote: "It was accordingly believed that, even if he did put an end to himself with a sword, his wound was cured, and his life preserved, according to that which was written regarding him, 'And his mortal wound was healed …'"
2. Gentry cites Revelation 13:10—"He that leadeth into captivity shall go into captivity: he that killeth with the sword must be killed with the sword. Here is the patience and the faith of the saints"—to show that the Beast who slays with the sword will himself be slain with the sword, and that this therefore refers to Nero.
3. Gentry cites the wound and states: "The mortal wound to *one* of the heads is a wound that should have been fatal to *the Beast, generically considered.* This explains why it is that after the wound was healed and the Beast continued alive, 'the whole earth was amazed and followed after the beast' (Rev. 13:3b)."

Gentry stresses the importance of understanding this passage in terms of relevance for the original audience and the history of the era. He believes that the death of Nero, which brought an end to the Roman Empire's founding family, the Julio-Claudian line of emperors, was an extremely "grave and serious matter to the Roman Empire." Following Nero's death "the Roman

Empire was hurled into civil wars of great ferocity and dramatic proportions ... the civil wars almost destroyed the empire, seriously threatening to reduce 'eternal Rome' to rubble."

Regarding point number one above, it is not a fact that Nero was revived. That Severus "associates Nero with the prophecy of Revelation" means no more than that this was the opinion of Severus. People are confused today, and people were confused in the past. This is one of the reasons why we must not identify Nero with the Beast of Revelation. Revelation 13:3 is not speaking about what people *erroneously believed,* but about what will actually happen. Though Gentry denies that he gives much credence to the place of the Nero redivivus myth, he seems to argue as though he finds it to be a helpful tool in the interpretation of Revelation 13. The Nero redivivus myth was the belief that Emperor Nero was invincible and would come to life subsequent to his death. After his death, animosity against him was so intense that some Roman citizens came to believe that Nero had not really died but had escaped to Parthia, from whence he would soon return to regain his throne. At any rate, whether it was believed that Nero had really not died and was going to return, or that he had died and was raised by mysterious powers, none of this has any place in guiding our interpretation of sacred Scripture. To ignore this is to turn the assertions of Scripture into nothing more than misguided belief.

The healing of the wound is a future fact, not a past myth, and it leads to universal worship. Revelation 13:4 states: "And they worshipped the dragon which gave power unto the beast: and they worshipped the beast, saying, Who is like unto the beast? who is able to make war with him?" This Scripture describes a twofold worship: worship directed to the dragon and worship directed to the beast. "Worship" is directed toward a perceived entity. Christians worship God because they perceive that He is God and worthy of worship. Worship of the dragon, in a similar way, can only come about if there is some discernible manifestation of his power and authority that evokes awe and admiration. No doubt, Satan was operative in and through Nero Caesar's career. But when we consider Nero's infamous and spineless career, it is hard to believe that worship would be given to such an irrational, hyper-emotional emperor who was suicidal, or that the satanic power energizing such an individual would evoke admiration.

Historians believe that Nero was a failure as an emperor. When Nero returned to Rome in A.D. 67, he was held in low esteem by the Roman senate. He had come to have a "playboy" image and his cruel acts of pomposity alienated the Roman people from imperial leadership. In May of A.D. 68 something else happened that was damaging to Nero's image: the governor of Gallia Lugdunensis, Julius Vindex, revolted. Though the revolt was put down, subsequent events further undermined Nero's image. By June 8, A.D. 68, when Nero was making plans to flee, his praetorian commander, Nymphidius Sabinus, deserted Nero. Feeling that Nero was a lost cause Nymphidius sided with Galba.

Does Roman History Fit the Biblical Description?

Preterists, such as Gentry, make the claim that the number of Roman emperors and their descriptions in the histories of Rome match the descriptions given in the Book of Revelation. Gentry, for example finds the mention of seven kings in Revelation 17:9—10 supportive of his preterist position. He argues that Nero was the sixth king and that the seventh, who according to Revelation 17:10 would reign for but a short time, must be Galba who, indeed, did reign for about a year. Gentry's case rests on his argument that Julius Caesar (49–44 B.C.) is the first of the Caesars, not Augustus (31 B.C.–A.D. 14). But does the line of the Caesars begin with Julius Caesar or with Augustus Caesar?

Several statements can be cited to show that it begins with Augustus. For example, the ancient Roman historian Seutonius (A.D. 69–140) records the words of Augustus who stated:

May it be my privilege to establish the State in a firm and secure position, and reap from that act the fruit that I desire; but only if I may be called the author of the best possible government, and bear with the hope when I die that the foundations which I have laid for the State will remain unshaken."

Furthermore, in commenting on the beginnings of the Roman Empire, J. C. Stobart writes: "Julius Caesar has usurped the credit of inventing that wonderful system, the Roman Empire. The credit really belongs to Augustus."

By 50 B.C. rivalry had developed between two leading generals, Julius Caesar and Pompey. In 49 B.C. Caesar crossed the Rubicon and pursued Pompey into the Balkans where Pompey was defeated at the Battle of Pharsalus in June of 48 B.C. However, while Caesar became the supreme leader of Rome, he failed to institute a truly workable government and was assassinated on March 15, 44 B.C. After his death there was a civil war in which his assassins were defeated by Marc Antony and Octavian, Caesar's adoptive son. With all the turmoil, it took several years for stability to be established. In fact, as Scarre points out, "the office of Roman emperor did not appear until the 20s B.C. ... and was essentially the creation of Augustus." Moreover, the titles Augustus applied to himself became the basis of the imperial titles of all subsequent Roman Emperors.

Events Leading Up to A.D. 70

The events leading up to A.D. 70 do not match with the Olivet Discourse. The historical destruction of Jerusalem was preceded by some very definite warnings of impending disaster. These were the years of the first Jewish revolt, a revolt that provoked the Roman overlord to use the cruelest means of putting an end to the rebellion. But regarding the cataclysmic events of the future referenced by Jesus in the Olivet Discourse we are told that it would be as the days of Noah—"they were eating and drinking, marrying and giving in marriage, until the day that Noe entered into the ark, And knew not until the flood came, and took them all away; so shall the coming of the Son of man be" (Matt. 24:38–39). If Jesus were talking about A.D. 70, the years immediately preceding the Roman invasion of Jerusalem should have been years of peace and tranquility, but that was not at all the case.

Beginning in A.D. 66, troops under Gallus marched south from Antioch and Tyre toward Caesarea Maritima. In the years 66–68 Vespasian, not yet emperor, devastated Jewish strongholds at Jotapata, Gischala, and Gamala. While the desert fortresses of Machaerus, Herodium, and Masada, were still holding out, the Romans were enjoying sweeping victories in the north and in the central part of Israel. Josephus records the events surrounding the fall of Jotapata:

> And on this day the Romans slew all the multitude that appeared openly; but on the following days they searched the hiding places, and fell upon those that were underground and in the caverns, and went thus through every age, excepting the infants and the women, and of these there were gathered together as captive twelve hundred; and as for those who were slain at the taking of the city, and in the former flights, they were numbered to be forty thousand. So Vespasian gave order that the city should be entirely demolished, and all the fortification burnt down. And thus was Jotapata taken, in the thirteenth year of the reign of Nero, on the first day of the month Panemus.

Revelation 17

Further doubts as to the legitimacy of giving the Tribulation of the Book of Revelation a first century date arise from a study of Revelation 17. Verse ten states: "And there are seven kings: five are fallen, and one is, and the other is not yet come; and when he cometh, he must continue a short space. "Gentry understands this "short space" as a reference to the short reign of Galba who reigned only seven months. This fits in with the preterist attempt to practice first century newspaper exegesis—find someone in first century news that fits with biblical prophecy. From this, preterists assume that the line of kings of Revelation 17 refers to a first century succession of Roman rulers and then declare Galba to be the emperor of Revelation 17:10. Johnson, however, raises some significant issues that become problematic for those who hold to a first century reference:

> To be sure there have been many attempts to fit the date of Revelation ... into the emperor lists of the first century ... But immediately there are admitted problems. Where do we begin—with Julius Caesar or Caesar Augustus? Are we to exclude Galba, Otho, and Vitellius who had short, rival reigns? If so, how can they be excluded except on a completely arbitrary basis? A careful examination of the historic materials yields no satisfactory solution. If Revelation were written under Nero, there would be too few emperors; if under Domitian, too many. The original readers would have had no more information on these emperor successions than we do, and possibly even less. How many Americans can immediately name the last seven presidents? Furthermore, how could the eighth emperor who is identified as the beast also be one of the seven (v.11)?

The text also reveals that these ten kings receive authority "one hour with the beast" (Rev. 17:12). Whatever is the precise meaning of "one hour," it signifies a short time of limited duration. For those undergoing persecution this would be a word of comfort. Their suffering from this hostile government is but for a short while. Yet a first century fulfillment can bring no such comfort. Following the destruction of Jerusalem there was no time of peace and acceptance for first century Christians. Rather, the persecutions grew more intense and spread to the entire empire.

Revelation 17:14 tells us of the outcome: "These shall make war with the Lamb, *and the Lamb shall overcome them:* for he is Lord of lords, and King of kings: and they that are with him are called, and chosen, and faithful."

Would the immediate readers of the Book of Revelation say that the destruction of Jerusalem in A.D. 70 was the fulfillment of this prophecy? Undoubtedly, preterists will answer in the affirmative. However, before accepting such an evasion, we need to remember that the years that followed the destruction of Jerusalem were years of trouble for both Christians and Jews. What kind of King can the Lord Jesus Christ be if the victory that He brings only leads to increasing persecution and martyrdom?

The years following the fall of Jerusalem did not bring peace either for Israel or for the church. Will Durant describes a great revolt that took place some sixty years later:

> Under the leadership of Simeon Bar Cocheba, who claimed to be the Messiah, the Jews made their last effort in antiquity to recover their homeland and their freedom ... For three years the rebels fought valiantly against the legions; finally they were beaten by lack of food and supplies. The Romans destroyed 985 towns in Palestine, and slew 580,000 men; a still larger number: we are told, perished through starvation, disease and fire; nearly all Judea was laid waste ... Thousands hid in underground channels rather than be captured; surrounded by the Romans, they died one by one of hunger, while the living ate the bodies of the dead.
>
> Resolved to destroy all vestiges of Judaism around which subsequent revolts might form, emperor Hadrian forbade several key Jewish practices such as circumcision, sabbath observance, and the observance of any Jewish holy day. All public Jewish rituals were banned. Jews were allowed to enter the city of Jerusalem on only one specified day of the year. New and heavier taxes were imposed on all Jews. The pagan city of Aelia Capitolina

was erected on the site of Jerusalem, along with shrines to Jupiter and Venus. The Council of Jamnia was disbanded and public instruction of the Torah was made illegal. Several rabbis who violated this legislation were executed.

The church also suffered following the Roman invasion under Titus and the destruction of the temple in A.D. 70. Initially Christianity was regarded by the Romans as a mere branch of Judaism which was held in contempt by many Romans but, nevertheless, a recognized and approved religion. However, with the rapid spread of the gospel and the success of the apostles and their disciples, Christianity posed a definite threat to the religion of Rome and consequently to the entire Roman Empire. Since Christians did not have statues and idols, they were regarded by many of the Romans as atheists. The various calamities that befell the empire from time to time— droughts, wars, and floods—were blamed on the Christian presence. Allegedly, because the church had been allowed to exist, the gods were angry at the Roman leadership for their laxity in allowing this.

The Roman emperor Decius brought persecution against the church to a new level of intensity. No longer was the persecution local and sporadic, but it became the official policy of the state and spread throughout the empire. Decius "resolved to root out the church as an atheistic and seditious sect, and in the year 250 published an edict to all the governors of the provinces, enjoining return to the pagan state religion under the heaviest penalties." The persecution under Decius "was properly the first which covered the whole empire, and accordingly produced a far greater number of martyrs than any former persecution."

Preterists give Christians and Jews absolutely no hope. If A.D. 70 is the fulfillment of all or most of the prophecies of the Book of Revelation and eschatological discourses of the synoptic gospels, God has miserably failed His people.

More Allegorizing: Should "Miracles" Cited by Church Historians Influence Our Eschatology?

With dogged preterist consistency, Gentry sees a past fulfillment of the sealing of the 144,000 of Revelation 7, and relates that scripture to the warning of Jesus in Matthew 24:16: "Then let them which be in Judea flee into the mountains ...?" He states that "the fact that an angel intervenes in order to prevent their being destroyed along with the land surely indicates the era prior to the devastation of Israel in A.D. 70."

However, Revelation 7 mentions the miraculous preservation of those who have been sealed. Are there any reported miracles which occurred around A.D. 70 that might fit the picture? Gentry finds one such deliverance recorded in the writings of the church historian Eusebius (A.D. 260–340). Eusebius writes:

> But the people of the church in Jerusalem had been commanded by a revelation vouchsafed to approved men there before the war, to leave the city and to dwell in a certain town of Perea called Pella. And when those that believed in Christ had come thither from Jerusalem, then, as if the royal city of the Jews and the whole land of Judea were entirely destitute of holy men, the judgment of God at length overtook those who had committed such outrages against Christ and his apostles, and totally destroyed that generation of impious men.

Here Eusebius tells of a "supernatural" warning that came "by a revelation" granted, evidently by God, to "approved men." Gentry refers to this as "an extremely interesting and famous piece of history" which "informs us that the Jewish Christians in Jerusalem escaped the city before it was too late, possibly either at the outset of the War or during one of its providential lulls." However, let's compare this "extremely interesting and famous piece of history" with Revelation 7:1–4 to see if there are really valid parallels or just surface similarities. This Scripture reads as follows:

> And after these things I saw four angels standing on the four corners of the earth [*ge*], holding the four winds of the earth, that the wind should not blow on the earth, nor on the sea, nor on any tree. And I saw another angel ascending from the east, having the seal of the living God: and he cried with a loud voice to the four angels, to whom it was given to hurt the earth and the sea, Saying, Hurt not the earth, neither the sea, nor the trees, till we have sealed the servants of our God in their foreheads. And I heard the number of them which were sealed: and there were sealed an hundred and forty and four thousand of all the tribes of the children of Israel.

It should be noted that there is nothing here that even remotely resembles the "revelation" mentioned by Eusebius and approvingly cited by Gentry. The means of deliverance in Revelation 7 was not by the faithful inhabitants of the city being commanded by a revelation, but rather by a Divine seal. Moreover, while Eusebius' account speaks about a special warning given to the inhabitants of the city of Jerusalem, Revelation speaks about a sealing that is far more extensive in its effects: "Hurt not the earth, neither the sea, nor the trees ..." Of course, since preterists overlook the details of prophecy, such discrepancies do not matter. Pre-millennialists, however, do not at all feel justified in taking such liberties with *any* text of Scripture.

There are other problems with identifying what is described in Revelation 7 with the events described by Eusebius. Revelation 7 speaks about the angels and "the four corners of the earth" and "the four winds of the earth." This is hardly terminology that can be limited to Jerusalem and environs. Alan Johnson states that these were expressions "used in antiquity among the Near Eastern nations much as we use 'the four points of the compass.'" Matthew 24:31 speaks of the elect being gathered "from the four winds, from one end of heaven to the other." Such language militates against a first century fulfillment. I must affirm that while there are some superficial parallels between events of the first century and the eschatological passages of the Gospels and the Book of Revelation, there is clearly no identity. Commentators must beware lest they find an identity where there is none. No doubt, there were some parallels between the fall of the northern kingdom and the fall of the southern kingdom—outsiders invaded, captives were taken, and people deported, many died—but the two events are not the same.

I have devoted no little amount of space to first century history. We need to know some particulars of the times to answer some very important questions:

1. Does imperial Rome match the descriptions of the final form of gentile world power mentioned in the book of Revelation?
2. Does Nero match the description of the Beast in the book of Revelation?
3. Do the conditions of the first century Roman world match the conditions described in the Book of Revelation?
4. Does imperial Rome match the government of the Beast?

There are a couple of possible answers. There is a simple "no." Then there is a simple "yes." In addition, another possible and, I believe, good answer is: "in some measure." This means that there is some measure of correspondence between Imperial Rome and the government of the Beast, but it avoids the preterist contention that the imperial government of Rome *is* the government of the Beast. This acknowledges that there are some distinct similarities between what happened in the first century with what is prophesied in the Book of Revelation without arguing for an absolute identity which, I believe, is erroneous.

Even granting an early date around the time of the Neronic persecution for the writing of the Book of Revelation, contemporary expectation doesn't fit a first century fulfillment. Christians were looking for a better day, not a worse day. Regarding the background and dating of the Book of Revelation, E. F. Harrison writes:

> It is quite understandable that just as the Hebrew people during the inter-biblical period, with little in current events to encourage them to think that a better day would soon appear, began more and more to pin their hopes on dramatic Divine intervention in an apocalyptic fashion, so the Christian community, under the pressure of incipient imperial persecution that seemed likely to increase rather than to diminish, turned its eyes heavenward in anticipation of a manifestation of divine power that would be at once a judgment and a deliverance, and did so the more readily since its Lord had already appeared on earth and by his redemptive work had laid the basis of his pledge of a second coming.

Chapter 10

Are We Really Living in the Kingdom Age?

By now the reader will realize the preterists are dead serious when they claim that we are now living in God's Kingdom Age. And they don't take this claim lightly. They do not believe that there is any future Kingdom period prophesied for planet Earth. We are now in the final kingdom. This is the age of God's victory. Israel has been cast aside and the church has now replaced Israel. The prophets of Israel spoke of this day and anticipated this day of Kingdom victory. If you don't believe it, you are a "pessi-millennialist" and hindering the Kingdom work of the church. For preterists Satan is now bound and it is up to Christians to be "covenantally faithful" in bringing all areas of life under the Lordship of Christ.

In this chapter we want to accomplish three things. First, we want to look at what Scripture says about the Kingdom of God. Secondly, we want to look at recent developments in technology, and then current events to see if the present time fits God's description of the Kingdom. We also want to deal with a nine-chapter section of the Old Testament that preterists can't handle.

The Kingdom of God

One of the main themes of the Bible is the Kingdom of God which, simply defined, means "the rule and reign of God." The word "kingdom" implies three essential elements:

1. A ruler—one who rules and exercises authority;
2. The ruled—the subjects under the authority of the ruler;
3. A realm—the sphere or jurisdiction of the ruler's authority.

Aspects of God's Kingdom Rule

Throughout the Scriptures God's rule takes different forms and is manifested in different ways. Before we can answer the question, "Are we really living in the Kingdom?" we must look at the different forms that God's rule takes.

1. God's General Authority Over All Aspects of His Creation
God is in control of all things by virtue of his providential Kingship. The change in the seasons, the rise and fall of the tides, the emergence of new nations, as well as the demise of old ones, are all under His general authority.

Belief in God's general authority over all aspects of His creation is what separates the deists from the theists. Deism sees God as having removed Himself from this world. He has wound it up like a big clock and now it is running on its own. Christian theism, on the other hand, sees God's continuing rule in all aspects of His creation: "For the LORD most high is terrible [awesome]; he is a great King over all the earth" (Ps. 47:2; Ps. 95:3–5). In this sense, we are in God's Kingdom at the present time,

2. God's Specific Authority Over Those Who Have Accepted His Lordship by a Childlike Commitment to Jesus Christ
One enters the Kingdom in this sense by a personal decision. Those who have put their faith in Jesus Christ have been translated into the Kingdom

of Christ (Col. 1:12–13). Though God's rule and reign does not need to be validated by a human decision, and His Kingship is not dependent on human consent, personal decision does determine one's relationship to the King. In this sense, all Christians are in the Kingdom.

To be sure, there *are* present aspects to God's Kingdom rule. He is currently exercising His sovereignty in the natural world as well as in the affairs of men. After his sanity returned, Nebuchadnezzar acknowledged God's present Kingship:

> And all the inhabitants of the earth are reputed as nothing: and He doeth according to His will in the army of heaven, and among the inhabitants of the earth: and none can stay His hand, or say unto Him, What doest thou?
> —Daniel 4:35

The Lord Jesus Christ is also presently exercising His Lordship in and through the church. "He is the head of the body, the church" (Col. 1:18). Because Christ is Lord of the church, He has the prerogative of ordering the affairs of His church, such as stipulating the qualifications for its leaders, requiring that "all things be done decently and in order" (1 Cor. 14:40), and stating requirements in other matters, such as giving (1 Cor. 16:1–4).

3. God's Messianic Rule Through His Son

Christ will one day return to earth to establish the rule and reign of God on earth. The Scripture speaks of world affairs following the Battle of Armageddon:

> And the armies which were in heaven followed him upon white horses ... And out of his mouth goeth a sharp sword, that with it He should smite the nations; *and he shall rule them with a rod of iron.*
> —Revelation 19:14–15

In the Old Testament, the seat of the Kingdom rule of God's Messiah is spoken of in terms of a "mountain."

> And it shall come to pass in the last days, that the mountain of the Lord's house shall be established ... And many people shall go up and say, Come ye, and let us go up to the mountain of the Lord, to the house of the God of Jacob ...
>
> —Isaiah 2:2–3

Though the Kingdom in the Church Age is personal and internal (Rom. 14:17), in the days of the messianic Kingdom, Messiah's rule will have a worldwide impact. "Nation shall not lift up sword against nation, neither shall they learn war any more" (Isa. 2:4).

It is in this latter sense that we are not yet in the Kingdom. While God rules providentially over the creation, and over His church, Satan is still very much on the loose in the world at the present hour. Hence, Jesus instructed His disciples to pray, "Thy kingdom come. Thy will be done in earth, as it is in heaven" (Matt. 6:10). We are instructed to pray that God's will be done "as"—i.e., to the same degree and extent as—it is done in heaven. This is something that is yet future and awaits the return of Christ. "When the Son of man shall come in his glory, and all the holy angels with him, then shall he sit upon the throne of his glory." It is only then that the King will say unto them on His right hand, "Come, ye blessed of my Father, inherit the kingdom prepared for you from the foundation of the world" (Matt. 25:31, 34).

Dispensational Distinctions Regarding the Kingdom

1. Church and Kingdom

A-millennialists and post-millennialists confuse the church with the final form of the Kingdom of God on earth. They believe that the church *is* the final form of the Kingdom. It is more in keeping with the Scriptures, however, to see the church as one phase of God's Kingdom program but certainly not the final form.

Though Jesus Christ is presently Lord of the church, the church is certainly not all that the Kingdom of God on earth is intended to be. The earthly Kingdom will be far more glorious and universal in extent than the church was ever intended to be.

The terms "church" and "kingdom" are never used interchangeably in the Bible. At His first advent, the Lord Jesus Christ came to offer Israel the Kingdom promised in the Old Testament. When Israel rejected her Messiah, the Old Testament Kingdom program was held in abeyance. It will, however, be established at the second advent when Christ will visibly rule over a restored and regathered Israel. When Jesus said, "I will build my church" (Matt. 16:18), He was speaking about an interim phase in the Kingdom program.

2. *Covenant and Kingdom*

A covenant may be defined as "a solemn promise made binding by an oath." It is by covenant that God promises a Kingdom. The Abrahamic Covenant guaranteed Israel a land. "In the same day the LORD made a covenant with Abram, saying, Unto thy seed have I given this land, from the river of Egypt unto the great river, the river Euphrates" (Gen. 15:18). This covenant promise will find complete fulfillment when Israel is restored to her land in the millennial Kingdom (see also Deut. 30:5–6).

3. *The Mystery Form of the Kingdom*

The interim form of the Kingdom program is also known as "the mystery form of the Kingdom." Matthew 13:11 speaks of "the mysteries of the kingdom of heaven." "Mystery" indicates "a hidden truth now revealed." In Matthew 13, Jesus revealed a body of truth about the Kingdom program never revealed before. He revealed that there would be a time period between the first and second advents characterized by apostasy and false professions. Judging from Scripture and from the defection from the faith apparent in so many churches and denominations at the present time, it would be more correct to say that we are in the Mystery Kingdom rather than in the final form of the Kingdom.

The Old Testament revealed much about the Kingdom of God, but Jesus here taught His disciples about a phase in the Kingdom program that would begin when Israel rejected her messianic King, and about the particular form the Kingdom program would take following that rejection.

Why is this phase of the Kingdom program identified as a "mystery"? Simply because the Hebrew prophets knew nothing about this phase. The Kingdom that they announced was the Kingdom of God on earth. It would be a Kingdom in which Israel and the messianic King ruling over an earthly Kingdom would be its prominent features (2 Sam. 7:8–16; Ps. 72; Ps. 88; Isa. 2:1–4; 35:1–10; Zech. 14). To confuse the Kingdom announced by the Old Testament prophets, John the Baptist (Matt. 3:2), and the Lord Jesus Christ (Mark 1:14–15) with the Mystery Kingdom, is to fail to recognize the marked differences between the two. In Matthew 13 there are several parables showing the characteristics of the mystery phase of the Kingdom.

The Parable of the Tares Among the Wheat (vss. 24–30, 36–43). Jesus tells a parable about a man who sowed good seed in his field. But while he slept, his enemy came and sowed tares. The man's servants observed the tares growing along with the wheat and asked the man if they could try to dig out the tares. But the man replied that they should not, lest they also uproot the wheat at the same time. They were to let both grow together until the harvest. Then the tares would be gathered and burned.

This parable is not a description of the world, but rather of the Kingdom in its mystery form. The point of the parable is that the Kingdom in its mystery form is of a mixed nature. The world will not be Christianized during this age, and even the church would have plenty of tares growing along with the wheat. This is a kingdom that is characterized by a mingling of the true and false professors of the faith, the good and the bad, the wheat and the tares.

The Parable Of the Mustard Seed (vss. 31–32). Jesus also compared the Kingdom of Heaven to a mustard seed, "which indeed is the least of all seeds: but when it is grown, it is the greatest among herbs, and becometh a tree, so that the birds of the air come and lodge in the branches thereof."

During this present age—the time period between the two advents—the Kingdom will show abnormal external growth. It will be like a herb that becomes a tree. Birds will come and nest in the branches. In the parable of the sower, birds represented evil, for they devoured the seed that had been sown (Matt. 13:4).

The mustard seed and its rapid growth into a monstrosity without substance is a picture of the church in this present age. "Churchianity" will grow in leaps and bounds. Many will make "professions of faith," but they will be devoid of substance.

The Parable of the Leaven (vss. 33–35). Jesus goes on to compare the Kingdom to leaven which has been hidden in three measures of meal until the whole batch was leavened. In Scripture, leaven uniformly indicates evil and impurity (Exod. 12:15, 19; 13:7; Lev. 2:11; Luke 12:10). In speaking of the danger of not dealing with a problem that requires discipline in the local church, the apostle illustrates how easily the evil of sin can spread through the entire fellowship when he writes, "Your glorying is not good. Know ye not that a little leaven leaveneth the whole lump? Purge out therefore the old leaven" (1 Cor. 5:6–7). In its mystery form, the Kingdom is like a lump of dough with yeast: evil and corruption proliferate.

The Parable of the Dragnet (vss. 47–51). In its mystery form the Kingdom is also like a dragnet, "which, when it was full, they drew to shore, and sat down, and gathered the good into vessels, but cast the bad away." At the end of the age there will not only be good fish, but also bad. "So shall it be at the end of the world: the angels shall come forth, and sever [separate] the wicked from among the just."

The erroneous belief that the gospel will pervade society and change society for the better until the Kingdom of God gradually blossoms forth in all its intended glory, has no basis in Scripture. Nowhere does leaven represent the good of the gospel. A converted world, ushered in by those who are seeking to fulfill the "cultural mandate," greeting Christ at His return, is contradicted by the tares among the wheat, and the bad fish among the good.

4. The Millennial Kingdom

After the awful judgments of the Tribulation, the Lord Jesus will return personally to earth (Zech. 14:4) to render judgment on the nations of the world preparatory to His rule and reign over them (Rev. 19:15–16). Christ will then establish Himself as King in Jerusalem (Isa. 2:1–3) and will rule from the throne of David (2 Sam. 7:16; Luke 1:32–33). Jerusalem will be the center of world rule (Zech. 8:3) and will be physically elevated to display its prominence (Zech. 14:10).

Scriptures describing the millennial Kingdom depict it as an age of worldwide peace between nations (Isa. 2:4; Mic. 4:2–4) and between animals (Isa. 11:6–9). Israel will be restored to her land (Matt. 24:31) and the Palestinian covenant fulfilled (Deut. 30:1–10). It will be a time when the full blessings of the New Covenant will be enjoyed by the nation of Israel (Jer. 31:31–34). Though covenant theologians like to praise their view of the Kingdom as being "spiritual," and lament the pre-millennial view of the Kingdom as being "carnal" because we look for a material and literal fulfillment of God's promises to Israel, the land and the people, there is nothing carnal about Israel's Kingdom promises. The Old Testament prophets, literally understood, speak of many spiritual aspects of God's earthly (millennial) Kingdom. It is a Kingdom characterized by holiness (Ezek. 43:12; Zech. 14:20–21) and by the fullness of the Holy Spirit (Joel 2:28—29; Ezek.

36:27; 37:14; Jer. 31:33). There will be praise, joy, spiritual power, and a radical inner transformation of Kingdom citizens (Isa. 32:15; 44:3; Ezek. 39:29).

This was the Kingdom John the Baptist announced when he cried out, "Repent ye; for the kingdom of heaven is at hand" (Matt. 3:2). This was the Kingdom Jesus offered Israel at His first advent (Matt. 15:25; 21:4–5).

This Kingdom Period Is Not the Church Age

Reformed theology equates God's earthly Kingdom with the church. Citing passages like Colossians 1:13, they claim that we are now Kingdom citizens in the fullest sense. Of course, their error is that they allegorize the Old Testament Kingdom promises and remove Israel from God's plan. Anyone who allegorizes the Old Testament Kingdom promises and removes Israel from God's plan will come up with the same conclusion.

In his *City of God,* Augustine (A.D. 354–430) identified the church with the Kingdom of God on earth. He was the first major Christian thinker to make such a bold identification.

With the passing of the centuries and the changes in belief and practice leading to the development of what is now known as the Roman Catholic Church, this seed idea presented by Augustine became a dominant concept. The "Church," i.e., the Roman Catholic Church, with its pontiff, ecclesiastical hierarchy, church courts, synods and councils, and control of secular governments, came to regard itself as possessing the power of the Kingdom. It sees no other earthly Kingdom. To be outside "the church" thusly defined was to be outside the Kingdom.

This erroneous notion has led to religious wars, the burning of heretics, religious crusades, inquisitions, book burnings, purges, and other vicious behaviors that ought never be equated with Christianity. Unfortunately, when speaking to nonbelievers, such behaviors perpetrated by armies bearing "Christian" banners have often provided a stumbling block to an effective witness. Sadly, there is a statement by unbelievers that is all too true: "If this is what Christianity is all about, I don't want anything to do with it." Neither do I.

The idea of associating the Kingdom of God with any ecclesiastical body is totally without biblical warrant. Such thinking comes from the error of exchanging the rule of King Jesus with the rule of man, i.e., the pope.

The Kingdom of God Will Not Be Established by Human Effort

Human fancy, based on the unscriptural notion of man's innate goodness, has equated the Kingdom of God with Utopia—a perfect society established by human effort. The theological optimism of nineteenth century liberalism saw the Kingdom as a society organized under the dynamic of love.

Such false optimism regarding man's potential was encouraged by Charles Darwin (1809-82) who espoused views that led to the notion that man is evolving upward. Evolutionary theory not only influenced thinking about human origins but was also projected into areas of philosophy and theology. In his allegedly upward evolution, man was becoming more fit to establish a perfect society on earth, i.e., you can have the Kingdom of God without God.

Others picked up on a related idea—that man is the master of his own destiny—and gave it new meaning and form. Karl Marx (181883) articulated the idea of the elimination of all economic class struggles. He hoped that in this way man could produce an age of peace and prosperity. This would be an "economic millennium" characterized by an egalitarian society. Men like Friedrich Nietzsche (1844-1900) saw this Utopia in terms of an idealized state controlled by the "super race."

History amply demonstrates that such optimism regarding man and his alleged abilities has led to unbelievable suffering and misery under totalitarian governments and egotistical tyrants. Such thinking completely ignores what the Bible says about human depravity, the outcome of history as prophesied in Scripture, and the Kingdom of God.

For these reasons we must not confuse earthly political structures, the spheres of national and ecclesiastical influence, and the civilizations of man, whether corrupt and ugly or Utopian and idealized, with the Kingdom of God. The Bible describes God's Kingdom in terms far too glorious for us to think that it is something developed by human ingenuity and potential.

The Kingdom In Its Glory Will Not Be Ushered In Prior to the Physical Return of Jesus Christ

All claims that the Kingdom has been realized and that we are now in the Kingdom must be rejected. Their problem: The King is absent.

According to the Scripture, it is the return of Christ to earth that brings about the destruction of the kingdom of man. The Kingdom in its glory will not be established until after Christ returns. Hence, His return is pre-millennial. "Thou sawest till that a stone was cut out without hands, which smote the image upon his feet ... and the stone that smote the image became a great mountain, and filled the whole earth" (Dan. 2:34–35). The Kingdom is not established by a gradual process of infiltration and permeation, but by a sudden and devastating blow. "And I saw heaven opened, and behold a white horse; and he that sat upon him was called Faithful and True, and in righteousness he doth judge and make war ..." (Rev. 19:11). The visible return of Christ to earth overpowers "the beast, and the kings of the earth, and their armies, gathered together to make war against him" (Rev. 19:19).

Where the Church Went Wrong

As we have already mentioned, Augustine's a-millennialism had a weighty influence in steering the church in the wrong direction. The way it all came about is fascinating and serves as a warning to us today. Let's look more closely at Augustine and his culture.

In his earlier years Augustine was involved in Manichaenism. Mani, who was born in A.D. 216, was a religious visionary who claimed to have visions and revelations. Much of what he taught was fanciful. He mixed Bible truth with esoteric ideas, but his was such a dynamic personality that he had great influence in the ancient Western world. Some of his ideas even took hold in the Far East.

Mickelsen traces the effects of Augustine's early Manichaenism on his thinking about biblical interpretation:

> Augustine ... was a Manichaean before he became a Christian. The Manichaean religious movement ... pointed with scorn at the anthropomorphisms of the Old Testament. "Look how literal interpretation results in absurdity," the adherents of Manichaeanism exclaimed ... Then came Ambrose who took Paul's statement that "the letter kills but the spirit makes alive" as a slogan for allegorical interpretation. In this approach Augustine found a way to overcome the objections of the Manichaeans to the Old Testament ... he himself allegorized extensively. For example, the Psalmist talks about lying down, sleeping, and rising again or awaking (Ps. 3:5). But what he really refers to is the death and resurrection of Christ!

The rapid development of the allegorical school of biblical interpretation and Augustine's adherence to that school's basic tenets brought the literal interpretation of Scripture into disrepute. Covenant a-millennialist Louis Berkhof writes:

> The allegorical interpretation of Scripture, introduced by the Alexandrian school, and sponsored especially by Origen, also had a chilling effect on millennial hopes. In the west the powerful influence of Augustine was instrumental in turning the thoughts of the church from the future to

the present by his identification of the church and the Kingdom of God. He taught the people to look for the millennium in the present Christian dispensation.

It is with statements such as these that we are able to understand some of the forces in the ancient world, as well as on the present scene, that are driving the popular move to cast aspersion on futurism. Connections with the Alexandrian school, the allegorical method, and the doctrines of Origen are a solemn testimony that no one can ignore.

Do Current Events Support the Kingdom-Now Idea?

Never before has there been a widespread departure from Christian values in America as at the present time. This departure is marked by the apostasy found in many of the churches.

In a recent book entitled *How the Clinton Clergy Corrupted a President*, author Moody Adams carefully documents how the antibiblical views espoused by President Bill Clinton can be traced to the teaching of his own pastors. The subheading of the book states the case all too well: "He was a bright young boy who walked a mile to church every Sunday, until ministers turned him into a moral tragedy." No doubt, Bill Clinton will be held accountable for his own sins, but the Scripture also testifies that those who preach error and lead their flocks astray will be judged even more severely (Jer. 14:14; 23:16–17; 5:31; James 3:1). Apostasy is hovering over the church like a funnel cloud, yet large numbers of Christians think that everything is the way it should be.

Our Youth

We can see the sharp decline in basic moral values by looking at the change in public [i.e., "government"] school disciplinary problems, as can be seen in the following comparisons:

1940s	1980s
1. Talking	1. Drug abuse
2. Chewing gum	2. Drinking alcoholic beverages
3. Making disturbing noises	3. Pregnancy
4. Running in hallways	4. Suicide
5. Stepping out of place in school lines	5. Rape
6. Wearing inappropriate clothing	6. Robbery
7. Not putting trash in wastebaskets	7. Assault

Indeed, young people are into some "heavy stuff." No doubt, human nature has not changed, but have you ever noticed how young people are becoming more involved in "adult" crimes? Laura Sessions Stepp, writing for the *Washington Post* (July 8, 1999) gave the following report. Here are the opening lines:

> The mother of an Arlington teenager will never forget the phone call she received from Williamsburg Middle School, where her daughter was in the eighth grade.
>
> "I'd like to invite you to a meeting about girls at risk," said Latanja Thomas, the eighth-grade school counselor.
>
> "What risk?" the mother asked. "Eating disorders?"
>
> "No."
>
> "Drugs?"
>
> "No."
>
> "Well, what is it?"

"Oral sex."

"I about dropped the phone," the mother recalled. "I was stunned."

News such as this is becoming all too common. Who are these middle schoolers? Are they from some depressed ghetto? No. The report indicates that they live in a mostly upper-income community of elegant brick homes, leafy sycamores, and extravagantly decorated lawns, The parents were totally unaware of what was happening, "Eager to avoid pregnancy and hold on to virginity, an increasing number of teenagers are engaging in oral sex, according to school and health officials."

The *Post* article indicates that some of the parents are upset—that their daughters are being singled out and being portrayed as "bad girls." "But where are the bad boys?" one mother asked. The parents tried to speak to their daughters, but the girls shrugged the whole thing off. "What's the big deal? President Clinton did it," one of the fourteen-year-olds stated.

The following was posted on the Internet in the summer of 1999 with no specific date or author given, but it is a penetrating commentary on today's youth:

> Whoa! What in the world is happening with our kids today? Let's see ...
>
> I think it started when Madelyn Murray O'Hair complained that she didn't want any prayer in our schools, and we said, "Okay."
>
> Then someone said you had better not read the Bible in school. After all, it says, "Thou shalt not kill, thou shalt not steal, and love your neighbor as yourself." And we said, "Okay."
>
> Then the Supreme Court said that we could no longer post the Ten Commandments in our classrooms because they might influence our children, in violation of the concept called "separation of church and state." And we said, "Okay."
>
> Remember Dr. Benjamin Spock, who said we shouldn't spank our

children when they misbehave, because their little personalities would be warped, and we might damage their self-esteem? And we said "Okay."

Then someone said that teachers and principals better not discipline our children when they misbehave. And other administrators said, "Whoa, no one in this school better touch a student when they misbehave because we don't want any bad publicity, and we surely don't want to be sued."

Then someone said, "Let's let our daughters have abortions if they want, and we won't even tell their parents." And we said "Okay." Then someone said, "Let's give our sons all the condoms they want so they can have all the 'fun' they desire, and we won't tell their parents." And we said, "That's another great idea!"

And then some of our top officials said, "It doesn't matter what we do in private as long as we do our jobs." And we said, "As long as I have a job and the economy is good, it doesn't matter to me what anyone does in private."

So now we're asking ourselves why our children have no conscience, why they don't know right from wrong and why it doesn't bother them to kill.

Probably, if we think about it long and hard enough, we can figure it out. I think it has a great deal to do with "we reap what we sow."

Whoa! What a concept!

Wars, and More Wars

Though many prophecies about the Kingdom Age speak about peace, we live in a world that is at war. Tom Raum, Associated Press writer, filed the following report on December 29, 1999, just a few days before the end of the twentieth century:

> The century is coming to a close with a third of the world's 193 nations embroiled in conflict, nearly twice the Cold War level …
>
> In its annual report, the National Defense Council Foundation blamed rising military coups and a backlash against democracy, a trend it suggested would continue for several years.

The foundation listed 65 conflicts in 1999, up from 60 the year before. It nominated Afghanistan as the world's most unstable state for 2000—followed closely by Somalia, Iraq, Angola and the breakaway Chechnya region of Russia …

In the past, small undeveloped nations posed no serious threat to the larger more technologically advanced nations of the world. However, with many of the smaller nations of the world stockpiling nuclear, chemical, and biological weapons capable of killing millions, even the smaller nations could inflict severe damage on a larger nation. Despite the optimistic projections of secular humanists and Kingdom-Now proponents who are anticipating a new century of victory over the forces of evil, human nature is still what it has always been, but the technology of destruction is far more available than ever before.

Moral Confusion

The degree of moral confusion in America and the world is increasing incrementally. In a report posted on February 7, 1999, by Prodigy we read:

> A prosecutor said Saturday he was appalled by an appeals court decision to overturn a prison sentence for a child rapist because the judge, when imposing sentence, had quoted from the Bible.
>
> In a 2–1 verdict, the Ohio First District Court of Appeals late Friday reversed a 51-year sentence of James Arnett, 33, who had pleaded guilty

on January 1998, to 10 counts of rape involving the 8-year-old daughter of his fiancée.

The report continues by stating: "In its majority opinion, the appeals court said Judge Melba Marsh clearly was influenced in her sentencing by a passage from the Bible." What passage from the Bible had Judge Marsh quoted that was so "damaging" to the rapist's rights to due process? The "offending" passage was Matthew 18:6 where Jesus says: "But whoso shall offend one of these little ones which believe in me, it were better for him that a millstone were hanged around his neck, and that he were drowned in the depth of the sea."

There have been other cases where justice has not been served for similar reasons. In the February 1999 Southwest Radio Church *Prophetic Observer*, I reported on the U.S. Supreme Court's refusal to reinstate a child molester's prison sentence, set aside by the highest court in the state of Nebraska, because a judge quoted Bible verses before imposing the man's punishment. In that case a twenty-five-year-old man, who pleaded guilty to sexually assaulting a thirteen-year-old boy, was set free by the Nebraska Supreme Court because the judge read a passage from the Bible condemning homosexuality.

With things like this happening, it is hard to believe that we are now living in the Kingdom Age. Isaiah 11:5–6 states: "And righteousness shall be the girdle of his loins ... The wolf also shall dwell with the lamb ... and a little child shall lead them." In a day when crimes against women, children, and the elderly are on the increase, and there is unrighteousness in high places, it is hard to believe that this present age can, in any sense, be called "the Kingdom Age."

Blame-Shifting

Since the beginning of recorded history blame-shifting has been a consistent practice. Now it is receiving official approval in the highest places.

The *Daily Oklahoman* for Monday August 2, 1999, featured a report entitled "First Lady Discusses Her Husband's Infidelity." The subtitle reads: "Clinton's Actions Blamed on Emotional Child Abuse." I quote from the article:

> Hilary Clinton reportedly told an interviewer from Talk magazine that, as a child of four, her husband was caught in a "terrible conflict" between his mother and his grandmother, who took care of him in Arkansas while his mother was studying to be a nurse anesthesiologist in another state. The First Lady is quoted as saying that she has been told by an expert that trying to please two women who are fighting over him is the "worst" possible scenario for a small boy... There's always a desire to please each one.

Edmund Burke has said that "men are qualified for liberty in exact proportion to their disposition to put moral chains upon their own appetites." It would follow then that if men—especially our leaders—cannot put "moral chains upon their own appetites," that men are not qualified for liberty. Lacking internal restraints, society can only function with the strictest of external restraints—and that is not liberty. The greatest casualty in this erosion of moral standards is liberty itself. The doors have now been opened for the strict surveillance of individuals, and mandated controls as the only way of getting people to behave responsibly.

Amazing Advances in Science and Technology

How advanced is science at the present hour? We have now arrived at the point of producing "goatwebs." E. W. Kieckhefer, writing a UPI release for May 18, 2000, reports the following:

> Canadian scientists have implanted spider genes in a herd of goats, resulting in the production of silky strands in goat milk that can be used for sutures

and other applications. The technique was perfected by Jeffrey Turner, a geneticist and president of Nexia Biotechnologies of Quebec. "We have combined the old and the new," Turner told UPI in a recent interview. "The old is represented by the goats and their milk, which is used to make cheese. The new is genetic engineering."

The webs are harvested from the goat's milk. The strands of "goatweb" are used to make sutures for eye surgery. The strands can also be used to reconstruct tendons and ligaments, and to repair bone. Companies like DuPont and 3M have been trying to duplicate spider web silk, but with no success.

Turner, the developer, is excited about the marketing possibilities for "goatweb." It could be used to make bulletproof vests and for the production of a waterproof covering for dome-shaped stadiums. There are also several applications in the aerospace and communications industries. Turner could be staring a fortune in the face. He estimates that the technology has a potential market of two billion dollars.

Genesis 1:11 states: "And God said, Let the earth bring forth grass, the herb yielding seed, and the fruit tree yielding fruit after his kind, whose seed is in itself." The Bible teaches a certain fixity of the species. Things reproduce after their own kind. This phrase appears ten times in Genesis 1. The seed was "programmed" for uniform reproduction of each kind through a remarkable mechanism known as the "genetic code." Goats that produce a web because of implanted spider genes seem to violate this principle, making man "the new creator." We may wonder what would happen if a goat gene was implanted in a spider. Will spiders grow horns and go "maaa"?

Changing Values

The coming reign and rule of the Antichrist will seriously affect Israel's most cherished religious institutions. Daniel 7:25 reminds us of the Antichrist's impact on Israel's religious practices. The Antichrist "shall speak great words against the most High, and shall wear out the saints of the most High, *and think to change times and Laws ...* " Are any "times and laws" being changed in Israel today as a prelude to this end-time development?

The *Jerusalem Post,* North American edition, for June 2, 2000, featured a front-page story entitled "Feminists Conquer Wall." Israel's High Court of Justice ruled that women can conduct their entire religious services at the Western Wall.

Prior to this decision, the women, who hold services on the first day of the Jewish month, have been reciting the morning prayer at the wall, but have moved to another location to read from the Torah. This ruling of Israel's High Court was seen as a victory for the women who had been engaged in a ten-year struggle to exercise what they believe to be their right.

Other reports also indicate that deep and profound changes are occurring in Israel's most basic and cherished institutions. In fact, there is what has been called "a quiet revolution" under way in Israel. Larry Derfner wrote a front-page article in the *Jerusalem Post,* North American edition, for September 10, 1999, entitled: "In a bind over books: New history textbooks challenging long-held assumptions about the state have been called a 'quiet revolution.'"

As the school year started, three new textbooks that challenge traditional biblical beliefs about Israel's history will be used in the ninth grade in the schools of Israel. The new textbooks, which were approved by the Education Ministry during the administration of Benjamin Netanyahu, use the term "Palestinian." This is a departure from standard practice. Older texts use the phrase, "the Arabs of the land of Israel." There are many other changes as well. This, of course, has caused deep furor in some Jewish circles. The "Palestinians" never had their own language or culture and there has never been a land known as "Palestine" governed by "Palestinians."

The *New York Times* also featured a story on the "rewriting of Jewish

225

history" entitled "In Israel, new grade school texts for history replace myths with facts" (August 14, 1999). From this title the *New York Times* has evidently concluded that traditional Jewish history is based on what it calls "myths." The Times story was later picked up by columnist Jim Hoagland who, writing for the *Washington Post,* applauded Israel for having the courage to engage in "admirable truth-telling, the beginning of coming to terms with a long suppressed Palestinian existence in history."

Some within the American Jewish community are drifting from their traditional Jewish roots. Rabbi Gerald L. Zelizer, who serves in a conservative Jewish congregation in New Jersey, authored a column entitled "Sanctify same-sex unions without marriage." Writing in *USA Today,* May 31, 2000, Rabbi Zelizer states that those who seek to avoid condemning all homosexual unions

> believe that the biblical verse that condemns homosexuality, when put in context, does not condemn homosexual relations under all circumstances. The same biblical chapter condemns all sorts of exploitative and deceptive heterosexual relationships, such as sex with a neighbor's wife or a father's wife.

Rabbi Zelizer goes on to state that

> the Bible abhors homosexuality, too, but only when it is deceptive and exploitative. When a homosexual union is genuine, not opportunistic, it is not within the parameters of the scriptural condemnation.

Ezekiel's Temple and the Kingdom

Another indication that we are not living in the Kingdom Age prophesied by Scripture is the absence of the Kingdom Temple. Ezekiel chapters forty through forty-eight speak about a future temple that will be the focus and center of worship in the Kingdom Age. It is the fourth and last earthly temple mentioned in the Scripture, coming after the Jerusalem Temple, the Restored Temple, and the Tribulation Temple. Preterists do not believe that it is a literal, future, earthly temple. Because of the vast amount of information given in the Scripture about this temple, their denial of the reality of this temple bears testimony to the weakness of their position. Let's look at some of the views concerning this temple.

Ezekiel's Temple is the first temple destroyed by the Babylonians in 586 B.C. However, the dimensions of Ezekiel's Temple do not match the dimensions of the First Temple. Furthermore, the First Temple never had a river flowing out of it that turned the salt water of the sea into fresh (Ezek. 47:8–9).

Ezekiel's Temple is the Restored Temple of the sixth century B.C. Once again, the details of the two do not match, Furthermore, if Ezekiel's Temple is the Restored Temple of the sixth century B.C., it is hard to imagine why Ezra, Nehemiah and Haggai do not mention it. They do not describe a temple that matches Ezekiel's Temple.

Ezekiel's Temple is a symbolic picture of the church as a fellowship of believers. This is a view that is quite popular with nondispensational writers. Its basic premise is that Old Testament prophecy is to be spiritualized. This would allow prophecy to be tailored to fit the church which, it is believed, is the inheritor of God's promises to Israel.

However, Ezekiel was not writing to Church Age saints, but to Old Testament Jews (Ezek. 40:4). Why would Ezekiel write to Old Testament Jews about the church? The entire passage shows that Ezekiel's Temple is associated with a time in Israel's future glory. This temple will be in existence at that future time when Israel's heart is changed, and the nation will no longer defile God's Holy name (Ezek. 43:7). There is repeated mention of the Jewish priesthood (Ezek. 44:10–11, 15–16). This is a *Jewish* temple with *Jewish* priesthood in a *Jewish* land. The church can only be found in the passage by willfully ignoring what is all too clear in the text.

Ezekiel's Temple is a symbolic picture of heaven as the dwelling place of God. This view also comes from allegorizing Scripture. There is absolutely nothing in Ezekiel chapters forty through fortyeight that refers to heaven. If it is speaking about heaven, why are there so many earthly details, such as the description of the boundaries of the land and the allocation of different portions of the land to the different tribes (47:13–23)? We are left with only one conclusion: This temple is a literal temple that will be built in Jerusalem during the millennial reign of Christ.

There are several unique features of Ezekiel's temple that show it to be different than earlier Jewish temples. The Ark of the Covenant, the central feature of the Tabernacle and the First Temple, is absent. Ezekiel's Temple has steps (Ezek. 43:17), something that was forbidden earlier by Moses. The reason for the prohibition: "That thy nakedness be not discovered thereon" (Exod. 20:26). The altar of Ezekiel's Temple is larger than in the earlier structures. It will be over twenty feet in height (Ezek. 43:13).

The Question of the Animal Sacrifices

An important element of millennial worship is the sacrificing of animals (Ezek. 43:18–27; 45:23). Since Christ has already made a perfect atonement for sin, how do we explain literal animal sacrifices in the future? This alleged problem is one of the reasons why some interpreters feel that they must spiritualize the passage. There is much confusion on this point because there is so much confusion regarding Old Testament sacrifices and the nature of worship. Consider the following points.

1. Old Testament Animal Sacrifices Were Never Meant To Take Away Sin, Nor Did They Ever Do So.
Those who find the animal sacrifices in the future temple a "problem"

usually reason that the Old Testament sacrifices took away sin, but that after the death and resurrection of Christ these sacrifices are no longer needed. This, however, is not correct reasoning. Animal sacrifices never took away sin (Heb. 10:4). The sacrifices had no power in and of themselves but were tokens of obedience and helped to establish the reality of one's relationship with God in the mind of the Old Testament believer. The temple sacrifices in the Millennial Age will be tokens of obedience and will serve as signs establishing the reality of one's fellowship with God. These sacrifices, thought of in these terms, do not violate any biblical principles.

2. Jewish Believers in Christ Living in the First Century A.D. Never Saw Any Problem with Temple Worship.

The Jerusalem temple continued to remain in existence during the first forty years of the church's existence. If temple worship in the Millennial Age contradicts apostolic doctrine, then one would expect that the early church would have argued against temple worship. Even after the resurrection of Christ and the outpouring of the Holy Spirit, Jewish Christians still frequented the temple (Acts 2:46; 3:1)

3. Even After the Death and Resurrection of Christ, Christian Obedience Still Involves the Outward and the External.

Some argue that all worship after the death and resurrection of Christ is purely spiritual, and consequently there is no place for outward rites or ceremonies, as would take place in the future Millennial Temple. Such reasoning is faulty. In the present age, symbolic actions which refer us to the death of Christ are still an important part of Christian worship. The church in the present age still has two ordinances, baptism and the Lord's Supper. The ritual actions of the Millennial Temple will be to the Jew of the future what baptism and the Lord's Supper are to the Christian today.

The Question of the Reestablishment of Mosaic Worship

Some would argue against the idea of a literal Millennial Temple on the basis that such a belief would require belief in the reinstitution of the Mosaic economy. However, while there are similarities in the worship of the Millennial Temple and Mosaic worship, there are some striking differences.

1. In The Millennial Temple, the Zadokite Priesthood Plays a Dominant Role.
Under the Mosaic system, the Levitical priesthood was in the center of things, but the Zadokites take that role in Ezekiel's Temple (Ezek. 43:19; 44:15; 48:11). As a whole, the Levites fell into apostasy, with the exception of one family within their ranks, the sons of Zadok. It is for this reason that they alone will be permitted to enter the Millennial Temple (44:15–16). The Levites will be given tasks of menial labor such as were formerly done by non-Israelites (Ezek. 44:4–14).

2. In the Millennial Temple, Several Features Characteristic of the Mosaic System Are Absent.
In Ezekiel's Temple there is no Ark of the Covenant, no pot of manna, no rod of Aaron that budded, no tables of the Law, no shewbread, and no temple veil. If the Millennial Temple is the reinstitution of the Mosaic system, one ought to expect to find the articles that were central of the Mosaic system in descriptions of the Millennial Temple.

3. In the Millennial Temple, Several Features Are Added to What Was Characteristic of the Mosaic System.
In the future temple the glory of God comes to abide for ever in the midst of God's people (Ezek. 43:1–9) and living waters flow from beneath the altar

(Ezek. 47:1–12). Verses ten and eleven provide details that strongly suggest that this is a literal earthly temple: the river flowing from beneath the temple that will sweeten the waters so that fishermen will spread their nets and catch many fish. Some salt marshes, however, will remain salty.

God devotes nine very detailed chapters of His Word to the Millennial Temple, and some of the material is given in painstaking detail. Why is the Millennial Temple so important? It is the climax of God's restoration of Israel. In the previous chapters of Ezekiel the prophet reveals that Israel will be regathered and spiritually restored (chapters 36 and 37) and that the Lord will supernaturally deliver His people from a northern confederation of invaders (chapters 38 and 39). The climax of all of this comes when God comes to dwell in the midst of His people.

The Millennial Temple of Haggai Chapter Two

Along with Ezekiel chapters forty through forty-eight, Haggai 2:6–9 also speaks of the Millennial Temple. This passage in Haggai could not have been fulfilled in the Herod's Temple because that temple had no glory associated with it. The Second Temple was the temple of first century Israel and, as we see in the New Testament accounts, the religious life of Israel totally lacked the power and glory of God. There was legalism, fleshly efforts at pleasing God, and hostility against the Gentiles. However, regarding the temple described by Haggai we read: "The glory of this latter house shall be greater than of the former" (Hag. 2:9). It is this temple to which the nations will come, and it will be filled with glory (vs. 7). Haggai's temple is not Herod's temple, but the temple of the Millennial Age.

Some preterists often try to argue that the second chapter of Haggai was fulfilled at the first coming of Christ and that He was the glory of the temple. Others push the view that Haggai chapter two is a reference to the church, or to the heavenly state of the redeemed. There is no warrant for this. The text shows a clear Jewish reference. The statement, "According to the word that I covenanted with you when ye came out of Egypt" (vs. 5), is a clear reference to Jewish bondage in Egypt. Furthermore, there is the promise that "in this place will I give peace" (vs. 9). Here is a special promise of peace for a special earthly place. Interpretations that find fulfillment in the church, or in the heavenly state, have to spiritualize this prophecy and virtually ignore the substance of what is promised.

The order of events outlined in Haggai 2 also suggests the future Millennial temple. The shaking of the heavens, earth, sea, and dry land (vs. 6) are all figures indicative of Divine judgment (see vss. 21–22). The statement "I will shake the nations" is reminiscent of the gathering of all nations together at the Battle of Armageddon and parallels the description of that event given in Zechariah 14:1–4. The pattern that emerges is Tribulation followed by "the glory of this latter house," and "peace" in this place. The patterns suggest a movement from a period of judgment followed by Millennial blessings.

From these considerations it is doubtful that the preterist contention that we are somehow in the Kingdom can be substantiated. Satan is now on the loose and going about as a hungry lion (1 Pet. 5:8). He interferes with the spreading of the gospel and hinders the work of edifying the saints (1 Thess. 2:18). It is no wonder that he is called "the god of this world" (2 Cor. 4:4) who puts obstacles in the paths of the lost and the saved (1 Thess. 3:5). It is impossible to be biblically literate and to equate the present Church Age with the period in which Satan will be bound so that he shall no longer deceive the nations (Rev. 20:1–6).

Some may think this view of the Kingdom is a pessimistic message, but pre-millennialists have a message that is supremely optimistic. God will establish His Kingdom on the earth, completely fulfill His promises to Israel, and bring in everlasting righteousness on the earth. Indeed, "this is my Father's world" and pre-millennialism doesn't surrender it to the devil.

Chapter 11

Preterism and the Old Testament Law

As we have seen in chapter three, in which we examined some of the fundamental beliefs of Covenant Theology, Covenant post-millennialism has a unique slant on the Old Testament Law. Preterists, especially those of Reformed persuasion, put the Christian under some aspect of Old Testament Law. This is not surprising since the Westminster standards—*The Westminster Confession of Faith*, *The Westminster Larger Catechism*, and the *Westminster Shorter Catechism*—all put a premium on Old Testament Law. Indeed, this is one of the hallmarks of Reformed Theology that leads Reformed theologians to claim that dispensationalists are antinomian—lawless—because we do not share their view of the Law as it pertains to the Christian life and sanctification.

To be sure, though there are moral and perpetually binding teachings in the Old Testament, the Old Testament scriptures were given to Israel and were to be Israel's rule of life. Covenant theologians will never understand this because of their artificial concept of God's one covenant of grace that supposedly extends from the fall of man to the return of Jesus Christ. Covenant theology is like colored glasses that filter out certain wavelengths on the spectrum. Those who wear those glasses are blind to certain colors.

Covenant theologians are blind to certain truths. Since this is almost always a primary point of error with preterism, we need to deal with this issue.

If we are truly to understand Scripture, we must rightly divide the Word. Though dispensationalists disagree on some of the particulars, all dispensationalists agree that different people at different points in redemptive history were given somewhat different obligations and requirements from God. Hutchings explains how this affects our understanding of the Bible:

> Paul likens the twofold project of God in the redemption of man and the salvation of the world to the building of a house in Ephesians 2:19–22, built on Jesus, the chief cornerstone, around which all the different components of the building fit neatly together, the foundation being the apostles and prophets. If you were building a house, you would not get a company that specializes in concrete foundation work to do the interior decorating. You would not get a man who specializes in cabinet making to put on the roof, nor would you hire a bricklayer to do the electrical wiring. You would hire the right man for the right job. God is no different in the building of His house. What if Noah, when God told him to build an ark, had taken his family up on Mount Sinai? ... What if Abraham had lacked the faith to leave his country and sojourn in a strange land? ... The important thing for us to recognize is that while all things pertaining to the redemption of man and the saving of the world, as given in the Bible, either point to or are built around Christ, God has given each generation, and to specific leaders, different jobs or missions ... The reason we have so many diverse Christian doctrines, churches, and denominations is that so-called spokesmen of God down through the centuries of the Church Age have continually tried to give the right people the wrong job.

Reformed preterists argue against this idea by explaining that the Old Testament Law can be broken down into three divisions. First, they like to speak of the *moral law*. By this they mean the Ten Commandments, or the Decalogue. Then they speak of the *civil law* and use this designation to refer to ancient Israel's rules and regulations regarding the Jewish society and the government of the Old Testament theocracy. Under this category is included a variety of regulations regarding laws of warfare, laws of property ownership, laws regarding crime and punishment, and so on. The third category is the *ceremonial law*. This is used as a reference to the ceremonies, washings, and laws of purification pertaining to the worship of God under the Old Covenant. The *Westminster Confession of Faith* states:

> God gave to Adam a law, as a covenant of works, by which he bound him and all his posterity to personal, entire, exact, and perpetual obedience ... This law, after the fall, continued to be a perfect rule of righteousness; and, as such, was delivered by God upon mount Sinai in ten commandments, and written in two tables; the first four commandments containing our duty toward God, and the other six our duty to man. Besides this law, commonly called moral, God was pleased to give to the people of Israel, as a church under age, ceremonial laws, containing several typical ordinances ... All which ceremonial laws are now abrogated under the New Testament. To them also, as a body politic, he gave sundry judicial [civil] laws. Which expired altogether with the state of that people ... (19:1–4).

In keeping with this, many Reformed theologians will emphatically state that while Christians are not under the civil law or the ceremonial law, they are under the moral law. They will say something like: "Surely, you don't deny that Christians are under the Ten Commandments, do you?" Not wishing to sound as if they endorse adultery, lying, stealing, disobedience to parents, and other violations of the Ten Commandments, most Christians will affirm that they believe in the Old Testament "moral law" and that the Ten Commandments are still binding on believers today. Of course, that immediately raises a thorny question: What about the fourth commandment, the command to keep the Sabbath? Most evangelicals will mumble something about Sunday being the "Christian sabbath," while others will become livid with rage and ask for proof that God has changed His holy day to Sunday.

Covenant Law

We will never understand the relationship between Law and grace, the dispensation of the Law and the dispensation of the church, unless we realize that the Ten Commandments constitute covenant Law. The commandments were God's specific requirements given to Israel under the Mosaic covenant. God entered into a unique and special relationship with the nation of Israel and Mount Sinai. This is why the Bible always ties the Ten Commandments to Israel and Mount Sinai, as I will seek to show. Though the New Testament scriptures do exhort Christians to obey the individual duties of nine of the Ten Commandments—the Sabbath commandment is excepted—it never puts the Ten Commandments as a body of laws on the church. In the following scriptures note how the Ten Commandments are always associated with Moses, the Mosaic Law, the Mosaic Covenant, Mount Sinai, and Israel.

> And the LORD said unto Moses, Write thou *these words:* for after the tenor of these words *I have made a covenant with thee and with Israel.* And he was there with the LORD forty days and forty nights; he did neither eat bread, nor drink water. And he wrote upon the tables *the words of the covenant, the ten commandments.*
> —Exodus 34:27–28

> And he declared unto you *his covenant,* which he commanded you to perform, even *ten commandments;* and he wrote them upon *two tables of stone.*
> —Deuteronomy 4:13

There was nothing in the ark save the two tables of stone, which Moses put there at Horeb, when the LORD made a covenant with the children of Israel, when they came out of the Land of Egypt,

—1 Kings 8:9

Significantly, a singular word, "testimony," was used to describe the Ten Commandments. "He took and put the testimony into the ark ..." (Exod. 40:20). This word is invariably associated with Moses and Mount Sinai: "And he gave *unto Moses,* when he had made an end of communing with him *upon Mount Sinai,* two tables of *testimony,* tables of stone, written with the finger of God" (Exod. 31:18; see also 34:29). John Reisinger, in his perceptive analysis of the relationship between the Old and New Testaments, states:

> It is significant that the word "testimony" is singular even though there were "Ten" Commandments written on the tablets. It confirms that the Ten Commandments are considered to be one single document, and the document is the covenant, or "testimony," between God and Israel.

The Ten Commandments and the Church

The Ten Commandments were not given to the church, nor were they given to any group other than Israel at a particular point in time. Though they embody universal and timeless principles and patterns of behavior, they were specific stipulations given to govern the relationship between God and Israel and were an important aspect of the "community charter" that God gave to that nation. Several scriptures clearly and irrefutably indicate the particular covenantal nature of the Ten Commandments:

> And he declared unto you *his covenant,* which he commanded *you* to perform, even *ten commandments* ...
>
> —Deuteronomy 4:13

> When I was gone up into the mount to receive *the tables of stone, even the tables of the covenant* which the Lord made with *you* ... And the Lord delivered unto me two tables of stone written with the finger of God; and on them was written according to all the words, which the Lord spake with you *in the mount out of the midst of the fire* ... And it came to pass at the end of forty days and forty nights, that the Lord gave me two tables of stone, *even the tables of the covenant.*
>
> —Deuteronomy 9:9–11

> And he hewed two tables of stone like unto the first; and Moses rose up early in the morning, and went up unto mount Sinai, as the Lord had commanded him, and took in his hand the two tables of stone ... And the Lord said unto Moses, Write thou these words: for after the tenor of these words *I have made a covenant with thee and with Israel*. And he was there with the Lord forty days and forty nights; he did neither eat bread, nor drink water. And he wrote upon *the tables the words of the covenant, the ten commandments.*
>
> —Exodus. 34:4, 27–28

As we have seen earlier, Reformed theologians like to speak of "different administrations of the one covenant of grace." It is in this way that Reformed writers deny that there are substantial differences between the Old and New Testaments, Israel and the church. On this basis, Old Testament Law becomes, in large measure, the rule for the church. However, these scriptures emphatically deny that there are "different administrations of the one covenant of grace." The Ten Commandments were themselves the rules and regulations for the Mosaic Covenant. The Mosaic Covenant is not a different administration of the *same* covenant. It is a *different covenant,* and the Ten Commandments were the stipulations of that particular covenant. Reisinger summarizes biblical truth:

If our system of theology did not teach us to think about the Commandments as a distinct and separate covenant then it did not teach us to think Scripturally. If we were taught to think of the Tablets of Stone as "the unchanging moral law of God," then we were taught wrong. Unfortunately, we were also taught, by default, to ignore the words and terms used by the Holy Spirit Himself. We may have done it unconsciously, but we nonetheless substituted erroneous theological terms in the place of Biblical terminology. Or even worse, if we were taught that the Ten Commandments simply could not be a separate distinct covenant but only a different administration of the so called Covenant of Grace, then we were taught to actually contradict the word of God. The Holy Spirit always relates the Ten Commandments, when considered as a unit, with the "words of the covenant" that were written on the Tablets of Stone at Mt. Sinai.

Notice, the author speaks of "the Ten Commandments, when considered as a unit." It is this unit that is covenant Law for those under the Mosaic covenant. However, moral elements in the individual commandments are still perpetually binding. That point must always be clarified and explained against possible misunderstanding. There is moral law in the Old Testament scriptures just as there is moral law in the Ten Commandments; but the *entire body* of these scriptures *taken as a unit* has non-moral elements that specifically pertained to Israel.

This becomes evident in those portions of the Commandments that relate to Israel. For example, Paul writes, "Children, obey your parents in the Lord … Honour thy father and mother … That it may be well with thee, and thou mayest live long on the earth" (Eph. 6:1–3). Exodus 20:12 says, "that thy days may be long upon the land," referring to the Promised Land. In this single commandment, the fifth commandment, we find both a moral and perpetually binding element—obedience to parents—as well as an ancient

Hebrew application—entrance into the Promised Land.

It must be reaffirmed, however, that taking a covenantal view of the Ten Commandments does not mean that I believe that the individual duties enunciated by the Commandments have been abrogated and that, therefore, it is perfectly permissible for Christians to violate the moral dictates of the Ten Commandments. This is not at all what I mean. The following illustration puts the entire issue in proper perspective.

> Perhaps it would be good to illustrate what has just been said. The American Colonies were under the constitution and laws of England up until 1776. On that date, the colonies became the United States of America. They united under the Constitution of the USA. From that moment they were "under a new rule." The laws of the constitution of England no longer had any legal authority over any American. The laws of England were totally null and void in respect to us as a nation. None of England's laws could be appealed to as the final authority on any matter whatsoever. America was under the authority of a new document or covenant. The Constitution of the USA was now the full and final authority over every American … It is very obvious that the Constitution of the USA carefully considered and used many of the laws of England when they wrote the new laws. However, that is not the point. The only point is the change from being "under the law of England" versus being "under the law of the USA."

There is much confusion over these issues. Christ perfectly fulfilled the Law of God for us and He is working to bring us into greater conformity to the eternal Law of God. This, however, does not mean that it is God's will that we put ourselves under the Law of Moses. That was for a different age and for a different people.

The idea that the church must be obedient to God by being covenantly faithful to the Mosaic Law has no basis in Scripture. Those who think that the

Law is the means by which the church will "Christianize" the planet prior to the return of Christ have substituted human fancy for scriptural truth.

Chapter 12

"The Blessed Hope" or "The Blasted Hoax"?

No discussion of preterism could be considered anywhere near complete without making mention of the doctrine of imminency—something clearly affirmed by pre-tribulationists, but ridiculed by others. When we state that the Rapture of the church is imminent, we mean that there is no prophecy that needs to be fulfilled before the Rapture can occur. Hence Church Age believers are not to be looking for signs, but rather for the Lord.

Preterism's denial of imminency is one of the most dangerous aspects of their teaching. DeMar insists that the majority of prophetic events mentioned in the New Testament were fulfilled in but a few years from their initial utterance. "Time texts" indicating that the prophecy is for "this generation" and that these events are "at hand" must be taken at face value, says DeMar. He believes that imminency is a manufactured doctrine which we have invented because of the necessity of our eschatological system. "Dispensationalists reject this literal approach to interpreting the time texts by fabricating a doctrine called *imminency*."

Looking For Him

In 1 Thessalonians 1:10 the apostle writes how, as a result of their conversion, the Thessalonians have turned from their idols to serve the living God, "and to wait for his Son from heaven, whom he raised from the dead, even Jesus, which delivered us from the wrath to come." We are waiting for God's Son, not looking for signs. Christians are therefore to be "looking for that blessed hope, and the glorious appearing of the great God and our Saviour Jesus Christ" (Titus 2:13). This is not a fabricated document, but a scriptural one.

Consistent with imminency is the belief that the "signs" that we are seeing at the present time are, strictly speaking, signs of the approaching Tribulation and Millennium to follow, not signs for the Rapture. An illustration should suffice. In the fall of the year, Christmas decorations that go up everywhere are not really heralding Thanksgiving. They are Christmas decorations. Nevertheless, signs reminding us of Christmas indirectly remind us of Thanksgiving, a holiday that precedes Christmas. In the same way, signs for events that follow the Rapture indirectly remind us of the Rapture, the event that precedes the Tribulation.

Predictably, Preterists Scorn the Rapture

Preterists hate the pre-trib Rapture and find all kinds of caricatures for it. John Noe, for example, ardent writer for the International Preterist Association (IPA) writes that "the prime motivation behind Western Christian fundamentalist advocacy of Israel is to precipitate the so-called Rapture." He sees pre-tribulationists as using their "pro-Israel" stance to somehow force God's hand. In addition, this stance "also fosters a legacy of hate, and doesn't have the best interest of the Jews, or of anybody, close to heart—i.e., reaching them with the correct Gospel message of love and grace." Noe stated this in a paper entitled "The Israel Illusion: 13 Popular Misconceptions about This Modern-day Nation and Its Role in Bible Prophecy." The paper was presented at the 52nd Annual Meeting of the Evangelical Theological Society, November 2000, in Nashville, Tennessee. Both Noe, and the Evangelical Theological

Society need to hide their heads in shame. That Noe's unsubstantiated and undocumented claims would be circulated at an ETS meeting certainly casts a shadow of doubt on the credibility of an organization that has been highly regarded in the field of biblical scholarship. Obviously, that organization has now stooped to presenting material that isn't fit to be printed in a cheap tabloid.

More credible than Noe is DeMar, who at least tries to support his preterist beliefs with Scripture. Of course, DeMar doesn't believe in imminency and argues for "immediacy" instead. He is confused in his reasoning, however, and misrepresents the pre-tribulational position. He quotes pre-tribulationist Gerald Stanton who correctly defines imminency as indicating "that something important is likely to happen, and could happen soon ... it is next on the program and may take place at any time." DeMar's critique of these words is revealing:

> Words such as "likely," "could happen," and "may take place" are nowhere indicated. If the biblical authors wanted to be tentative in the way they described future events, they would have equivocated by using words expressing probability.

Contrary to DeMar, advocates of imminency do not see the return of the Lord for the church as something that "could happen." The uncertainty is not about the Lord's coming, but the time of His coming. The biblical authors were "tentative," to use DeMar's own word, not about the event, but about when it will occur. I checked the source of DeMar's quotation to see if Stanton really believes that Christ's return is tentative and, of course, he doesn't. Stanton writes that "we sing with expectation, 'Jesus is coming to earth again, What if it were today?'" Stanton goes on to state: "In the midst of trials and sorrows, the hope of Christ's imminent return never fails to encourage a troubled heart." There is nothing tentative about that.

The Bible never calls into question Christ's return, but it repeatedly leaves the time uncertain—something that chronic date-setters need to consider. Jesus said, "Take ye heed, watch and pray: for ye know not when the time is" (Mark 13:33). He then explains in greater detail:

> For the Son of man is as a man taking a far journey, who left his house, and gave authority to his servants, and to every man his work, and commanded the porter to watch, Watch ye therefore: for ye know not when the master of the house cometh, at even, or at midnight, or at the cockcrowing, or in the morning: Lest coming suddenly he find you sleeping. And what I say unto you I say unto all, Watch.
>
> —Mark 13:34–37

The command to "watch" is found in several scriptures dealing with end-time events. In 1 Thessalonians 5:6, Paul exhorts: "Therefore let us not sleep, as do others; but let us watch and be sober." The whole context is a call for being on the alert.

> For yourselves know perfectly that the day of the Lord so cometh as a thief in the night. For when they shall say, Peace and safety; then sudden destruction cometh upon them, as travail upon a woman with child; and they shall not escape.
>
> —1 Thessalonians 5:2–3

The command to "watch" is a command that benefits us. The One who gave Scripture has no doubt about the exact time of the Lord's return and did not make tentative statements about the time of His return because He was in ignorance of the exact time. The Lord wants His people to stay awake, "lest coming suddenly he find you sleeping." There must be some intrinsic benefit in not knowing the exact time of the Lord's return. The whole drift of these passages, and many others like them, is that we must rest our hope on Christ and on the fact of His imminent return. The Lord, through these Scriptures, is cultivating a special attitude in the hearts of His children. He wants us to realize that we stand in danger of missing His best for our lives if we fail to heed the injunction to "watch." This is one of the great tragedies of preterism. There is no need for watchfulness since, according to preterist belief, everything has already come to pass. There can be no sense of expectation or carefulness for those who believe that the exhortations to "watch" must of necessity be addressed to the Lord's immediate disciples and their contemporaries.

Were the Virgins Preterists?

Preterism runs rough shod over the Olivet Discourse. One of the tragedies of preterism's treatment of Matthew 24 is that it affects one's understanding Matthew 25, where we are told the parable of the Ten Virgins (vss. 1–13). The emphasis here is on watchfulness, and the section concludes with the Lord's exhortation: "Watch therefore, for ye know neither the day nor the hour wherein the Son of man cometh" (vs. 13). There is a significant contrast between Matthew 24 and Matthew 25. In Matthew 24:43–51, the exhortation is the need for watchfulness in case the Lord returns *sooner* than anticipated. In Matthew 25, however, the exhortation focuses on the need for watchfulness in case the Lord returns *later* than anticipated. The foolish virgins took no oil and were unprepared for the delay.

In stressing immediacy instead of imminency, preterists have limited the need for spiritual watchfulness only to Jesus' immediate contemporaries. This is no empty criticism. DeMar cites several scriptures where the Lord says, "I am coming quickly," or where scripture states, "the time is near," and then relates those scriptures to the first century. "These passages and others like them," writes DeMar, "tell us that a significant eschatological event was to occur in the lifetime of those who heard and read the prophecies." If all of these warnings referred to the first century, then they are not for us today. That things of momentous significance are about to happen ought not, then, to lead us to watchfulness because they have already occurred! Rather than this being an "eschatology of victory," it is an "eschatology of slumber." It is also an "eschatology of despair." As Tim LaHaye observes, if imminency is not true, then instead of singing, "Glad Day! Glad Day! ... Jesus may come today," we ought to be moaning, "Sad Day! Sad Day ... Jesus can't come today."

The idea of a spiritual coming of Christ in judgment upon Israel in the first century as a fulfillment of Rapture passages certainly provides us with little more than a "blasted hoax" instead of "the blessed hope," and it would have been scorned by the first century church. When Jesus spoke about His return, it was a return *for the purpose of bringing believers to Himself.* "And if I go and prepare a place for you, I will come again, and receive you unto myself; that where I am, there ye may be also" (John 14:3). Preterists resort to a tortured explanation for their defense of a spiritual coming. It may appeal to them, but believers are looking for a coming that translates them from this world to the next, not one that makes for nice reading in history books.

An Attitude of Expectancy

Preterists go wrong when they look to date prophecy. Statements in Scripture that are addressed to churches in the first century must, in the preterist mindset, limit the time of fulfillment to a first century date. But is this phenomenon a deliberate teaching of Scripture, or is it something that arises from the fact that Scripture was written in the first century to first century Christians?

Using preterist "logic," 1 Thessalonians 4 must teach an immediate resurrection of the dead. In verse one Paul writes to his contemporaries and says, "Furthermore then we beseech you, brethren, and exhort you by the Lord Jesus, that as ye have received of us how ye ought to walk and to please

God, so ye would abound more and more." There is an immediacy to these words. Paul, the missionary pastor, is writing to a local congregation on earth at that time. Why shouldn't there be an immediacy to his words? However, he continues with the same language later on in the chapter when he speaks of the descent of the Lord and the raising of the saints.

> For the Lord himself shall descend from heaven with a shout, with the voice of the archangel, and with the trump of God: and the dead in Christ shall rise first: Then *we which are alive and remain* shall be caught up together with them in the clouds ... *so shall we ever be with the Lord."*
> —1 Thessalonians 4:16–17

This is a future event, yet Paul includes himself and his readers.

One of the great resurrection chapters of the Bible is 1 Corinthians 15. It "preaches well" at funerals and demonstrates that we have a well-grounded hope. But if we allow a preterist understanding to be imposed, then the resurrection of believers has already occurred. "Behold, I shew you a mystery," writes Paul to the church at Corinth. "We shall not all sleep, but we shall all be changed" (vs. 51). No doubt, we shall all be changed by the resurrection of Jesus Christ; but Paul says, "We shall not all sleep." "Sleep" is a euphemism for death (see 1 Cor. 11:30). Paul is including himself with the word "we" and saying that there are some hearing this letter who will not die because we will hear the trumpet and we will be raised incorruptible.

The same language is found in 2 Peter 3. Peter wrote about the time when "the heavens shall pass away with a great noise, and the elements shall melt with fervent heat, the earth also and the works that are therein shall be burned up" (vs. 10). However, Peter includes his immediate readers in these events:

> Nevertheless we [Peter and his first-century audience], according to his promise, look for new heavens and a new earth, wherein dwelleth righ-

teousness. Wherefore, *beloved,* seeing that *ye* look for such things, be diligent that ye may be found of him in peace, without spot, and blameless.

—2 Peter 3:13–14

Expectancy is clearly the attitude that Christians are to have regarding the Lord's return. Knowing that the Lord's return is imminent means that He could come at any moment—unannounced and quite by surprise. Many of the views that are circulating today, and winning adherents have one thing in common: they deny imminency. "The pre-Tribulation Rapture ... is the only one that provides Christians with an at-any-moment expectancy ... all other views leave something more to be accomplished before Jesus can return" For those in the pre-wrath camp there must first be the appearance of the Antichrist. For post-millennialists it is the worldwide preaching of the gospel that leads to the Christianization of planet Earth. Sadly, more and more are being deceived into believing that Jesus can't come at the present time.

There is a definite immediacy in the language of prophecy, not because there would be a first century fulfillment, but because the Holy Spirit of inspiration is more concerned with keeping God's people in a continual attitude of watchfulness and expectancy than in dating when these events will take place. Words such as "you," "ye," and "we" do not always indicate immediate fulfillment. Rather, they are used to remind Christians that we need to live every moment as though it were our last—because it very well could be.

This same phenomenon can be observed in the Old Testament. God speaks through His prophets and seems to speak as if there will be an immediate fulfillment, but by examining the actual fulfillment of past events we know that at least several hundred years have elapsed before the actual fulfillment. The Mosaic Covenant ratification ceremony with appended blessings and curses well illustrates this. It is directed to the Jewish nation of Moses' day, yet it speaks about events far in the future. Deuteronomy 28:36–37, 49 states:

> The LORD shall bring *thee,* and thy king which thou shalt set over thee, unto a nation which neither thou nor thy fathers have known; and there shalt *thou* serve other gods, wood and stone. And *thou* shalt become an astonishment, a proverb, and a byword, among all nations wither the LORD shall lead *thee* ... The LORD shall bring a nation against *thee* from far, from the end of the earth, as swift as the eagle flieth; a nation whose tongue thou shalt not understand ...

Verses thirty-six and thirty-seven probably refer to the invasion of Samaria by Assyria in 721 B.C.—some seven hundred years after these words were addressed to the original audience. In verse forty-nine the reference to "the eagle" is probably a reference to the invasion of Jerusalem under Nebuchadnezzar. Here are references to events seven hundred years and nine hundred years in the future yet using a preterist understanding of prophecy we would have to conclude that God was addressing that generation of Jews and that they, along with Moses, would literally see the Assyrians and the Babylonians.

Will the Church Lose Its Heart for Prophecy on the Eve of the Rapture?

In the last few years many Christians have lost their hunger for the study of biblical prophecy. When hostilities were growing in the Persian Gulf and "Operation Desert Shield" had America glued to the television, many believed that the world was on the brink of Armageddon. When hostilities erupted into "Operation Desert Storm" and images of the night sky over Baghdad were flashed on the TV news showing skies filled with exploding antiaircraft artillery shells, the growing apocalyptic fervor was fueled by prophecy teachers who wrote books and produced videos. Mindful of the fact that the prophetic scriptures describe end-time events in the Middle East—the same area where the conflict was growing in intensity—millions of Christians in America and in other parts of the world, especially those who were pre-millennial in their outlook, were seeking to trace the events of the early 1990s in the prophetic scriptures. President Bush's statement about the coalition that was fighting Saddam Hussein being a demonstration of the "new world order" seemed to be another indicator that the events described in Revelation 13 were about to unfold in the immediate future.

Bill Clinton's two terms in office, his obvious hatred of biblical morality and constitutional safeguards, plus his attempts to weaken America's sovereignty, likewise looked like an important piece of the puzzle for the end-time scenario. Millions of Christians were outraged that he was allowed to engage in "government by decree" as he issued one executive order after another and went unchallenged by Congress.

And then came Y2K—which seemingly passed with a whimper. When it turned out to be a non-problem, many felt let down, deceived, and disappointed. They blamed Christian ministries and various prophetic writers for creating a hoax so that they could make a fortune selling books and videos. But while Christian ministries were taking the heat, the critics conveniently failed to realize that it was the secular media that started the Y2K alarm in the first place. On June 13, 1998, CNN reported that Senator Chris Dodd (D-Conn.) stated: "We are no longer at the point of asking whether or not there will be any power disruptions, but we are now forced to ask how severe the disruptions are going to be." A few days later, on June 15, 1998, Senator Robert Bennett (R-Utah), chairman, Senate Special Committee on the Year 2000 Technology Problem stated: "In the event of a Y2K induced breakdown of community services, that might call for martial law."

Y2K did not turn out to be as severe as anticipated, but it did have some side effects that were downplayed and all but ignored except by a few of the more discerning. In a book that I coauthored with Noah W. Hutchings entitled *Y2K=666?* we raised the question if Y2K could lead to a universal computer system controlled by a single entity. Many thought the idea was ridiculous. We even caught flak from those within the Christian community. However, a report in *USA Today* (January 3, 2000) quoted John Koskinen, President Clinton's top Y2K adviser. Koskinen's statement shows that our assessment was right on target. Koskinen stated:

> When somebody asked me after my first congressional testimony in April 1998 "How big is your staff?" I told them it was me and three other people. I thought it was pretty neat to show that I could run the world with four people. This has been an appropriate first battle of the new millennium, but only the beginning of a need for global cooperation.

Many are unaware of the true significance of current events. Dismissing Y2K and other epoch-making events as not really important, millions are debunking disaster and scoffing at the nearness of the Lord's return. Anyone who speaks about the Second Coming, the Rapture, the Tribulation, and the Russian invasion of Israel, is dismissed as an alarmist, a far-out conspiracy theorist who is "selling fear." Scoffers love to point out that there was "millennial madness" around A.D. 1000. At the close of the first millennium wild speculations arose that Jesus Christ would appear shortly. He didn't. Nor did He appear on December 31, 1999. Of course, reputable prophecy teachers never said that He would, nor have reputable Bible teachers equated Y2K with Armageddon. We certainly didn't, but scoffers don't like to mention that fact.

Evidence for Delay

Impatience is something from which we all suffer. Many things in life take much longer than is acceptable to those who are impatient. Every gardener knows the feeling. Wouldn't it be nice to see those seeds sprout the day after they were planted? James 5:7–8 uses an agricultural illustration to exhort us to patience.

> Be patient therefore, brethren, unto the coming of the Lord. Behold, the husbandman waiteth for the precious fruit of the earth, and hath long patience for it, until he receive the early and latter rain. Be ye also patient; stablish your hearts: for the coming of the Lord draweth nigh.

This is a pertinent bit of advice because people will look at the times and wonder why the Lord is delaying His return. People who are impatient will ask, "Why hasn't He yet come?" And every day of apparent delay will only increase the number of scoffers of whom Peter speaks. In fact, the presence of scoffers in the last days is something that is of primary importance. "Knowing this first, that there shall come in the last days scoffers" (2 Pet. 3:3). "First" means "of first importance." Some two thousand years ago people were impatient! And today we are still waiting. No wonder Peter states that knowing about the coming of scoffers is of first importance.

But why this apparent delay? Why have two thousand years elapsed, and still the Lord has not come? Peter, by inspiration, helps us to get the true picture: "The Lord is not slack concerning his promise, as some men count slackness"—meaning that God is not behind schedule because He is unable to bring His promise to pass—"but is longsuffering to us-ward, not willing that any should perish, but that all should come to repentance" (2 Pet. 3:9). In other words, there is an explanation for the Lord's apparent slowness. It must be understood from the perspective of Divine love. The fact that God's timetable is different than ours in the sense that "one day is with the Lord as a thousand years" (2 Pet. 3:8) and that God's nature is gracious, is the real reason for the apparent delay. This truth allows us to say that the Rapture is "imminent," and His return is "soon."

No doubt, as world events become more tumultuous, some will set a date for the Lord's return, as many have done in the past. Yet belief in imminence does not require date-setting. In fact, imminence and date-setting are mutually exclusive. If you really believe in the imminent return of the Lord for the church, you cannot be a date-setter. If there are no predicted events to precede the Rapture, date-setting is futile and vain. This, however, does not deny that a "season" for the Rapture can be discerned, and that its approach may be indicated by a variety of events. Ice and Demy state:

> Although date-setting is clearly prohibited in God's Word, we believe it is valid to understand that God is setting the stage for His great end-time program. What does that mean? As we mentioned earlier, the rapture is a signless event, thus it is impossible to identify specific signs that indicate its nearness. This is why all attempts to date the rapture have had to wrongly resort to the application of passages relating to God's plan for Israel to the church. An example of this misuse would be those who say Israel's feasts (i.e., Rosh Hashanah) relate to dating the rapture … However, since the Bible outlines a clear cast and scenario of players, events, and nations involved in the end-time tribulation, we can see God's preparation for the final seven years of Daniel's 70 weeks for Israel … Dr. Walvoord correctly says, "There is no scriptural ground for setting dates for the Lord's return or the end of the world … [but there is] a remarkable correspondence between the obvious trend of world events and what the Bible predicted centuries ago."

The study of biblical prophecy is both rewarding and informative for those who believe that there is still much unfulfilled prophecy that yet awaits fulfillment. We can only really understand the present by having an insight into the future. Preterism, however, with its insistence that virtually all prophecy has been fulfilled, sees the future as a vast uncharted sea. Since all prophecy has been fulfilled, we can virtually know nothing about the future. Is this how God operates? Since God has consistently revealed His prophetic will to His people in the past, are we to believe that He has said nothing to us about tomorrow?

The Bible speaks about growing apostasy in the church. Hearts will grow cold as church members seek to find their fulfillment in material things. Increasing numbers of church members are going to the polls and voting their pocketbooks rather than their consciences.

Are we really living in the last days or, as preterists teach, are the last days past days? As more and more Christians buy into preterism, it may very well be that the church will lose its heart for prophecy on the eve of the Rapture.

Addendum

Prophetic Gaps

In this section I want to set forth a few things about prophetic gaps. At the outset let me say that this has nothing to do with the "gap theory" of creation, a theory teaching that between Genesis 1:1 and 1:2 is a gap of an indeterminate period of time—perhaps millions of years which allows room for the geological ages postulated by unbelieving scientists—between the original creation and the creation week. I do not hold to that view and do not want to give the impression that I do.

When I speak of "prophetic gaps" I am referring to the phenomenon observed in the prophetic writings of the Bible in which prophetic events are not fulfilled in rapid successive order. The Hebrew prophets were not always aware of time in the way we are. For example, in some Old Testament passages, both the first and second advents of Christ are spoken of as though they are successive, but from our perspective, greatly enriched by having a completed Bible, we know that there is at least a two-thousand-year period between the advents. The reader will quickly see how the denial of such gaps is a very convenient device for preterists. Without such gaps, everything must have been fulfilled rather quickly. On the other hand, if there are gaps, futurists would be able to maintain that there are some prophecies that yet await fulfillment.

To give one example, we will look at Daniel 9:24–27, which speaks of

Daniel's "seventy weeks." Preterists argue that they are fulfilled consecutively, meaning that the final fulfillment was in the first century A.D. Futurists, on the other hand, speak about a gap between Daniel's sixty-ninth and seventieth weeks. We argue that the passage can be divided into three segments. The first segment consists of seven weeks (forty-nine years), and the second sixty-two weeks (four hundred thirty-four years). Both of these segments of time total sixty-nine weeks, or four hundred eighty-three consecutive years—all of which were fulfilled before the death of Christ. The final week of seven years, however, has been postponed and does not begin until a future time. This gap between the sixty-ninth and seventieth weeks corresponds with the Church Age. Following the Rapture, the seventieth week—the Tribulation period—will begin.

If biblical prophecy does not contain gaps, but is fulfilled in rapid successive order, then such an interpretation would, to say the least, be strange and forced. On the other hand, if prophecy does contain such gaps, a postponement of Daniel's seventieth week is not at all unusual. The following are a few of the Scriptures that show the existence of prophetic gaps.

Isaiah 61:1–2

This passage is referred to in the New Testament by the Lord Jesus Christ. I will quote both the Old and New Testament passages to make an important point. The numbers in parenthesis indicate the verses. In Isaiah 61:1–5 we read:

> (1) The spirit of the Lord God is upon me; because the LORD hath anointed me to preach good tidings unto the meek; he hath sent me to bind up the brokenhearted, to proclaim liberty to the captives, and the opening of the prison to them that are bound; (2) To proclaim the acceptable year of the LORD [gap], and the day of vengeance of our God; to comfort all

that mourn; (3) To appoint unto them that mourn in Zion, to give unto them beauty for ashes ... (4) And they shall build the old wastes, they shall raise up the former desolations, and they shall repair the waste cities, the desolations of many generations. (5) And strangers shall stand and feed your flocks, and the sons of the alien shall be your plowmen and your vinedressers.

When we read this passage, it appears that everything is in close succession. However, when the Lord Jesus Christ read this passage in the synagogue in Nazareth and applied it to Himself, He didn't read the whole passage because the whole passage was not applicable to the first advent. In Luke 4:16–21 we read:

(16) And he came to Nazareth, where he had been brought up: and, as his custom was, he went into the synagogue on the sabbath day, and stood up for to read. (17) And there was delivered unto him the book of the prophet Esaias. And when he had opened the book, he found the place where it was written, (18) *The Spirit of the Lord is upon me, because he hath anointed me to preach the gospel to the poor; he hath sent me to heal the brokenhearted, to preach deliverance to the captives, and recovering of sight to the blind, to set at liberty them that are bruised,* (19) *To preach the acceptable year of the Lord.* (20) And he closed the book, and he gave it again to the minister, and sat down. And the eyes of all them that were in the synagogue were fastened on Him. (21) And he began to say unto them, This day is this scripture fulfilled in your ears. [Italics supplied by author.]

Jesus opened the scroll and deliberately "found" this particular reference. Jesus had come to Israel to proclaim, "the acceptable year of the Lord." This was the time that "the kingdom was at hand" and God was commanding His people to repent and to receive their Messiah. Jesus was not heralding the

Tribulation. "The day of vengeance of our God," mentioned in Isaiah 61:2, would come later.

Isaiah 9:6–7

This much beloved passage presents the first advent (Jesus comes as the Child) but also the second (when He takes the government of the world).

> (6) For unto us a child is born, unto us a son is given: and the government shall be upon his shoulder: and his name shall be called Wonderful, Counseller, the mighty God, The everlasting Father, The Prince of Peace. (7) Of the increase of his government and peace there shall be no end, upon the throne of David, and upon his kingdom, to order it, and to establish it with judgment and with justice from henceforth even for ever.

In verse six the reference is to the first advent. A Child was born in Bethlehem in accordance with the prophecy of Micah 5. By the time we get to verse six, however, there is at least the suggestion that more than the first advent is in view. The Child's government is going to increase, and it is going to be established with "judgment" and with "justice."

Isaiah 40:3–5; Malachi 3:1–3

These are two prophecies which use similar language and illustrate both multiple references and prophetic gaps.

Isaiah 40:3–5
> (3) The voice of him that crieth in the wilderness, Prepare ye the way of the LORD, make straight in the desert a highway for our God. (4) Every valley shall be exalted, and every mountain and hill shall be made low: and

the crooked shall be made straight, and the rough places plain: (5) And the glory of the LORD shall be revealed, and all flesh shall see it together: for the mouth of the LORD hath spoken it.

Malachi 3:1–3:

(1) Behold, I will send my messenger and he shall prepare the way before me: and the Lord, whom ye seek, shall suddenly come to his temple, even the messenger of the covenant, whom ye delight in: behold, he shall come, saith the LORD of hosts. (2) But who may abide the day of his coming? and who shall stand when he appeareth? for he is like a refiner's fire, and like fuller's soap: (3) And he shall sit as a refiner and purifier of silver: and he shall purify the sons of Levi, and purge them as gold and silver, that they may offer unto the LORD an offering in righteousness.

The passage from Isaiah 40 is applied to the first advent (Matt. 3:3; Mark 1:3; Luke 3:4; John 1:23). The context in Isaiah is thoroughly Jewish and speaks about Jerusalem and that "her iniquity is pardoned" (Isa. 40:2). Verse four speaks about the physical features of the land being changed. This did not happen at the first advent but is prophesied for the second (Zech. 14:4—5).

Malachi 3 has similar references. Verse one speaks about "the messenger" who is going to prepare the way for the Lord. The first prophet of the New Testament is John the Baptist, and we may assume that there is some reference to him in these verses. But then we are told that "the Lord shall suddenly come to his temple" (Mal. 3:1). Jesus presented himself in the temple when He was twelve (Luke 2:46), then at the beginning of His public ministry (John 2:13–21), and still later at the close of His public ministry; yet none of these match all the descriptions of this prophecy. Malachi 3:3–5 speaks about the Lord purifying the sons of Levi so that "the offering of Judah and Jerusalem be pleasant unto the Lord." Verse five speaks about the establishment of justice in the Millennial Age:

And I will come near to you in judgment; and I will be a swift witness against the sorcerers, and against the adulterers, and against false swearers, and against those that oppress the hireling in his wages, the widow, and the fatherless, and that turn aside the stranger from his right, and fear not me, saith he LORD of hosts.

Though preterists try to get around these scriptures by saying that the prophets were describing New Testament realities in Old Testament language, this is not the language of the Church Age, neither in form nor in content. This is a nice way of saying that they are having extreme difficulty in making the Bible "fit" into their preconceived ideas about what it should really say.

Micah 5:2, 10–15

(2) But thou, Beth-lehem Ephratah, though thou be little among the thousands of Judah, yet out of thee shall he come forth unto me that is to be ruler in Israel; whose goings forth have been from of old, from everlasting. (10) And it shall come to pass in that day, saith the LORD, that I will cut off thy horses out of the midst of thee, and I will destroy thy chariots: (11) And I will cut off the cities of thy land, and throw down all thy strong holds: (12) And I will cut off witchcrafts out of thine hand; and thou shalt have no more soothsayers: (13) Thy graven images also will I cut off, and thy standing images out of the midst of thee; and thou shalt no more worship the work of thine hands. (14) And I will pluck up thy groves out of the midst of thee: so will I destroy thy cities. (15) And I will execute vengeance in anger and fury upon the heathen, such as they have not heard.

Verse 2 is a clear reference to the first advent (see Matt. 2:3–6), yet it also states that Jesus is to be "ruler in Israel." Though He is currently Lord of the church, He is not yet "ruler in Israel." There are other features of this prophecy that were not fulfilled at the first advent. God will one day remove the pagan practices and graven images and will bring renewal to the land and people of Israel. The "groves" where pagan fertility rites were practiced by apostate Jews will be removed. Since the time of Christ, and even before the first advent, Israel has been in apostasy. While some Jews have accepted Israel's Messiah, the kind of national revival that is predicted here awaits a future time for fulfillment.

Zechariah 9:9–10

(9) Rejoice greatly, O daughter of Zion; shout, O daughter of Jerusalem: behold, thy King cometh unto thee: he is just, and having salvation; lowly, and riding upon an ass, and upon a colt the foal of an ass. (10) And I will cut off the chariot from Ephraim, and the horse from Jerusalem, and the battle bow shall be cut off: and he shall speak peace unto the heathen: and his dominion shall be from sea even to sea, and from the river even to the ends of the earth.

Matthew 21:4–5 applies verse nine to the entry of Jesus into Jerusalem on "Palm Sunday." At the first advent, and during our Lord's entire earthly ministry, He truly was the One "having salvation," and He appeared in Jerusalem "lowly and riding upon an ass." Verse ten, however, speaks about a great battle, and the Lord establishing His dominion all over the earth.

It is by observing prophetic gaps and by taking God's promises to Israel literally that we see how some prophecies may have a far distant fulfillment, even though the immediate context may suggest a fulfillment in ancient times.

The metallic image of Daniel chapter two reveals four empires that hold sway over the land of Israel. The kingdoms are easily discernible, both from the explanation given in the text and from a general knowledge of ancient history. In Daniel 2:36–38 we are told that King Nebuchadnezzar is the head of gold. Verse thirty-nine shows successive fulfillment: "And after thee shall arise another kingdom inferior to thee, and another third kingdom of brass" (vs. 39). Three kingdoms are mentioned: the Babylonian, the one following (Medo-Persia), and then a "third kingdom of brass," the Grecian Empire under Alexander the Great.

The first three kingdoms are mentioned in summary form, but we immediately notice something special about the fourth, or the Roman kingdom: Daniel spends far greater time in explaining the parts of this aspect of the vision. While the preceding three kingdoms are presented in the short space of three verses (vss. 37–39), the fourth kingdom is given verses forty through forty-five for description and explanation.

If this passage were given in the New Testament era, preterists would explain the focus on the fourth kingdom by saying that the Roman Empire was in authority at that time and therefore much more is said about it. However, Daniel was taken into captivity in 605 B.C. Inasmuch as Jerusalem was destroyed by the Babylonians in 586 B.C., the dream and its interpretation, as recorded in Daniel chapter two, occurred many centuries before Rome came into the ascendancy. Daniel's focus on the fourth empire must be explained on the basis of its significance in world history.

Pre-millennialists have long noticed that on the basis of a successive presentation of prophetic events, the fourth kingdom would appear to be the ancient Roman Empire. However, pre-millennialists have also noticed that the fourth kingdom is presented as the final form of gentile world power which is destroyed by the Smiting Stone. And, according to Daniel 2:35, "the stone that smote the image became a great mountain and filled the whole earth." While preterists will argue that the Kingdom of God was established through the events surrounding the first advent of Christ, it must be remembered that at the end of His earthly ministry Jesus Christ was put to death by the sentence of an official working under the auspices of this fourth empire.

No Smiting Stone destroyed the fourth kingdom in the first century A.D. Moreover, while the church did enjoy a measure of success in the first century through the outpouring of the Holy Spirit and the powerful preaching of the apostles, it is also true that there was growing opposition to the gospel in various parts of the empire. Persecution of the church became the official policy of the Roman hierarchy throughout the empire under Decius in A.D. 250. It is hard to believe from a reading of Daniel chapter two that the fourth empire suffered a devastating defeat in the first century. On the contrary, every indication is that just the opposite occurred. No doubt, this was not something that caught God by surprise, or something that He wanted to change but could not; nevertheless, it was not in His good time to establish the Kingdom and fulfill the prophecies of Daniel 2, and other portions of Scripture, in the first century A.D.

It is important to notice that the final form of gentile world power will end suddenly by a catastrophic, devastating blow, and that only after the demise of gentile world power does God establish His Kingdom on the earth. This is diametrically opposite of the post-millennial scheme which sees a gradual infiltration of society and culture by the gospel over a period of perhaps hundreds or even thousands of years. Gentile world power does not exist alongside God's Kingdom. Rather, gentile world power comes to an end suddenly and decisively, and it is only after that event that the Kingdom of God is established on the earth.

Where is the Church Age in Daniel chapter two? It does not appear in this vision because the Church Age is a mystery that was not revealed to the Hebrew prophets (Eph. 3:1–6). The interposition of the Church Age was a "mystery" revealed later through the apostle Paul. The Smiting Stone, therefore, must not be equated with the church, as dominionist and Kingdom-Now writers hold. The church was never given the task of destroying gentile world power.

Gaps also appear in New Testament passages speaking of Rapture and resurrection. Death came by Adam, but "in Christ shall all be made alive" (1 Cor. 15:22). A few verses earlier the apostle wrote that Christ has "become the firstfruits of them that slept" (1 Cor. 15:20). The firstfruits were the first installment of the crop and were regarded as a guarantee that the entire crop would be forthcoming. But the whole crop doesn't come forth at the same time. "But every man in his own order: Christ the firstfruits; afterward they that are Christ's at his coming" (vs. 23). "Afterward" indicates a gap of at least two millennia. The resurrection of Christ occurred many years in the past. The resurrection of those who are in Christ will occur at the time of the Rapture—something that has not yet occurred. Verse twenty-four states: "Then cometh the end, when he shall have delivered up the kingdom to God ..." "The end" is to come a considerable time after the Rapture. The word "then" means "after that." It is a translation of the word *eita*. Interestingly, *tote* is the usual Greek temporal adverb for successive events, normally meaning "then." The fact that Paul uses *eita* instead suggests that "the end" doesn't follow immediately. In Mark 4:17 *eita* indicates something that occurs after a lapse of time: "Afterward [*eita*], when affliction or persecution ariseth for the word's sake, immediately they are offended."

No doubt, preterists do not like to acknowledge the existence of multiple prophetic references (see chapter eight) or prophetic gaps. Both, however, are recurring phenomena of biblical prophecy that have important ramifications for our understanding of the timing of prophetic fulfillment and scheduling of end-time events.

How To Receive Jesus Christ

1. Admit your need (I am a sinner).
2. Be willing to turn from your sins (repent).
3. Believe that Jesus died for you and rose from the grave
4. Through prayer, invite Jesus Christ to come in and control your life through the Holy Spirit (receive Him as Lord and Savior).

What To Pray

Dear Lord Jesus,

    I know that I am a sinner and I need Your forgiveness. I believe that You died for my sins. I want to turn from my sins. I now invite You to come into my heart and life. I want to trust and follow You as Lord and Savior.

In Jesus' Name. Amen.